THE LITERARY LIFE OF THE EARLY FRIENDS

THE LITERARY LIFE

OF THE

EARLY FRIENDS

1650~1725

BY

LUELLA M. WRIGHT

WITH AN INTRODUCTION BY

RUFUS M. JONES

AMS PRESS, INC.
NEW YORK
1966

TO MY FATHER

DAVID SANDS WRIGHT

PREFACE

As a group the Quakers have always manifested an interest in writings of autobiographical nature. In the following chapters the personal note in the literature of The Religious Society of Friends has been employed as the center of interest. This study purposes to direct attention to a descriptive analysis of the Quakerly and literary qualities dominating the writings of the seventeenth and early eighteenth-century Friends. The literary tenets, the peculiar social traits that brought Quaker literature into prominence, and the various types of writing which the Friends employed have all been examined. Wherever possible the authors have been allowed to state in their own words their personal and group aims, to narrate their sufferings under persecution, to describe their attempts to adopt the Quaker way of life, and to reveal their discouragements and aspirations in their religious confessions. This personal note is not only apparent in such narratives as these, but dominates many of their controversial tracts, and almost all of their historical, meditative, and poetical endeavors.

Until very recently critics and literary historians have given but scant attention to the thousands of tracts issued by the early Friends; and up to the present time they have contented themselves by relegating these productions to the scrap heap of seventeenth-century journalism. Though it is natural that critics should recognize the shortcomings in Quaker literature, yet on the other hand the contribution made by Friends between 1650 and 1725 deserves more recognition than it has hitherto received. This is true on account of its large corps of authors and especially on account of its contemporaneous record of thought current in the England of Cromwell and the later Stuart rulers. A few detailed histories of English literature mention *The History of the Life of Thomas Ellwood* because of the latter's connection with Milton, note the *Works* of William Penn, and refer to *The Journal of George Fox*. Henry Craik in his prose anthology and likewise Quiller-Couch in *The Oxford Book of English Prose* include only two Quaker writers, Penn and Fox.

Lately, however, certain indications point to a widening recognition of the literary work of the early Friends. The editors of *The Cambridge History of English Literature* have devoted an entire chapter to Quaker writings during the Restoration. In this article Mr. Edward A. Grubb has given an admirable introduction to the chief literary monuments of the early Friends. He stresses the mystical strain in such writers as Isaac Penington, the didactic elements in Penn's *No Cross, No Crown,* and the aphoristic wisdom of the latter's *Fruits of Solitude,* and he calls attention to the most important autobiographies, stressing particularly *The Journal of George Fox,* which for originality, spontaneity, and unconscious power of "sincere expression," he asserts is "probably without a rival in religious literature." He devotes considerable space to Robert Barclay's *Apology for the True Christian Divinity.* Mr. Grubb has here presented a thoughtful approach to the literary endeavors of the first two generations of Friends.

Then too, in his recent survey of English literature the French critic, Dr. Louis Cazamian, has voiced a plea for the writings of the Friends. In discussing the evolution of ideas current during the Commonwealth and post-Commonwealth period he declares that "literary history cannot neglect" the early Quaker records and that "the numerous writings in which these men defend themselves, tell their story, and spread their faith are of the utmost importance to the historian of ideas and sentiments."

During the early part of this century John Wilhelm Rowntree mapped out a series of Quaker historical studies which have been elaborated upon by representative Friends in England and America. Prominent among them are those of W. C. Braithwaite and Rufus M. Jones who from an historical point of view have made ample use of the stores of early Quaker documents, manuscripts, and tracts which have been treasured with zealous care in Friends' libraries. This undertaking is, I believe, the first attempt to study and classify the writings of the Friends as literature, and I think I am safe in adding, of any nonconformist group originating in the seventeenth century. H. M. Dexter in his *The Congregationalism of the Last Three Hundred Years as Seen through its Literature* was almost wholly interested in the theological aspects of the Independent tracts which he examined.

My work has been greatly facilitated by the Rowntree History Series and by the libraries at Swarthmore College, Haverford College, and the Friends Reference Library. Especially am I grateful to Dr. Dean Lockwood and Miss Amy Post, who for two summers gave me the key to the library at Haverford College and to the Jenks Collection of Tracts, and permitted me to work in the Quaker alcove; and also to Mr. John Nickalls and Miss Muriel Hicks, who allowed me to make use of the large collection of tracts and manuscripts housed in Friends Reference Library in London. In a different way I am grateful to a Lydia C. Roberts fellowship, which enabled me to continue my studies for two years at Columbia. To the members of the English department at Columbia University I acknowledge further indebtedness, especially to Dr. Ashley H. Thorndike, to Dr. W. Haller of Barnard College, who offered invaluable criticism, and to Dr. George Philip Krapp under whose direction this work was carried on. I have further thanks to offer to my colleague Dr. Margaret Alterton; and to Dr. Norman Penney, who read my manuscript in its early stages, and has generously replied to numerous letters, and furnished much valuable data. I also wish to express my appreciation to Dr. Henry J. Cadbury for reading the book in proof, and for his comments, and especially to Dr. Rufus M. Jones for his initial suggestion as to the direction which this study should take and for his writing the foreword to this book.

I am indebted to The Macmillan Company for kind permission to quote from the works of W. C. Braithwaite, and of Dr. Rufus M. Jones; to E. P. Dutton and Co. for the privilege of quoting from the Tercentenary edition of *The Journal of George Fox,* and to the John C. Winston Co. for one quotation from the Cambridge edition of Fox's *Journal.*

L. M. WRIGHT

UNIVERSITY OF IOWA
  IOWA CITY, IOWA
  March, 1932

CONTENTS

INTRODUCTION

Luella M. Wright has made a notable incursion into a somewhat unexplored field of human interest and she has come upon live, palpitating people. The mounds of Babylonia and Palestine, the tombs of Egypt, the sites of buried Troy and Mycene and Gnossos, the ruins of Mexico and Central America are revealing the life and habits of ancient civilizations and every piece of pottery, every inscription, every implement, that comes to light out of the darkness of lost centuries is precious because it brings us back into living contact with men and women like ourselves, who lived and loved and struggled and suffered with hopes and aspirations and passions like our own.

But here in an environment much closer to our time and nearer to us in faith and ideals, Doctor Wright has brought to light the inner life, the high hopes, the dreams of new heavens and a new earth of a group of men and women whose personal confessions and whose biographical revelations of themselves have remained largely unknown to the general public. Quaker leaders and students here and there have broken into this world before her and have been stirred with feelings of fellowship and unity of spirit for the founders of their beloved community, but until now no one armed with spade and sieve has dug into this vast heap of remains to appraise with impartial mind its human worth and its literary value.

In the period covered by this book, 1650-1725, four hundred and forty Quaker writers produced no less than two thousand, six hundred and seventy-eight separate pub-

Chapter I

THE FIRST FOUR HUNDRED
AND FORTY

1

The earliest contemporaries regarded the members of the new Quaker sect as radicals and dangerous innovators, bent upon overturning orthodox and time-honored principles of religion. In sharp contrast to this view the world of today generally thinks of the Quakers, or as they prefer to be called The Religious Society of Friends, as a small protestant body, devoted to passivism and to the ideals of world peace. This decided change in popular esteem has not resulted wholly from the growth of religious toleration during the last three hundred years, but has been due largely to changes within the Society which tended toward conservatism. Even before 1725 the early aggressiveness of the Quakers had shifted to a quietistic view of the place of religion in life. Despite this obvious and growing conservatism within the Society between 1650 and 1725, the entire trend of Quaker beliefs and of Quaker literature was, nevertheless, stamped upon the group by its leaders of the first and second generations. Strong conviction, untiring energy, and unbounded religious fervor in both preaching and writing characterized the earliest stages of the Quaker movement.

During the Commonwealth Quaker men and women, preaching after the fashion of the modern Salvation Army, attracted great crowds in market places and upon highways, lications. Some of them no doubt, may as well remain buried and forgotten, for they are no longer quick and vital, but in this amazing output of life and thought there is much that possesses permanent human interest. The English Commonwealth period was one of the most virile and creative epochs in English history. It was a time of new births. It seethed with religious enthusiasms and with democratic hopes. Out of the ferment a new experiment in democracy and in mystical life emerged in the form of the Quaker Movement. Fortunately nearly all the pillar leaders of the movement wrote autobiographical journals or left material out of which biographies could be made. These revealing journals are prominent in this study. In many respects this confessional literature was a new type of self-revelation and today it is interesting both as a literary *genre* and as source-material for the inner life of the epoch out of which it came.

This study is rather a unique instance of the interpretation of life and the autobiographical story of persons who belong, not in the list of trained scholars, but rather in the ranks of "the common man." A few of these documents of confession were written by men of the type of Penn and Keith and Barclay, but most of them came from very humble pens. We have a chance here to see "the common man" who was "no orator" and who had no artifices of persuasion, writing his plain unsophisticated story and defending his precious truth in straight-forward and simple style.

Doctor Wright has done an extensive piece of research. She has shown scholarly insight and she has put all of us who are interested in this great mutation period of English life, and in genuine human nature, deeply in her debt.

RUFUS M. JONES

HAVERFORD COLLEGE
HAVERFORD, PA.

and by their language and remarks created antagonism among Anglicans, Presbyterians, and Independents. In addition the Quaker press, issuing tract after tract in which Calvinistic views were ruthlessly assailed, raised storms of disapproval. In upholding the Quaker way of life, both preachers and writers tenaciously upheld certain principles that were novel in their day and thoroughly disapproved of by their critics—principles of democracy, of philanthropy, of inwardness in religion—which have since had a permanent influence upon later social and religious thought and practices.

Opposition from many quarters confronted the Quakers. The civil wars and the unstable political conditions of the interregnum made officers of the law peculiarly apprehensive of radical measures. For this reason judges often ruled that Friends were subversive to the best interests of the Parliamentary government when Quaker street preachers openly argued against the payment of tithes, and likewise held them guilty of contempt of court when Friends refused to remove their hats before the bar of court, or when under arrest, to take legal oaths before trial. Often officers took occasion to arrest itinerant Quaker preachers and throw them into jail under charges of vagabondage when they addressed assemblies in such unheard of places for worship as barns, churchyards, or country roadsides. Serious opposition of a different type came from rival church men—Anglicans, Presbyterians, and Independents—who in no uncertain language denounced the Quakers as proselytizers, heretics, and Jesuits in disguise.

In spectacular ways the earliest Friends sought to gain popular attention. Fully convinced of the truth and truths of Quakerism, they allowed no obstacles to stand in their way. A Quaker, stoned from an English village by an excited mob, was apt to re-appear on the next day and complete his sermon. William Dewsbury for instance, in 1653, "after sounding the day of the Lord in the steeple-house" at Abbey

Holme, was dragged first into "the grave yard" and immediately driven from the town with violence. As soon as he recovered strength, however, "he stood upon a little hill," where according to an old record, "he cleared himself by speaking to the people."

In this period during the commonwealth they drew into fellowship with them many Anglicans, at that time deprived of their regular clergy; and they openly proselytized from the congregations of the Presbyterians and the Independent sects; they themselves refusing any remunerations for preaching, not infrequently called upon ministers of other denominations in their homes or publicly berated them for receiving hire for ministerial work. During the Commonwealth Quaker preachers entered churches to show either by silence or by remonstrance their disapproval of the service, or of the doctrine taught; if forbidden entrance, they awaited the congregation in the churchyard; and if arrested and sent to prison, they frequently seized the opportunity presented for preaching to jailer and fellow prisoners.

For delivering their sermons these early Friends chose places which seemed incongruous to churchmen, reared on Laud's "beauty of holiness," and which also raised the ire of conservative Presbyterians, such as Edwards, Prynne, and Pagit. The founder of Quakerism, George Fox, reasoned that if Christ had preached on the Mount of Olives, then he and other religious men of the seventeenth century could not do better than follow the example of their Master. Fox himself once preached from a craggy eminence on a mountain side,[1] and in the early days of his ministry, after maintaining a silence for several hours that his hearers might be "famished for words," he addressed "a great audience of professors from a haystack."[2] Other Quakers in their first missionary endeavors spoke in meetings arranged for them in private homes, upon hill tops, and in barns, and more than once spoke from windows of hay chambers and of jails.[3] These missionaries traveled in all directions upon foot, on horseback, and upon sailing vessels to distant countries, preaching and distributing tracts wherever they journeyed.

With consternation the religious bodies of the time watched George Fox's little handful of followers steadily annexing new recruits until a half century later the "despised Quakers" became not only the largest sectarian group in England, but in 1700 actually equalled in number the four next largest organizations dissenting from the Church of England. Nothing daunted these Children of the Light, as they first designated themselves. For "conscience' sake" they endured floggings, property losses, imprisonment and banishment. Before the Restoration over three hundred Friends had died either in prison or from the effects of prison confinement.[4] These early Quakers were terribly in earnest and not "at ease in Zion." The more the Friends endured persecution, the more their converts multiplied; and the more the turnkeys flung open the doors of Bridewell, Newgate, and provincial jails to receive "the rebel Quaker saints," the more widely heralded became the Quaker message.

2

A survey of the literary contribution, made by the Friends and other nonconformists between 1650 and 1725, rounds out and illumines for students of the period many cross-sections of English life which Clarendon and Burnet passed over with little notice; in fact the majority of English historians, since they have been principally interested in the relationship of the English church and state, have as a rule given scant attention to the literature of nonconformity. The ecclesiastical chroniclers of the Friends, such as Croese, Penn, Sewel, and Besse, present a changing panorama of social conditions—of the road from Highgate to Saint Albans beset by robbers, of women preachers flogged at Cambridge, of prison ships on the Thames, and of courts of law. The personal literature—letters, confessions, and journals —vividly portrays experiences of mystic nature, men summoned by an inward Voice from the plow or shop to preach an untaught gospel and whole assemblies moved by a power which they likened to Pentecost. It shows too, "all manner and conditions of men"—tradesmen, sailors, young children in Quaker boarding schools, justices, jailers, courtiers, and kings.

The historian, interested in the evolution of ideas, finds in Quaker documents a distinct contribution to the growth of democratic ideals and of the spirit of religious toleration. A full century before the French revolutionists were hoarsely shouting their cries of liberty, equality, and fraternity through the streets of Paris, the Friends, always with a hope in view for the immediate amelioration of society, were endeavoring to inculcate these very principles into daily life and were advocating them in their tracts. Since the Friends maintained the equality of all men in the sight of God, in their dealings with their fellowmen they put this democratic principle into actual practice. They refused to acknowledge any degrees of inferiority and superiority, and therefore were unwilling to remove their hats as a token of deference, or to address any individual, citizen, justice, or king with a title of any description.

Even more vigorously the Friends asserted as their unrestricted right the privilege of worshipping when, where, and as they chose. In order that their beliefs might gain wider publicity, they, at the risk of imprisonment and confiscation of presses, persisted in defying licensing enactments. Whenever the views of the Quakers came into conflict as they often did, with ecclesiastical and civil laws,[5] the Friends submitted to distraint of property and imprisonment with merely "passive resistance." The tenets of the Society forbade opposition by physical force but no inhibitions interfered with the Quakers' employment of often virulent and explosive tracts and epistles as weapons of remonstrance. The incessant activity of the Quaker press from 1653 to 1689 kept in circulation popular demands for freedom of speech, of the press, of belief, and of worship, and by so doing assisted substantially in creating a type of public opinion which could only be appeased at the accession of William and Mary with the Act of Toleration, an act permitting all dissenters in England to worship without fear of disturbance by officers of the law.[6]

A unified determination that the Quaker idea of practical Christianity should prevail actuated both speakers and writers among the Friends. The acute political and religious crises of the seventeenth century forced strong convictions upon individuals and upon groups. During the interregnum, men almost perforce took sides politically with either the parliamentary or royalist party, and religiously with Presbyterians, Anglicans, or with one of the numerous sects.

3

The Quaker movement rose into prominence almost at the very middle of the seventeenth century. In 1647 George Fox, a young religious enthusiast, twenty-three years of age, began teaching individuals and groups in the north of England that he had discovered in the doctrine of the inner Light the very secret of apostolic Christianity. He, furthermore, taught that God, through the inner Light, was still revealing himself to men as he had done to the Hebrew prophets, and later to the apostles, St. Paul and St. John. George Fox centered his teaching about the inner Light—

the belief that a spark of divine essense dwells in each human being, and that if obedience is yielded to this inner Light or Word that man can be led into all Truth and thus possess a guide for the intricate problems of daily living and for the conduct of life. In the spreading of this belief the Friends desired to awaken their age to a realization of its spiritual barrenness both in its attitude toward religious observances and in its perception of a spiritual relationship between God and man. They desired to turn people from being "half believers in a casual creed" to a deep-seated faith in a religion whose basic principle was spirituality.

Almost immediately there rallied to the side of George Fox an energetic band of young men, ready and eager to carry the message of their founder to the English speaking world and beyond. From that time on until 1700 the growth of the Quaker movement was phenomenal. As in apostolic days, sometimes alone, but oftener traveling in pairs, these first "gospellers" to the number of seventy—among them William Caton and John Stubbs, John Audland and John Camm, Edward Burrough and Francis Howgill—set forth to preach the doctrine of the inner Light in the three British kingdoms. Even before the death of Cromwell in 1658 the Friends, as preachers and pamphleteers, had invaded every shire in England,[7] and their emissaries had crossed the seas and reached the Mediterranean countries, the West Indies, and the American Colonies. Estimates show that at the Restoration the Friends numbered "upwards of sixty thousand."[8]

4

No one who read the first few Quaker tracts as, with black print and a liberal use of italics for emphasis, they issued from the presses in 1653,[9] could have anticipated that within half a century the Friends would become a powerful adjunct

to the ranks of nonconformity, and that they would disseminate literally thousands upon thousands of tracts. Today when in England and in America, the Friends represent
statistically a very small protestant body, it is difficult to
realize that at the beginning of the eighteenth century the
membership conjecturally "in the three kingdoms reached
the number of a hundred thousand"[10] and in England,
"equalled the combined strength of the Roman Catholics,
Presbyterians, Independents, and Baptists."[11]

In addition, this large Quaker aggregation produced a
proportionately numerous quota of writers. Contact with the
teachings of George Fox almost invariably turned the more
educated converts into vigorous defenders of Quaker faith
and practices. Within seven decades after 1653, four hundred and forty writers became propagandists of Quakerism,[12] and produced 2,678 separate publications,[13] varying
in length from the single broadsheet to folios of a thousand
pages. Quaker tracts multiplied in numbers. Twenty-three
were issued in 1653, forty-three the following year and
seventy in 1655. The total number of separate publications
mounted to four hundred and sixty-eight before the Restoration.[14] Many of these were reprinted in issues of a thousand
copies; no opportunities were neglected for giving them
wide circulation. Many were reprinted and re-edited. The
total number of Quaker tracts circulated before 1725 has
been variously estimated. Some authorities state that in these
years the Friends issued two and a half million tracts while
others insist that the number did not fall below four million.[15]

The first four hundred and forty writers among the
Friends represent a level of culture far above the average
for England and America during the Commonwealth and
later Stuart periods. Though many authors had received
little formal education and were devoid of skill in writing, a

fairly large number of the leaders had been trained at Oxford and Cambridge; a few like Giles Barnardiston and William Penn had been sent abroad to complete their education with foreign travel. Some like Samuel Fisher and Francis Howgill had studied divinity for the purpose of taking orders in the Church of England, and after becoming dissatisfied with Anglican doctrines, had preached for Independent congregations before joining the Friends. To their support of Quakerism such men brought the zeal that fresh inspiration and novel intellectual views can furnish as well as minds that had already been trained to organize and express thought. The stylistic superiority of the Quaker polemics in comparison with much of the political and religious propaganda of the day is to be accounted for by the superior training which many converts brought to the Society of Friends.

Writers as well as preachers among the early Friends courted publicity. Avoiding only satire, light verse, and drama, they forced their way into every field open to contemporary journalists and littérateurs. To themselves they appropriated all the popular controversial measures of the day: the one page fly-leaf, the journalistic tract written in dialogue form, and the more formal tractate. The Friends of the first generation turned almost spontaneously to the press in order to further the aims of the newly organized sect; those of the second, however, displayed a marked degree of conscious effort in designedly employing the press in the education of their constituency, in unifying their membership, and in the censoring of their own publications.

Three closely related aims motivated both the pioneer writers and their followers in the next generation. Both groups firmly believed that as the Hebrew prophets had formerly been commissioned by Jehovah, they likewise were divinely inspired to preach to all men the gospel of the inner Light. In the first place, then, they endeavored to awaken their age to a firm belief that Christianity could be practical, and living in this world a spiritual experience. This desire led to the writing of meditations, verse, and advisory epistles.

In the second place, the Friends, with profound faith in their belief and their mission, desired to propagate their social and religious principles. This motive produced the bulk of their literature. In tracts, in petitions, and in folio volumes the leaders defended every major and minor tenet of the Society. In tract form, they presented *apologiae* for Friends and their principles, pleas for their co-workers in prison, or expostulations against the spoken and written assertions of their Anglican and Calvinist opposers.

In the third place, by revealing in confessional form the steps by which they had been led to accept Quakerism and to find peace in the mystic power of the inner Light, they hoped to convert others to their views. In making popular appeals to their auditors and readers, both preachers and writers employed the confession of their personal experiences as an expedient method for convincing others of the power of the inner Light in their lives.[16] In point of priority of time the written confession of the Friends is the chief contribution which the Quakers made to the history of English literature. These confessions are, furthermore, noteworthy documents because in them the Friends as a group embodied a degree of subjectivity that, except sporadically in individual memoirs, was not again employed (the Methodist group possibly excepted) until modern psychology opened up the present day interest in the examination and the recording of the inner life.[17]

Group consciousness characterizes the entire Quaker literary contribution. This element becomes most conspicuous in the personal writings, especially in the Quaker religious

confessions of which the Friends, during the first eight
decades of Quakerism, produced upwards of ninety.[18] Of
these about half were published as separate tracts by the
first generation of Friends, and the rest were incorporated in
the complete memoirs of the second. These confessions are
unmistakably dominated by a prevailing consciousness of
the group mind. The dominance of the Society intervenes
between the personality of the writer and the mind of the
reader. The Quaker memorandist constantly played a double
rôle. As an individual, recounting the events of his life, he
stressed those that duplicated the experiences of others
within the group; as spokesman for the Society, he subordinated personal episodes in his own life to those shared
by the group. These confessions, since they reveal men and
women facing life problems and struggling toward a definite
goal, transcend the sectarian field; and since they deal with
man's interest in himself and God, they become contributions of universal import in the literature of autobiography.

CHAPTER II

THE MYSTICAL SECTS

1

Unsettled political and religious conditions during the Commonwealth fostered the growth of the Independent sects. Some of these sprang into existence teaching fantastic doctrines, lasted a few years and disappeared; some like the Muggletonians have survived up to the present with a meagre membership, and others like the Baptists later developed into strong centers of nonconformity. These sects came into being because they fulfilled a need of the times. They were attempts, sometimes fanatical and sometimes sound, to satisfy the questionings of persons who had been cast religiously adrift when the Church of England during the interregnum was functioning at lowest ebb, or to meet the needs of those who had become dissatisfied with all existing types of organized religion in their age.

An independency of mind, strengthened by the Reformation and by the Englishman's natural inclination toward democracy, also contributed to the emergence of the sects and accelerated their growth. Particularly among the middle classes, this independence displayed itself in antagonism to Laudian tendencies in the Church of England and later to autocracy in Presbyterian policies. It formed the basis of Winstanley's efforts through the Diggers and of Lilburne's through the Levellers to awaken Englishmen to independent thinking. Sectarianism, or nonconformity as it was termed in England after 1660, had inherited its determined resistance to authority from the Reformation. Everywhere the sectaries were re-asserting Luther's plea that each individual possessed the right to interpret the Scriptures as he saw fit, and to reject priestly mediation between himself and his Creator.

In England the middle years of the seventeenth century were marked by strife. Everything, socially, politically and religiously, swirled in a state of flux. In 1653 Cromwell became Lord Protector of England and inaugurated an experiment unprecedented in English history. The public mind was still agitated over questions which the Commonwealth with all its efforts since 1642 had manifestly been unable to solve. Conflicting views were as rife as they had been eleven years before when the Long Parliament had closed the theatres and banished the bishops. On every hand dissatisfaction was intensified by the disillusionment which had followed the first civil wars and the later campaigns of Cromwell in Ireland and Scotland during the years 1649 to 1652. Men who had thrown themselves into these conflicts with religious fervor or with high hopes for the social or political amelioration of the nation were bewildered. Neither the decrees of Parliament, nor the successive executions of Strafford in 1641, of Laud in 1645, or of Charles I in 1649 had succeeded in bringing to England any degree of equilibrium. In 1642 Englishmen had seen the Established Church give way before the Presbyterian, the Anglican clergy[1] silenced and presbyters installed in place of bishops, and a little later the universities under Parliamentary control.[2] Now they saw in the present supremacy of Cromwell a victory for the Independents. Many people with troubled thoughts were surveying the religious dilemma about them. Some, torn from old traditional moorings of Anglican uprearing, were tempest-tossed, and forced into questioning what they had been taught and what they should believe. Some who had frequented parish churches from their childhood found these closed or occupied by puritan lecturers expounding Calvinism and denouncing liturgy. Still others, brought up under Puritanism, upon searching the King James Version for themselves, discovered new interpretations which they felt to be irreconcilable with their childhood instruction. Not infrequently these searchers established or joined new Independent sects.

During the interregnum many men and women turned successively from the Anglican to the Presbyterian fold,[3] and from the latter to one or more of the newer sects, which for several decades had been multiplying with rapidity. Some, like the Seekers, gathered into little groups to await a prophet who could direct them into right ways of thinking and living;[4] others, like Milton, withdrew from church affiliations. The rising power of the Independents and the loosening of inhibitions hitherto imposed by the strongly centered Anglican and Presbyterian hierarchies added difficulties to the situation. Out of war-weariness and out of religious and civic disillusionment, sectarianism steadily gained in strength. Constantly there continued to rise other denominations, which felt it incumbent upon themselves to deduce from scripture drastic solutions and to apply them to existing conditions.

2

Out of these circumstances the Quaker movement developed. The Friends represented a constantly enlarging group of religiously-minded men and women who demanded something more from religion than they had hitherto experienced.[5] They sought for solutions which could satisfy their doubts concerning ritual, theology, and the moot question of entire separation of church and state. After various attempts to find spiritual satisfaction in Anglican liturgy and Calvinistic creeds, they turned to the principles of the young George Fox who since 1647 had been teaching the possibility of finding inner peace in this world through the inner Light.[6] God, he taught, was even then directly revealing himself to all who voluntarily surrendered their wills to the divine Will.

During the first five decades of the seventeenth century, the growing insistence that man could have direct recourse to God was further strengthened by the mystical teachings of the Dutch and German spiritual reformers whose beliefs for more than fifty years had been slowly filtering into England through the Anabaptists, Mennonites, and Behmenists. Puritanical and mystic teachings frequently became the basis of separation both of fanatics and of sober minded people into distinct religious groups, such as the Ranters, the Etheringtonians, the Familists, and the Muggletonians. From among these at the very middle of the century emerged the Friends, destined to become numerically the largest of the mystical groups and the most prolific producers of ephemeral and journalistic tracts, thus offering through the Quaker way of life a solution for the troubled conditions in the nation.

Although less directly effective than the practical mysticism which descended to the sects through the continental spiritual reformers, philosophical mysticism also contributed to the growth of these sectaries. These two types of mysticism may be differentiated by noting that the practical mystic is either intermittently or constantly aware of a greater consciousness impinging upon his own, toward which he turns for direction in the conduct of life. The philosophical mystic, on the contrary, concerns himself with questioning the source of this mystic sensation and its relation to the universe, God, and man. Many Jacobean, Carolinian, and Commonwealth writers[7] had inherited from the Renaissance Platonic and Neo-Platonic doctrines concerning the unity of all creation and concerning the harmonious relation of the finite with the infinite. Spenser, Drummond, and Sir Thomas Browne delighted in losing themselves in mystical speculations as did Henry More and the Cambridge Platonists. Donne and Crashaw infused into their poetry the mystic glow of the medieval saint, Vaughan, something of Wordsworth's feeling for nature, and Keats's worship of beauty,[8] and Traherne meditated in prose and verse upon the immanence of God.

Many of the mystical sects shared with the Friends the beliefs which had come down to them through various channels from Plato and from the apostles Paul and John, and later from Peter Waldo, Meister Eckhart, Kasper Schwenkfeld, Jacob Boehme,[9] Menno Simons, and Henry Nicolas (or Niclaes). The exhaustive inquiries of Dr. Rufus M. Jones in his *Studies in Mystical Religion,* and in *The Spiritual Reformers of the 16th and 17th Centuries* have shown that Quakerism, in stressing spiritual values in religion, was the result of a "slowly maturing movement."[10] Light has very recently been thrown upon Fox's immediate sources of contact with these mystical sects through the discovery of a manuscript list of the books owned by George Fox at the time of his death. This document was found in the library at Friends House in London by Dr. Theodor Sippell of Marburg, who annotated some items.[11] His work has been further enlarged upon and edited by Mr. John Nickalls, present curator of the library, who asserts that this discovery now establishes the fact that Fox had in his possession books on mystical themes written in pre-Quaker days by Sebastian Frank and Henry Nicholas.[12] Since Fox is now known to have owned two hundred and twenty-seven other volumes in addition to the list recently discovered, and though he himself was unable to read the text in the original, he may easily by means of his personal library have had contact with the writings of Hans Denck, and of Menno Simons.[13] Intense and minute study of the Scriptures affected the life, thinking, and writings of the sectaries. Hebraic phraseology, patriarchal greetings, and prophetic utterances became a part of everyday speech and aided materially in forming the texture of their verse and of their prose. Life, for instance, was metaphorically defined by one Friend as a long travail from the Babylon of this world to the Bethel of the one to follow. As soon as the King James Version became a popular possession, individuals began to interpret the Bible with an avidity that had never before been possible. Such questions as the Pauline instruction that women should keep silence in the churches, baptism, and communion were all points for common study, consideration, and zealous advocacy.

3

Conservatives among the Anglicans and especially among the Presbyterians under the Commonwealth surveyed the overthrowing of traditional observances with genuine alarm. Even before 1642, the former had seen their congregations grow smaller; the latter resented open attacks upon Calvinistic dogma and turned to the press in order to check the obstreperous sectarian reactionaries, who by 1644 were already appearing in Parliament with petitions for greater religious freedom. In an age when a man's beliefs were of utmost importance, all forces turned to the polemic. According to Neal, the most "furious writer against the sectaries was Mr. Thomas Edwards," a Presbyterian, whom Milton, when objecting to the oppressors of conscience in Parliament thus scorned:

> Men whose life, learning, faith and pure intent
> Would have been held in high esteem with Paul
> Must now be nam'd and printed heretics
> By shallow Edwards.

In 1646 Edwards published his *Gangraena or a Catalogue of the Discovery of many Errours, Heresies, Blasphemies, and Pernicious Practices Vented and Acted in England in the Last Four Years.* In this vitriolic attack he listed sixteen sects and one hundred and seventy-six heresies; before the year was out however in an additional section of the book he had brought the number of heretical beliefs up to three hundred.[14] In the same year Ephraim Pagit in his *Heresiographie* exhibited deep distress over the "numerous company of heretics suddenly descending upon London like locusts." Among these he cited the "unpure Familists, who pretend to be godified like God; the illuminated Anabaptists, the Independents with their excess of Liberty . . . the Millenaries, who believe in the reign of Christ and his Saints for a thousand years . . . and an atheistical sect, who affirm that men's souls sleep with their bodies until the Day of Judgment."[15]

The early Friends surpassed the other mystically inclined separatist bodies, as the next chapter will show, in centralizing all their beliefs and practices about the doctrine of the inner Light. Two other groups, the Ranters and the Seekers, in both origin and faith bore affinity to the Friends. Each, however, interpreted its cardinal belief in widely different respects. By experience the Friends soon discovered the necessity of holding a *via media* between the extremes of pantheism as taught by the Ranters and the absolute lack of definite creed among the Seekers,[16] and thus preserved an integrity which outlasted most of the mystical sects originating in the period of the Commonwealth.

The Ranters became trouble makers for many sects, particularly for the Friends.[17] It was an easy matter under the unsettled conditions of the Commonwealth for belief in inward revelation to degenerate into fanaticism and license. In a pantheistic manner the Ranters declared that their actions were sanctified because a spark of divine essence was indwelling in each soul. On this account they insisted that their members "were above such beggarly things as ordinances," and also "above sin" and therefore personally infallible. Since they claimed to be instructed by the Spirit, they insisted that "all other teachings either by Scripture or otherwise were of no use to them," holding that the Scriptures represented a "tale, a history, a letter, fleshly history, and a bundle of contradictions ... and the cause of all mystery and divisions in religious and civil affairs."[18] Lack of balance and restraint, however, inhibited the Ranters from securing any degree of unity, with the result that they failed to attain longevity. Certain pronounced similarities of belief, especially reliance upon the inner Light and the subordination of the Scriptures to a less important place than that assigned by the Calvinists, made it an easy matter for the Ranters to be identified in the popular mind with the Friends.[19] The latter were continually decrying the Ranters who attacked them in print, and with boisterous conduct[20] disturbed their silent meetings for worship.

With the Seekers the situation was entirely different. The name Seeker itself defines the constant aim of these groups. They were a spiritually minded people,[21] who, in the chaotic conditions of the Commonwealth, earnestly sought to find God, and who never formally organized themselves into a sect. George Fox in his earliest ministry had not infrequently found the ground prepared for his message of the inward Christ, and in some places found the people waiting for a prophet who would be a revealer of religious truths. These Seekers, spiritually minded, bent on discovering the will of

God, had reached the conclusion that man could only wait until God saw fit to initiate action in the worshipper.[22] In this respect they anticipated the quietistic tendencies of eighteenth century Quakerism.[23] According to John Saltmarsh,[24] a contemporary mystic, the salient characteristic of the Seekers "was their waiting in silent prayer. By themselves they felt incapable of infallible interpretation of the Scriptures and were waiting for an apostle or some one with a visible glory and power, able in the spirit to give demonstration of being sent."[25] Since in respect to the inner Light and silent worship, the Seeker attitude of mind concurred with that of the Friends, many isolated Seekers willingly turned to George Fox and his First Publishers of Truth as prophets who could give "evidence of being sent." Larger groups of Seekers very soon became strong nuclei for Quakerism in Westmorland,[26] in Bristol, and in London.[27]

4

The development of lay ministry greatly aided the constantly increasing separatist bodies in circulating their demands for congregational church government and for the right to draw up creeds as they chose. Declaring that the command, "Go ye into all the world and preach the gospel" referred not only to a consecrated order of priests but to Christians generally, the sects encouraged lay preaching, which became increasingly more popular from 1642 to 1660. Some lay preachers, called messengers by the Baptists, and Publishers of Truth by the Friends, had formerly served as Anglican clergymen; some had been puritan lecturers, and many others with no divinity training whatsoever assumed to themselves the right to preach and expound the Scriptures.

Under the Commonwealth, preachers were legally permitted to speak to congregations other than their own and to declare their views after the regularly installed pastor had completed his sermon. Though forbidden to speak from the pulpit, they could rightfully testify from the floor, call upon the incumbent minister to furnish further proof, or they could refute his statements.[28] Many Friends availed themselves of this privilege and on some occasions after speaking were dragged into the churchyard. Others were listened to with the greatest respect.

The pulpit reached its highest elevation in the formulation of religious thought in the seventeenth century.[29] In early Jacobean and Carolinian days, from both populace and court, sermons and preaching received considerable attention. Conservative forces in the Established Church, however, systematically discountenanced all puritanical efforts toward allowing the sermon to dominate or supplant the more ritualistic parts of the church services. The Presbyterians and the sectaries insisted upon centering their devotions about the sermon.[30] As early as 1622 the high church party, fearing that the lecturers might either employ their influence for political propaganda or mislead the populace[31] through ignorance or unsound theology, endeavored to check the power of the puritan lecturers, who, because they were not attached to any one living, could not be easily subjected to ecclesiastical discipline.

Lay preaching, as the century advanced, continued to gain favor with the populace. Even though Baxter and Milton complained bitterly of the condition of the clergy in their youth, the Anglican and also the Presbyterian Church in comparison with the independent sects favored a highly trained and educated ministry. Most sects of the Commonwealth, however, took the stand that theological training at Oxford or Cambridge could not prepare for a truly spiritual ministry. They stoutly maintained that the power to minister to souls was "God-given" and could not be conceived as a "man-made" or "state-made gift."[32] Through lay preaching, therefore, the sectaries aimed a definite blow at all types of priesthood fostered by civil authority, whether they were Roman, Anglican, or Presbyterian. This position, earlier assumed by the Baptists and Independents, the Friends carried to unprecedented limits by allowing women to preach and by asserting that every person belonging to the Quaker constituency was a potential minister.

Anglicans who remained in England during the interregnum and Presbyterians who felt that their power would be curtailed by fanatics and zealous Independents, grew fearful. Ephraim Pagit in 1646 saw great cause for alarm in an unlettered ministry where "everyman that listeth turneth preacher" and where cobblers, "ostlers" and buttonmakers were intruding into pulpits and "venting strange doctrines tending to faction, sedition, and blasphemy."[33] In the army of Parliament during the civil wars, prophesying or lay preaching gained further popularity. Thomas Edwards, a partisan Presbyterian, in his *Gangraena*, deplored extemporaneous preaching and the "seraphical tendencies" existing in Cromwell's army, proclaiming with rancor that these army preachers were not purely Independent but "higher flown . . . and compounded of Anabaptisme, Antinomianisme, Familisme, all these errours and many more too, sometimes meeting in the same persons, strange monsters, having their heads of Enthusiasme, their bodies of Anabaptisme, their hands of Arminianisme, and Libertinisme, as the great vein going through the whole."[34] All unlettered preachers as well as the sectaries to whom they preached were anathema to Edwards.

The utilization of the press for propagating sectarian views alarmed Anglican and Presbyterian conservatives fully as much as did the sectarian system of lay preaching. For several decades after 1653 the Friends followed the system and forms of protest which their puritan precursors had employed. These predecessors had remonstrated against every reflection of Roman Catholic symbolism, and against veneration of the saints, and of the Virgin,[35] and at a later time against the Acts of Supremacy and Uniformity,[36] which respectively made Elizabeth supreme ruler in civic and ecclesiastical affairs,[37] and required every clergyman to employ the *Book of Common Prayer* in religious services.[38] Under James I came further protests such as the Millenary Petition, and under Charles I, the Petition of Right. Pamphleteering had already become popular for ridicule, for satire, for propaganda, for abuse, and for serious discourse. The Friends in their early literature not only reflected the spirit of protest but they also adopted the controversial tract of the puritans for asserting their views and for refuting those of others.

5

Floods of tracts appeared throughout the first half of the seventeenth century in which Anglicans, Presbyterians, and Independents counter-attacked and heaped abuse upon one another, or with great dignity pleaded for toleration on high grounds, such as Jeremy Taylor employed in his *Liberty of Prophesying*. When Quaker journalists entered the field, the separatist sects were utilizing the press for defensive and for offensive propaganda. In broadside ballads and scurrilous tracts Cavaliers, scoffing at puritan prejudices against music and dancing, had ridiculed their puritanically inclined countrymen. The Roundheads, in their turn, rushed through the press pamphlets and books in which they upheld their principles, their right to protest, and their personal views of politics and religion. The middle classes during the central decades of the seventeenth century became suddenly articulate. Independent thinking impelled them to express their ideas and to disseminate their beliefs in printed form. For the most part, in preparing tracts for the press, they had in mind a reading public of mental calibre equivalent to their own. They felt not the slightest need for the highly Latinized style of Sir Thomas Browne, the rhetorical periods of their contemporary Jeremy Taylor, or the flowing grace and deliberation of Isaak Walton.

Intense conviction motivated the majority of these sectarian pamphleteers. They felt deeply. Writing under emotional stress, they were far more concerned with what they had to say than with their manner of expression. The result was the emergence of a simpler prose style than English literature had heretofore known, a style that borrowed its imagery from the homely and simple metaphors of everyday life and from the Old Testament psalmists and prophets. At its worst it degenerated into overwrought appeals where in prophetic language the nation was urged to repent in sackcloth and ashes, or it partook of the embittered and virulent spirit of current controversy. At its best in the hands of such Quaker writers as James Nayler, Francis Howgill, and Isaac Penington, it sometimes reached heights of impassioned prose seldom attained by Richard Baxter and above the level of much of Jeremy Taylor's controversial writings.

In an open epistle addressed to the churches of England and Ireland, attributed to the early Quaker preacher, James Nayler, and reprinted in his complete *Works,* occurs a passage in which the growth of conscience is told in the form of a parable. Its rhythm, its repetitions, and its phraseology are essentially biblical.

Was not there a Plant planted amongst you once, a tender Plant, which had a little rooting in a tender Ground, which began to appear out of the Earth, more in Beauty than all the

Wild Trees of the Forest; it also did begin to Blossom, and some tender Grapes did appear; and the Roots and Branches began to spread, and to bend towards him that planted it, and made its appearance towards Heaven; and there were great hopes of a Blessing in it, and that it would have covered the Earth with its Comeliness that was beginning to be put upon it; insomuch as the Oaks and Cedars, and all the rest of the Trees, the Briars and Brambles, began to envy its Appearance, and gathered in Counsel against it in great Strength: But the Maker thereof, seeing it bending to him, in that straight undertook to make Room for it, cutting down some, and plucking up others by the Roots, even of the tallest and strongest that withstood its spreading, until he left scarce a Briar to hinder the Fruitfulness thereof. Then he looked that it should arise, and spread, and bring forth Fruits, according to its own Nature, Tender and Good; and this was that which bare the Name of *Tender Consciences,* and indeed did so prevail in many, as nothing was to be compared with it, nor valued like it, whose Fame was spread in the World.[39]

For the most part they chose a diction that was easily comprehended. Not infrequently passages of mystical import were written in metaphorical language with grave dignity. Much, however, of their tractarian literature bore the earmarks of journalism in that it was designed primarily to deal with burning questions of the moment; it was, however, admirably adapted for conveying beliefs and explanations to a rapidly enlarging, if not highly cultivated, reading public. Fortunately for the disseminating, interpreting, and publishing of the Quaker gospel, many of Fox's converts brought to early Quakerism minds that had been trained to express themselves in pulpits, and pens that had been developed by earlier literary and controversial work. Convinced as they were of the belief that, in the inner Light, they had rediscovered the apostolic Christianity of the first two centuries, these converts bent every energy to send forth this message and its Quaker implications in faith and practice to the world.

CHAPTER III

THE INNER LIGHT

1

The very simplicity of the doctrine of the inner Light, with its absolute freedom from liturgy and from formal creeds made it, in the 1650's, readily communicable and acceptable to numerous seekers after religious truths who in the "Lo, here," and "Lo, there," of the times were bewildered and confused. As the doctrine was evolved by George Fox and put into practice by the Friends, it first of all demanded from the convert apartness from the world, often deprivation and suffering; but paradoxically on the other hand, it promised to the spiritually distressed, peace of mind. Almost every book, tract, or epistle written by an early Friend drew its chief inspiration from belief in the inner Light. Since the writers were convinced that the Friends had been divinely commissioned as "a remnant chosen from the people" to renew apostolic Christianity among the nations, they designed their tracts to defend and to explain to the world[1] their newly found gospel.[2]

Quakerism came into existence, historically speaking, through the conjunction of two trains of thought, the one puritanical, and the other mystical. With Calvinistic doctrines and a Presbyterian theocracy it stood at variance. Its puritanical strain, descending directly from the Reformation, manifested itself in a renewed insistence upon individual liberty of conscience, and in a tendency both to protest against any infringement upon religious rights, and to emphasize rigor in the conduct of life. Desire for religious freedom made the Friends champion the congregational system of church government—the goal toward which all the Independent sects of the Commonwealth were striving. So far as the conduct of life was concerned, in respect to plain dress, and plain speech, and attitude toward amusements, the Quakers outpuritaned the Puritans.

As distinguished from the Puritan, the Quaker was essentially mystical, centering his teachings upon the belief of the Christ indwelling in each heart. Dr. Rufus M. Jones has defined normal mysticism as a "type of religion which is characterized by an immediate consciousness of relationship with God." All mystics, the Friends included, uniformly assume an attitude of mind whereby they look upon all creation as a consummate unity of which each person is a component part; they, therefore, believe that "nature, man, and the heart of man" are expressions of the great Reality. Since unity embraces all things in the universe, the commonest objects are symbolic of the omnipresence of divinity, and the whole earth is sacred. The mystic desires "to find God, to be like God, and to have the experience of God."[3] This searching becomes the dominant factor in his life, for he believes that he is a co-sharer with the great beneficent Power of the universe, that is, in "omnipotent Love, Beauty, or Power."[4]

This mystical conception of man's relationship to God became the fountain head of the Quaker's desire to make living in this world sacramental and at the same time to be mindful of an unseen world as well as the visible one. To this general ideal the Friends added also the element of practical mysticism, that is, they turned to the inner Light for guidance in every episode in life. They sought contact with God in order that through inner revelation[5] they might secure directing power for the needs of life; and because of their consciousness of God, they felt little necessity for rationalizing their practical mysticism into a creed or a philosophy.[6] In fact they would have preferred, like the Seekers, to remain creedless and individualists.[7]

The experiences and ideas of George Fox acted as a fusing element in welding together the mystical strains in seventeenth century thought with the ancient puritan spirit of courageous protest. George Fox, pre-eminently a religious genius,[8] endowed with a psychic temperament, executive ability, strong personality, and transcendent faith, taught his contemporaries a way of life whereby they might penetrate to a spiritual worship of God which, according to his belief, lay at the center of all things. Through his study of the Bible, which it is said he knew by heart,[9] and through his mystic "openings" he believed that he had touched the secret power of primitive Christianity.[10] To his early converts he appeared almost as a second John the Baptist, teaching mankind that Christ was at hand and could be found, not in creeds or liturgy but in the heart of man. Had the age, however not been prepared by antecedent forces, both puritanical and mystical in nature, for his presentation of spiritual religion, the Friends could not have carried their teachings in one generation to the entire English speaking world and beyond, nor could they have enlisted, as they did, four hundred volunteer writers as missionaries and as interpreters of their experiences and beliefs. The originality of Fox's religious genius did not lie in novel ideas emanating from his intellect but from his ability to synthesize about the doctrine of the inner Light a coherent body of beliefs and practices, and to render these transmissible to others. The Quaker way of life, as it was tried out in the seventeenth century, became one of the world's great experiments in practical Christianity.

2

Directly or indirectly, belief in the inner Light became the pivotal center for Quaker life and literature, about which every philosophical thought, all religious experiences, and all habits of life turned.[11] Acceptance of the inner Light involved first of all individual experience in religion, and secondly a new appraisal of traditionally accepted values in religion, including a new conception of the Trinity, of the sacraments, and of the inspiration of the Scriptures.

All three of these then novel interpretations of protestant Christianity developed out of the basic mysticism underlying Quaker beliefs, and consequently figured conspicuously in the controversial tracts and in the confessions and memoirs of the Friends. This Light, as Quaker authors constantly reiterated, was not an abstract theorem to be perceived by means of the intellect or reason,[12] but ideally a living and enduring personal experience.[13] Acceptance of this Light, since it implied an introspective view of self, an examination of motives for action, and a surrender of the will to the leadings of the Spirit, frequently required a complete orientation in the convert's estimation of his former religious views and of the place that religion should hold in life.

This adjustment to new standards was not a conversion in the sense of its being an isolated experience, but resulted in the gradual development of an habitual attitude of mind wherein the convert displayed an intense willingness to wait for guidance, and to act only after a careful weighing of the directions of the Voice within. George Fox wrote and preached of the constant necessity of a minute examination of the heart to see that its motives were right and prompted not by self but by God;[14] and he frequently repeated, as a corollary, that after the heart had once been set right the main objective of the Friends was "to keep in the Light."

3

Essentially mystical were George Fox's early religious experiences. Only after a long apprenticeship with current beliefs and with spiritual travail had he been able to attain the assurance that spiritual peace could be achieved in this world. His *Journal,* both a personal record and a faithful presentation of Quaker beliefs and history, contains a vivid account of his search for religious truth. Mystic invasions, "openings" he called them, brought him certainty of the truth, vouchsafed to him, and of his own mission in the world. As with Paul on his Damascus journey or with Rousseau on his way to Diderot, they brought all the forces of his being to center upon a single purpose in life.[15] With Fox this centralizing purpose was the promulgation of an untaught social and religious gospel. Fox's first great "opening" throws light upon what he himself meant by a religion based upon experience of God. From his twentieth to his twenty-fourth year, as a restless youth, Fox had wandered about England seeking help from one religionist after another, constantly fearing that all "professors" and creeds were going to fail him. Almost without hope, after fasting and wandering about in lonely places, he suddenly was given a new insight into spiritual living. According to his account, in the depth of his being he became aware of a Voice which brought assurance to "his despairing condition." The episode is thus related in his journal:

And when all my hopes in them [teachers and professors of religion] and in all men were gone so that I had nothing outwardly to help me, nor could I tell what to do; oh! even then I heard a Voice which said, 'There is one, even Christ Jesus, that can speak to thy condition'; and when I heard it my heart did leap for joy. Then did the Lord let me see why there was none on earth that could speak to my condition . . . and this I knew experimentally.[16]

This first opening of his with the declaration, "There is one, even Christ Jesus that can speak to thy condition," proved to be a transforming one of lasting nature; henceforth he felt that his life work was mapped out for him. He firmly believed he had been in rapport with Divinity and had been receptive to the message of God. He would, no doubt, have repudiated any suggestion that the answer he had sought so long was one which had been slowly maturing in his mind. Other revelations concerning the universal significance of the inner Voice or Light followed. Through them, he saw that this inner Power belonged to all men,[17] everywhere; and that he himself had been singled out as a divinely commissioned prophet to carry the gleam of the "inner Light into the dark places of the world" which to him seemed "thorny and briery." He saw, furthermore, that he was to direct people not to a mere collection of biblical writings, but to the Spirit that gave forth the Scriptures, and that he was to condemn the falsities in all contemporary worship that did not possess the Spirit of Truth in its inward parts.[18]

In his personal teachings he made constant use of three expressions, which breathe the very spirit of Quakerism. They are "waiting for guidance," "experiencing religion," and "knowing God experimentally." Early Quaker literature contains, perhaps, no better explanation of these processes than the suggestions which Fox sent in a letter to Lady Claypoole, the favorite daughter of Oliver Cromwell, shortly before her death.[19] The first step in "waiting," he indicated, implied an active striving of the will to shut out human desires and intellectual activity. This accomplished, the soul could then become aware of divine leadings. He wrote,

Friend,—Be still and cool in thy own mind and spirit from thine own thoughts, and then thou wilt feel the Principle of God to turn thy mind to the Lord. . . . That is It which works up . . . into stillness, into staidness, into quietness, up to God, with his power. Therefore mind: that is the word of the Lord God unto thee . . . that is It which keeps peace, and brings up the witness in thee. . . . Therefore be still a while from thy own thoughts, from searching, seeking, desires, imaginations; and thou wilt find Him to be a God at hand. . . . From thy own will, that is, the earthly thou must be kept. Then thou wilt feel the power of God . . . and so come to know the Seed of God . . . that ye may feel the power of an endless life, the power of God that is immortal.[20]

The key to an understanding of the controversial and personal literature of the Friends turns on the practical and basic mysticism of the Quaker way of life. In the preaching and writings of the Friends, personal experience in religion was the first requisite upon which they insisted. No desideratum was valued higher than that of spiritual peace— the knowledge that the motives and actions of the individual were in harmony with divine creation.[21] In comparison with other dissenting bodies, the strangeness and novelty[22] of the Friends' reliance upon the inner Light lay in their making it the core of their living, preaching, and writing to the extent that they were willing to suffer distrainment of property, imprisonment, and even to surrender their lives in proof that inward revelation could be made a reality in human experience and in the conduct of life.[23]

4

Acceptance of the inner Light not only made the Quaker convert introspective, but in addition it forced him to readjust his thinking to a new conception of the Trinity, of the sacraments, and of scriptural inspiration. This thinking, especially when it conflicted with Arminian and Calvinistic views, produced seemingly endless verbal and printed controversies. The Quaker insistence that in human experience the power of the Holy Spirit transcends that of the other persons in the Godhead was anathema to the Anglicans and particularly to the Presbyterians and to the Calvinistic Baptists, all of whom charged the Friends with blasphemy.[24]

In differentiating the three views of the Trinity held by the Calvinists, Anglo-Catholics, and Friends, some one has said that the Calvinists magnified the first person, the Hebraic conception of a God of awfulness and power; that the Anglo-Catholics stressed the second person, the Christ, the union of the human and the divine; and that the Friends exalted the importance of the third person,[25] the Holy Spirit. The application of the remark to the first two cases is not pertinent to the study in hand; to the Quakers, however, it is apt and fitting. To them God was a spirit to be worshipped in spirit and in truth, and necessarily, they reasoned, the heart of man was the place in which He was to be worshipped.[26]

The assumption of the Friends that the inner Light was an authoritative guide in life was derided in non-Quaker tracts as misguided enthusiasm, and deemed blasphemous. George Fox, James Nayler, and many other First Publishers in the early 1650's faced blasphemy charges and suffered imprisonment and floggings for upholding the belief that God was indwelling in them.[27]

5

While all Friends did not formally discard the doctrines of the fall of man and of the atonement, yet on account of their belief in the efficacy of the inner Light they relegated such theological conceptions as these to a less important position than they held in the eyes of the Calvinists.[28] The greater share of the Friends reasoned that if God were indwelling, then man could not be hopelessly depraved and fallen.[29] In this respect they anticipated certain aspects of the theory of man's essential goodness, which Law and Rousseau embodied in their philosophies in the century following. The Friends considered it a matter of prime importance for a worshiper, if he longed to become a sharer in omnipotent love, to put himself into right relationship with God.[30] They reasoned that if man came into close relationship with his Creator he would have little need for theoretical conceptions of God or for such instruction in divinity as was taught in the universities. With them the atonement, therefore, tended to represent an at-one-ment of the individual with spiritual Power.

The Friends antagonized their religious co-temporaries in their position on the ordinances. As a corollary to the inner Light, the Friends taught that the sacraments of baptism and communion,[31] as commonly observed, were unnecessary. They took the position that if spiritual power were limitless, they had no need of "outward helps" in order to renew their strength. They furthermore desired that nothing tangible should intervene between themselves and Reality.[32] A recent authority on the faith of the Quakers has noted that the Friends have never been strong in symbolizing power.[33]

Such heresy as the rejection of baptism and the eucharist naturally became, in the world of seventeenth-century journalism, an occasion for much bitter controversy.[34] Very early, the Friends had revolted from a tendency in these ordinances, first designed as aids to worship, to become themselves objects of worship and hence a barrier between the worshiper and God. Going one step farther, they did away with priestly ministration.[35] They not only refused to remunerate their preachers, but did not allow a minister to assist officially at funerals or marriages, though at either any Friend might speak if he felt that he had a message. Marriages were performed by the simple ceremony of the participants taking each other as man and wife in the presence of witnesses.[36] The Friends insisted that a deeper spiritual communion was possible through contact with the inner Word than that symbolized by water from the baptismal font, or bread and wine from the altar, or from priestly mediation.

Though the Friends valued the Scriptures highly, they provoked storms of hostile tracts by advocating continuous as opposed to closed revelation. No innovation of the Friends occasioned more hostile criticism from Calvinistic circles than that of placing intuitional guidance above the authority of the Scriptures.[37] Fox in his *Journal* and doctrinal works made his position clear that true biblical interpretation was possible only when men and women in the study of the Scriptures were willing to submit to the same Power by which the biblical writers had in ages past been inspired. He did not look upon revelation as something infallible, shut within the covers of a book to which nothing had been added for centuries,[38] but as something accessible to all spiritually minded people.

Fox in his *Journal* appeals to his own experience as proof, writing, "I saw in an opening, that none could interpret John aright and a true understanding of the scriptural words but [those who were] in the same Spirit by which John spoke them. . . . Yet I had no small esteem of the Holy Scriptures, but they were very precious to me, for I was in that Spirit by which they were given forth."[39] That the followers of Fox held the Scriptures in high veneration is patent from the omnipresence of biblical language in every thing they wrote, and from numerous defense tracts[40] wherein the ministering or "public" Friends openly upheld their reverence for the Scriptures.

6

Reliance upon the inner Light not only subjected individuals to spiritual experience and orientated them to novel theological ideas, but it dominated all group assemblies of the Friends—their meetings for business as well as for worship. In both the Friends strove to establish what a modern Quaker has termed "a spiritual democracy." In meetings for business, the democratic spirit was and is carried almost to the point of unanimity. No vote was, or is, taken at the close of discussions. Agreement or lack of it is freely expressed, and if harmony seems to prevail the clerk reports the "sense of the meeting"; if otherwise, the matter is dropped, or deferred until concurrence seems assured.

The "spiritual democracy" was even more marked in the meetings for worship where the group assembled to await the guidance of the Spirit. Every member was ideally a potential minister and theoretically shared the responsibility of the service whether it were a marriage, a burial, or a First or Fourth Day Meeting.[41] Each participant "obeyed" when the call came to prophesy, preach, or pray. In practice, however, as Dr. Jones has pointed out, the ministry fell on spiritually-minded participants whose "psychical temperaments were so suggestible"[42] that they "responded to telepathic states in those about them."[43] Meetings were begun in silence, a silence often pregnant with prayer, in which the members were not unmindful of the corporate needs of the group assembled. No tapestries, no stained glass windows picturing saints and gospel scenes, no music pealing from organs either aided their worship or distracted their thoughts. No Quaker poet rose to give immemorial utterance to the mysticism of their faith, but their early prose writers not infrequently reached high poetic levels in a dignified and cadenced rhythm which reflected their authors' intimate knowledge of the King James Version.[44]

A quotation from a tract of Isaac Penington,[45] one of the saintliest souls attracted to early Quakerism, will explain the highly mystical import of the silent meetings and the attitude of the Quaker worshiper:

And this is the manner of their worship. They are to wait on the Lord, to meet in the silence of the flesh, and to watch for stirrings of his Life . . . in the breaking forth of that power they may pray, speak, exhort, rebuke, sing or mourn, according as the Spirit teaches, requires, and gives utterance. But if the Spirit do not require to speak and give to utter, then every one is to be still in his place . . . feeling his measure, feeding therefrom into his spirit what the Lord giveth. . . .

For absolutely silent meetings we know not; . . . but we wait upon the Lord, either to feel Him in words, or in the silence of the Spirit without words, as He pleaseth.[46]

In establishing congregational church government Fox and the early Friends went beyond most of the Independent sects in banning a paid ministry. With the inner Light foremost in his consciousness, George Fox looked upon the ideal church as one composed of a group of believers in which every man and woman, through the guidance of the Spirit, might become his own teacher.[47] Fox, an indefatigable student of the Bible, basing his plan on the New Testament epistles, attempted to build in so far as possible an "invisible church."[48] In his search he found no distinction in apostolic days between clergy and laity, and he therefore removed ministers from his scheme of church government, and permitted women to preach.[49] Fearing that formalism might inhibit the development of spirituality, he would have preferred no system of intercommunication such as he later established with monthly, quarterly, and yearly meetings. The demands, however, of missionary propaganda, discipline, and especially the need for inter-relating the smaller groups with the larger units made some sort of organization for the growing Society imperative.[50] The system, as he worked it out, while binding the units together by the thread of group interests, has been kept democratic, and at the same time each unit has been allowed a large amount of congregational autonomy.[51]

Though more obvious in questions of faith and worship, the influence of the inner Light underlay the customs that differentiated the Friends from other sects, subjected them frequently to caricature, and rendered them "a peculiar people." Insistence upon simple garb, the use of "thou" not the plural form "you," for the singular pronoun in the second person,[52] the puritanical attitude toward amusements and the stand on peace—all represented the social challenge of Quakerism against prevailing conventions. Because of the indwelling "spark within the clod," belief in the essential dignity of man led the Friends to democratize not only their meetings for business and for worship, but also their social contacts with members of the Quaker group and with outsiders in the affairs of everyday life. The conception of the innate worth of all mankind influenced them, too, in their refusal to use titles and to remove the hat as a token of deference[53] to their supposed superiors in social rank and office, or to royalty. The so-called "hat honor" tested the sincerity of the converts, particularly those who entered the fold from the genteel classes.[54]

The Quaker belief that all phases of church life should result from spiritual motivation made them object to supporting a traditional ministry connected with "steeple houses", "hireling priests" and the payment of tithes.[55] On this point, both under Cromwell and Charles II, the Friends came into direct conflict with governmental authority, which considered the Friends' refusal to pay tithes as revolutionary in character and subversive to law. Neither government was sufficiently stable to look with favor upon any sects whose tenets forbade them to pay tithes or to take oaths in court.[56] By the Friends, swearing was considered unnecessary and also forbidden by Scripture. Ethically the Friends had been instructed that in family, trade, and social affairs their Aye should be Aye, and their Nay, Nay.[57] In addition they maintained that oaths were expressly forbidden by Christ in his Sermon on the Mount.

A practical mysticism pervades the controversial and personal writings of the Friends. Though the literature records manifestations of psychopathic states,[58] visions,[59] prophetic warnings,[60] divine healings,[61] and whole assemblies shaken by a power which they likened to Pentecost,[62] they seem not to have sought these excitable or rapt states for the experience itself. Their mysticism expressed itself in seeking for spiritual guidance in matters that concerned their personal contact with men and women both within[63] and without the group,[64] and with law and government.[65] In practice it permeated thought and activity, and for that reason it became the ground work of Quaker controversies, verse, and confessional literature.

The combined work of Quaker preachers and writers, however, would have failed in its power to sweep thousands of people from other religious persuasions into the Quaker way of life, had not the simplicity of the inner Light in the midst of the current unrest of the day satisfied the religious questioning of many English men and women. Like Mahatma Gandhi today, George Fox and the earliest Friends felt that they were vitalized by the firm belief that the source of their teaching was derived directly from infinite Power. Adoption of the inner Light promised the worshiper freedom from current distrust of dogma and ritual, the ability to be at peace with "the seen and the unseen world," and gave him a sense of mystic relationship with God.

CHAPTER IV

CONTROVERSY

1

As progressives of the seventeenth century the Friends rebelled against the conservatism and fundamentalism of currently held religious views. It is worthy to note that in its own theological thinking the Religious Society of Friends has had to make fewer adjustments to the inroads of so-called modern higher criticism than have other protestant denominations. In the 1650's, however, its pronouncedly startling views on the sacraments, and the inspiration of the Scriptures, brought the Friends into open conflict with Calvinistic Presbyterians and Baptists.

Presbyterian and Independent ministers, aroused by views which they deemed radical and heretical, inveighed against the Friends from the pulpit, denounced their principles, and invoked laws against them; furthermore they utilized the press to assail the unconventionality and fanaticism of the Quaker preachers. In addition they made it unmistakably clear that they objected not only to Quaker doctrines but to their methods of attracting public attention. They objected particularly to several Quaker leaders who denounced them as ministers of Antichrist, called their teachings heathenish, and publicly berated them for preaching for hire.

The intense convictions of both groups of these journalistic pamphleteers can scarcely be realized today when tolerance, approaching unthinking indifference, prevails everywhere. Some of these articles provoked as many as six replies and counter replies. An alliterative title such as *The Boasting Baptist Dismounted and the Beast Disarmed* with its counterblast of *The Quaker Quashed and his Quarrel Quelled* illustrates the bitterness that interpenetrated these warring polemics.[1] The "virulent controversy of the period," remarks Braithwaite, "was the mark of an age which was entering into the enjoyment of religious liberty. It was a great advance for polemic, however violent, to replace persecution."[2]

By 1653 the Friends, in their endeavors to make Christianity practical, had formulated their social and religious theories, and during the following seven years of the Protectorate the Quaker movement gained its first great momentum. The First Publishers, numbering twenty-five in 1652,[3] had increased in the northern counties alone to seventy in 1654,[4] and a little later to two hundred and thirty-one in the nation. Of these one hundred ninety-eight were men and thirty-three women.[5] These itinerant missionaries not only uttered their ideas in retired meetings for worship, in disputes "with professors of religion," and shouted them in the court room, but many of them developed into indefatigable journalists. Wherever they went they carried their quill pens and inkhorns, writing prolifically in wayside taverns, on shipboard, in prisons,[6] and oftentimes after returning to their occupations they wrote laboriously into the night after long hours spent in the harvest fields or in the shop. Even before the first generation of Friends had passed away, the members of the Society looked back upon the 1650's and the decade following as a time when the entire group, close to the fountainhead of an inspired leadership and of soul-stirring experiences, had been welded together into a close federation. After the death of George Fox in 1691 the new leaders, fully realizing that the Society had lost its early vigor, constantly referred to the primitive work of the organization as the "golden age of Quakerism."

2

Between 1650 and 1725 the literary aspirations of the Friends were necessarily affected by the problems which the first generation and their successors of the second faced. Especially before the Act of Indulgence of 1672 the necessity of forcing Quaker beliefs upon the public in the face of undisguised hostility confronted the writers of the early period. From the first the strong bond of a vitalizing belief and the necessity of a unified stand against civic and ecclesiastical persecution welded the Friends into a solid group. They felt themselves under divine commission to demonstrate to an unbelieving world that they were preaching by word of mouth and through the press a gospel by which increasing thousands could live; that they could sustain a rapidly increasing membership without ritual, or sacraments, or a paid ministry; and that with only passive resistance they could endure and survive persecution. On this account the Quaker press became a strong bulwark in the altercations into which the First Publishers were plunged at the opening of Cromwell's rule as Protector.

The leaders of early Quakerism naturally became its literary exponents. Since controversy necessarily arises out of an immediate situation, it generally results in ephemeral or journalistic literature, and only on rare occasions does it reach the level of *belles lettres*. In a study of the literary life of the early Friends, controversy, at the very least, demands the space of a single chapter. This is true first of all because controversy gave Quaker authors a training in advocating both their own ideas and those of the group which they represented; and secondly, as nothing else can, it illuminates for readers of today the groundwork out of which the later controversial and the more literary Quaker endeavors evolved.

Prior to their conversion to Quakerism, several of the First Publishers of Truth had been exceptionally well trained at Oxford and Cambridge. Foremost among these stand Edward Burrough[7] and his close associate, Francis Howgill;[8] Thomas Taylor, pastor of the group of Seekers, who in a body joined forces with Fox in 1652;[9] and Samuel Fisher, who, according to an old Quaker record, "forsook his great benefice of several hundred pounds per annum for the Truth's sake."[10] Of these the last three were not only Oxford men but had served as pastors for Independent congregations. Still other ministerial acquisitions were Thomas Yarwood, John Wilkinson, William Bayly, and John Audland. Mr. E. E. Taylor in compiling a study, based on the early records of the First Publishers of Truth and first printed in 1911, discovered that "half of the first seventy may be described as being in good material position in life, as having a superior education, and as possessing wide influence in the districts in which they lived."[11] Fox, though practically an unlettered man himself, possessed remarkable executive capacity for enlisting in Quaker causes the services of men superior to himself in formal school training and in writing ability.[12]

3

Fox, in collaboration with Edward Burrough and others, compiled upwards of two hundred and fifty separate publications. Of these many were reprinted and translated into Dutch, French, and Latin. In 1831 they were collected into eight portly volumes and published in Philadelphia. *The Journal of George Fox* fills the first two volumes, *The Great Mistery of the Great Whore*, the third, and Fox's *Doctrinals* and *Epistles* complete the eight. Many pages in these collected *Works* today hold only the attention of the historian, interested in the development of the larger implications of dissent in England. Two of Fox's works which are notable for other points beside controversy, his curious *Battle-Door for Teachers and Professors to Learn Singular and Plural* and his *Journal*, regarded by Mrs. Burr as a very important study of self in English will be taken up for consideration in later chapters.[13]

The polemical writings of Fox partake of the vagaries and the virulency of the times, and also of the intense sincerity of the man; they contributed much toward setting the mould for contemporary and subsequent Quaker journalism. Fox's first important effort at putting the doctrine of the inner Light into a permanent form was entitled, *To All who would Know the Way to the Kingdom . . . A Direction to turn your Minds within where the Voice of God is to be heard, whom you Ignorantly Worship as afar off; and to wait upon Him for the True Wisdom.*[14] This was printed in 1653. In the same year he published *Saul's Errand to Damascus with his Packet of Letters from the High Priests against the Disciples of the Lord,*[15] at once a defence of the inner Light and a refutal of blasphemy charges which had been brought against him at the Lancashire sessions in 1653.

In the midst of a busy life spent in preaching and in journeying, Fox managed to keep specifically informed in respect to all the attacks made on the Society of Friends. In 1659, with the aid of the untiring and devoted Edward Burrough, Fox answered a hundred of the most important onslaughts brought against the Society by such prominent ministers as John Bunyan, Richard Baxter, and John Owen, Chancellor of Oxford. The long title, couched in apocalyptical language, suggests its content: *The Great Mistery of the Great Whore unfolded; and Antichrist's Kingdom Re-*

vealed unto Destruction, In Answer to many False Doctrines and Principles which Babylon's Merchants have traded with . . . sent forth from time to time, against the despised people of the Lord, called Quakers, who are the Seed of that woman who hath long fled into the Wilderness. In the eyes of Fox and Burrough the merchants of Babylon represented the present ministers of Antichrist who were both deceiving the people with a false gospel and criticizing the Quakers for bringing to their age the needed Truth of the inner Light. The long introduction, largely the work of Burrough, gives one of the most comprehensive expositions of Quakerism written before the Restoration. These answers of Fox and Burrough to a hundred contentious Presbyterian, Baptist, and other sectarian critics upheld with equal zeal the Quaker position on the ordinances, continuous revelation, and a religion based upon experience. Fox and Burrough employed the current method of first printing a query and following it with an appropriate reply; or of excerpting a quotation from an opposing tract, and in a paragraph or two proving the assertion, at least to their satisfaction, false, defamatory, or unjust.

For nearly forty years Fox kept a controlling hand upon the writings of the Friends, urging defenses, censoring manuscripts submitted to him, and dominating the spirit of the work. In 1689, two years prior to his death, he wrote a treatise in which he outlined for critics the Quaker mode of worship, beliefs, hopes, and plan of church government. He chose an opportune time for restating Quaker aims, for the efforts of James II from 1685 to 1688, to foster the interests of the Roman Catholics in England, had been thwarted by the arrival of William and Mary. At their accession both Anglicans and Dissenters felt an imperative need for reasserting the claims of their respective beliefs

—an opportunity which the astute George Fox seized in defending the Friends in his tract entitled *Concerning the Antiquity of the People of God Called Quakers.*

4

In Edward Burrough, a young man barely twenty years of age, George Fox found his first able assistant in replying to the criticism heaped upon the Friends. For allying himself with "the despised Quakers," among whom young Burrough confessed his soul discovered "full satisfaction, joy, and content," the boy was immediately disowned by his family. From 1652 until his death from a wasting prison fever in Newgate prison in 1662, Burrough, with unflagging enthusiasm preached and wrote for the new Quaker sect. A folio volume of nine hundred pages, entitled *The Memorable Works of a Son of Thunder and Consolation,* contains the extant writings of Edward Burrough. Though the author died in 1662, on account of the enforcement of the laws against seditious printing and the difficulty of securing the *imprimatur* of the licenser, the Friends considered it unsafe to publish Burrough's collected *Works* until 1672, the year in which Charles II issued the Act of Indulgence.

In spite of the fact that prolixity characterizes many of Burrough's tracts, a deep emotional tone pervades all of his epistles, his prophetic entreaties in which he besought England to repent, and his own religious confession, called strangely enough, *A Warning to Ye Inhabitants of Underbarrow.* On occasion Burrough bristles with puritanic rage. Nowhere does he show this emotional undercurrent better than in an explosive tract in which he expressed disapproval of the elaborate ceremonies accompanying Cromwell's interment in Westminister Abbey. On the morning of the funeral, as the young Quaker was attempting to cross the thoroughfare at Charing Cross, his horse was halted by officers who were keeping the street clear for the cortège of the Protector. The magnificance of the trappings and particularly the effigy of Cromwell borne in state toward Westminster filled the youth with anger. Upon his return to his lodging he poured forth his feelings in *A Testimony Against a Great Idolatry*. In this he lamented in prophetic language the fact that the people of England were turning from the one God who could be found within the heart to gods similar to Baal.

Perhaps the most famous of Burrough's opponents was John Bunyan, whose first book vigorously attacked the Quaker view of the inner Light. Bunyan, then twenty-eight years old, and a deacon and preacher of a group of Baptists at Bedford, published in 1656 a tract entitled *Some Gospel Truths Opened . . . and also Answers . . . against those blustering Storms of the Devil's Temptation which do at this Day, like so many Scorpions, break loose from the Bottomless Pit.* Burrough lost no time in replying with *The True Faith of the Gospel of Peace Contended for, in the Spirit of Meekness . . . Vindicated in the Spirit of Love against the Secret Opposition of John Bunyan, a professed Minister in Bedfordshire.* Bunyan in his turn wrote a retaliatory vindication to which Burrough again contributed a rejoinder in 1657 with *Truth . . . Witnessed forth in the Spirit of Truth against all Deceit.* The long title drastically continues to condemn Bunyan as "one of God's Army" yet the perpetrator of "above a 100 foul dirty lyes and slanders." Burrough's style varies from the plainest of unvarnished prose to vigorous invective, and to an occasional passage of highly emotional power, especially when he was "moved" to write of his mystical experiences with the inner Light.

5

In 1653 James Nayler, a man of great personal charm and a brilliant preacher, met with unusual success in London, a success scarcely equalled by the founder of Quakerism. In his ability to handle written language Nayler far excelled Fox. James Nayler, "the reproach and the glory" of early Quakerism, however, permitted his belief in inward revelation to carry him to excesses more characteristic of the Ranters than of the Quakers. His "fall" at Bristol in October 1656, attracted wide attention and brought the Friends into great disrepute. Accompanied by a group of women, chanting, "Holy, holy, holy, Lord God of Sabaoth," Nayler, in a moment of ecstatic fervor, allowed himself to be led into Bristol on horseback in imitation of Christ's triumphal entry into Jerusalem. For thus assuming identity with God Nayler was charged with blasphemy and after a spectacular trial before Parliament, he was sentenced to the pillory by that body, and further punished by having his tongue bored with a red hot iron, by being branded with the letter B, and by being whipped through the streets of London before he was consigned to Newgate.[16] After his imprisonment and retraction up to the time of his death in 1660, he continued both in preaching and writing to exemplify the basic spirituality of the Quaker way of life. Without doubt Nayler's "fall" ultimately produced good results in checking unrestrained enthusiasm and fanaticism among the early followers of Fox.

Nayler's writings are singularly free from the rancour which characterizes the Quaker and non-Quaker polemics of the day—much freer in this respect than the writings of either Fox or Burrough. In a personal manner, Nayler frequently refers to his own spiritual states. His collected *Works*, published in 1716, give ample evidence of a close familiarity with the rhythms, repetitions, and phrasings of the Old and New Testament.[17] Nayler's *How Sin is Strengthened*, a summary of Quaker beliefs, was frequently reprinted and given wide circulation during the seventeenth century. His ideas blending together into sermonized meditations are generally put into essay form. The simplicity of his diction and the depth of his spirituality are revealed in the following passage, where he quietly endeavors to explain the efforts of the Friends to bring apostolic Christianity to seventeenth-century England:

Indeed we read in the Scriptures of Truth of the Gospel Preaching, but it was not limited to one House, nor by an [hour] Glass, but from House to House, City to City, and that by the Spirit, and their [the apostles'] Worship was in Spirit; they prayed with the Spirit, and they sung with the Spirit, and he that had a Psalm sung it with the Spirit, and with Understanding also; and they worshipped and preached in Fields and Mountains and Streets, and Schools, and Markets, and they prayed by Seashores, or in any Place where God moved and led them by the Spirit of Jesus: And all this we [the Quakers of this day] own, which the Scriptures testifie to. And this is it that we would have all brought to tryal, and that worship owned which Christ and the Scriptures own, and none forced against it, by any means whatsoever, which are come up since the Scriptures were written, and the Apostles Times.[18]

The name of Francis Howgill figures conspicuously in early Quaker annals. Like George Fox in his youth, he had questioned many "professors of religion" and after considerable training at Oxford had united with two distinct sects before he was "reached" and "convinced" by Fox's preaching in 1652. Travelling often in company with his close friend Edward Burrough, he became one of the foremost early Publishers. On account of his education, his former training as an Independent minister, his ready skill in handling the pen, and his unfailing devotion to Fox and his principles, he was a valuable asset in forwarding Quaker interests. His spiritual distress and his prolonged search for a satisfying form of religion are portrayed in his autobiographical account, *The Inheritance of Jacob Discovered after his Return out of Aegypt,* a full account of which will be taken up in the chapter on Quaker confessional literature.[19] Sincerely spiritual by nature, he took little delight in reviling his opponents with strong names but preferred to present in language of mystic nature the advantages of the inner Light over prevailing forms of worship, and to point out the necessity for all religious people to take up the cross of Christ. Between 1653 and 1668 Howgill wrote upwards of fifty tracts. Some of these were collected and published in 1676 in a small and now rare folio volume which fittingly bore the title of *The Dawnings of the Gospel Day and its Light and Glory Discovered.*

6

Quiet in contrast with the writings of Nayler and Howgill stands the more pugnacious work of Samuel Fisher, Master of Arts from Oxford in 1630. Before casting in his lot with George Fox and his Publishers in 1655,[20] he had been in succession an Anglican rector, a puritan lecturer, and a Baptist minister. During the decade preceding his death from the plague in 1665, Fisher wrote constantly in behalf of the Friends. His complete *Works,* the *Testimony to the Truth Exalted,* fill a large folio volume. The most important of these, *Rusticus ad Academicos,* covers seven hundred fifty of these pages.

This treatise, caustic in its casuistry, represented the defiant answer of Samuel Fisher to a group of polemicists whom, not without a touch of insolence, he addressed as the "Four Foremen of the whole Fraternity of Fiery Fighters against the true Light of Christ and his Children." These "foremen" were John Owen, Dean of Christ's College, Oxford, Thomas Danson, minister of Sandwich in Kent, John

Tombes of Leominster, and Richard Baxter but recently of Kidderminster. This diatribe with its long title of nearly two hundred and fifty words, beginning, *Rusticus ad Academicos ... the Rustic's Alarm to the Rabbies or the Country Correcting the University and Clergy*, and closing with the words *By Samuel Fisher, who sometimes went Astray, as a lost Sheep among the many Shepheards, but is now returned to the Great Shepheard, and Overseer of the Souls*, dealt with one of the great points of contention maintained not only by the Friends but by many contemporaneous sects. Fisher in his defence of Quaker views asserted that the Friends or rustics were able through the intimate guidance of the inner Word to confute the rabbis, the learned, university and divinity-schooled adversaries of the Quakers. This book, according to a modern historian, shares the faults of an "age entering into the enjoyments of religious liberty" which "made headway not by persecution but by polemic."[21]

Fisher interlarded his arguments with quotations from the Bible, the classics, and the church fathers, and in mid-seventeenth century fashion made ample use of marginal notes. He followed the enumerative method of reprinting opposing statements verbatim and fitting to each its respective reply. Through fantastic metaphors and excessive alliteration, he drove his points home with sarcasm and on some occasions with personal invective. In attempting to justify the more liberal attitude of the Friends toward the inspiration of the Scriptures as opposed to the verbal plea urged by the Calvinists, Fisher became a seventeenth-century higher critic. He thus attacked the "Four Foremen of the Whole Fraternity of Fiery Fighters" and the thousands whom they represented:

And because we [the Friends] do not with the misty ministers of the meer letter . . . own the bare External Text of Scriptures (which they themselves [the schoolmen] confess to be corrupted, vitiated, altered and adulterated in all Translations) entire in every Tittle, Letter, Vowel, Syllable, and Jota . . . but say it suffered much more than Vowels . . . yea even of whole Epistles and Prophesies of inspired Men . . . ; especially because we own not the said alterable and much altered Text and letter, but [own] the Holy Truth and inward Light and Spirit . . . to be the Word of God, which is the Living Foundation of all Saving Faith . . . therefore they [the Calvinists] cry out against us as siders with the Jews, Papists, Atheists, and all Scripture Haters. . . . Yet the Scriptures are owned by us in their true place . . . the letter acknowledged by us to have been written by Men moved by God's spirit and to be useful, profitable, serviceable, etc., to be read and heeded.[22]

A more exhaustive treatment of the early Quaker controversialists would include a survey of the tracts of Richard Farnsworth; of Richard Hubberthorn, "slow of speech yet of great reliability and sound judgment," at one time a preacher in Cromwell's army; of William Dewsbury, worthy the name of "Quaker saint," who for "conscience' sake," spent twenty years in English prisons; and the writings of the boy martyr, James Parnell, who died of neglect and abuse in Colchester Castle in 1656. One name, however, cannot be omitted, that of Isaac Penington, who came into fellowship with the Friends in mature life. Well educated, scholarly by nature, and trained in surroundings of culture, he added a distinctive note to early Quaker writings. After his "conviction" to belief in the inner Light, he devoted his life to the interpretation of Quakerism particularly its mystical phases. His treatises, collected in 1681 and published as *The Works of the Long Mournful and Sorely Distressed Isaac Penington,* contain many purple patches of rare beauty.

7

In contradistinction to the early pioneers, the second generation, in part made up of descendants of Friends, in part of converts or "convinced Friends," faced new conditions within and without the Society. By the time of George Fox's death in 1691 the name Quaker, instead of standing as a term of opprobrium, had gained respectability. The Quaker's integrity in business, his Aye signifying Aye and his Nay, Nay, his plain dress, his simple house furnishings, and his few amusements were all conducive to thrift. As the Friends increased in wealth, and as they grew more conservative, the badge of Quakerism—plain speech, the foregoing of oaths, salutations, titles, and "hat honor"—ceased to set the Friends as sharply at variance from other dissenting bodies as it had formerly done.

This changing attitude was fraught with subtle dangers for the Society. To offset these, the leaders sought new means for consciously maintaining the integrity of the group, which had hitherto been almost spontaneously synthesized. To accomplish this end they turned their literary efforts definitely and deliberately into sectarian channels. With clarity they saw that even though the Friends had gained concessions through the Act of Toleration, and no longer feared that their meetings would be broken up and the attendants carried off to prison, yet in these very concessions they perceived that they faced new and grave dangers. Two of the ties, which in earlier days had cemented the Society into a close federation, were weakened. Formerly the convert to Quakerism had been forced to "renounce the world." Now he had less to forego when he met with little or no resistance from "the world's people," and therefore he felt less instigation to fight for the people of his adoption and for their tenets. In the next place with the ceasing of persecution a second bond weakened. It was no longer necessary for the Friends to support by voluntary contributions the families of wage earners, imprisoned for conscience' sake, or to offer to lie "body for body" for sick or dying prisoners. The leaders saw that the previous ties of sympathy, of

sacrifice, and of measures for common defense against persecution were weakening rather than strengthening after
1689.

The new writers, since they sensed more clearly than
their predecessors what Quaker literature had accomplished
and the ends it could serve, began to adapt their literature
to the developing needs of the Society. They desired to free
the Society, so far as they were able, from previous charges
brought against it—charges of enthusiasm, prophetism, and
fanaticism. With growing consciousness they strove to find
means for uniting outlying meetings with the London Yearly
Meeting, to educate youthful Friends in the history and
beliefs of the Friends, and in every way to deepen the sectarian interests of the Quaker group. Controversy, of course,
continued, for the Act of Toleration, while it granted greater
freedom of worship and of the press, had not released the
Friends from taking oaths in court. In addition, strong trini-
tarians and churchmen still looked askance at the heretical
emphasis which the Friends placed upon the guidance of the
Spirit, and disregard of the sacraments. The energy of the
first generation was spent upon controversy and upon religious confessions. Later chapters of this book will consider
in detail the more literary forms of history, essay, verse,
and autobiography in which the second generation of Friends
engaged.

Controversy did not cease with the Act of Toleration. The
newer leaders, William Penn, Thomas Ellwood, and the
veteran George Whitehead, whose lifetime extended over
both periods, continued to answer every criticism directed
against the Friends. The former violence, as well as the allegorical and scriptural titles, tended to disappear, but even
these died slowly. In the minds of contestants, pamphlets
still needed replies, and additional replies fitted to these. In
1696 an Irish non-juring clergyman, Charles Leslie, sum-

marized the literature hostile to the Quakers in *The Snake in the Grass*. George Whitehead responded to this in the following year with *An Antidote Against the Venom of the Snake in the Grass*, a tract designed to refute the "gross abuses and calumnies" of Charles Leslie and to "detect the author's malice and persecutions" against the Quakers. In the last year of the century, when a third edition of *The Snake in the Grass* was published, Joseph Wyeth issued his *Anguis Flagellatus:* or, *A Switch for the Snake*, to clear up, as he said, "the misrepresentations and perversions" of the Truth "doctrinely delivered" by the Friends. Old moot questions persisted. Thomas Ellwood, John Gratton, and William Penn discussed at length the Quaker attitude on tithing, on the ordinances, and upon intuitional guidance. Whereas the earliest criticisms against the Friends had been launched largely by the Presbyterians, Baptists and other sects, for the most part those at the close of the century were produced by Anglican churchmen.

The most scholarly presentation of Quaker principles came from the pen of Robert Barclay, a young Scotchman of gentle birth, educated in the schools of Aberdeen and the Scots Theological School of Paris.[23] He purposed in *The Apology for the True Christian Divinity* to present Quaker principles in contrast to the theology of Rome and of Geneva, in both of which he had been thoroughly trained, particularly in the latter. Dr. Rufus M. Jones regrets that Barclay's training had not aligned him with the thought of the early spiritual reformers on the Continent and of the Cambridge Platonists. With both of these groups Robert Barclay had innate sympathy.[24] Since the *Apology* answered proposition by proposition the Westminister Confession and the Shorter Catechism,[25] it became a useful handbook for the itinerant "public" Friends traveling in the three kingdoms and the American colonies, who frequently had to meet the theological arguments of their better trained opponents. Voltaire after reading Barclay's *Apology* said that it was as good a book as that kind of book could be.[26] Not all of the reasoning of the First Publishers of Truth was sound, and in the first dynamic energy that came from adventuring in new realms of experience and thought, the Quakers undervalued authority and learning, which they termed "outward helps,"[27] or as Braithwaite has written, they failed to recognize that "the intellect is rather a province of man's spiritual nature than something that stands apart from it."[28]

No treatise of Quakerism has had the influence which Barclay's *Apology for the True Christian Divinity* exerted upon the subsequent policies of the Society of Friends. Written first in Latin and published in Amsterdam in 1678, it was "Englished" and printed in London two years later, where it passed through five editions before 1703. Besides these before 1710 it was twice printed in Latin, twice in Dutch, once in French, twice in Spanish, and part of it in Arabic.

His main plea is that religion cannot be based upon dogmatic theology but must come directly from God to the human heart, and that God's spiritual power is able to transform human nature. Barclay goes minutely into all phases of Quaker thought and activities from a discussion of the inner Light, which he calls a *vehiculum dei,* to the Quaker prejudice against the reading of romances and theatre attendance. Barclay's style is clear, free from lengthy theological terms, and also free from any studied attempt at felicity of phrasing. It is the clearest exposition of Quakerism that was written for nearly two hundred and fifty years, and has only been superseded by the comparatively recent work of W. C. Braithwaite, A. Neave Brayshaw, T. Edmund Harvey, and Rufus M. Jones.

CHAPTER V

THE LITERARY PRINCIPLES

1

A marked homogeneity of content and style characterized early Quaker literature. The first generation of Friends, with little consciousness that it was producing a prose style, turned spontaneously to the press, and adapted to its needs several guiding principles which the second generation later recognized as *loci critici* for Quaker writings.

In securing an understanding of the Quaker mind lying back of these literary endeavors, three of these previsions assume large importance. The first two deal directly with style. In the first place the Friends scrupulously avoided a display of learning, and in the second rigorously excluded from their pages all types of ornamental phrasing and diction. The third principle cannot be stated so concisely as the other two, yet it lies at the very heart of the Quakers' faith in the press, for in literature as in religion and life, the Friends desired to penetrate or "to reach" the spiritual basis of man's nature. In their eagerness to exalt intuitional Guidance, they minimized the power of the intellect, holding it to be a snare rather than a guide to right action. They, therefore, sought through appeals of emotional and spiritual nature to acquaint readers with the inner peace which they themselves had attained. Each one of these critical opinions can be traced back to puritanical and mystical origins inherent in primitive Quakerism. By the close of the seventeenth century these literary principles had become so ingrained that readers of Friends' books were warned not to expect a display of learning, an ornamental style, or food for the intellect alone.

In 1703, just fifty years after the publication of the first Quaker tracts, these three cautions or negative aims just enumerated were clearly defined by William Penn. For some months during 1703 the Second Day Morning Meeting, the official board for reviewing and censoring Quaker publications, had been occupied in collecting and editing the scattered tracts of John Whitehead, an early Publisher of Truth. As this committee neared the completion of its task, William Penn was requested to prepare a title and preface for these works.[1] Later the Meeting gave formal approval to the name submitted, *The Written Gospel Labours of John Whitehead*.

As usual in such prefatory "Notes to the Reader," Penn seized the opportunity of restating the religious and ethical aims of the Society; but with a touch of originality and insight he also included a survey of the literary aims of the Friends during the preceding half century, a task which no Quaker before him had attempted. In this chapter the critical pronouncements of William Penn and his comments upon them will be used as a basis for examining the literary principles which Quaker writers, with varying degrees of consciousness, employed during their first five decades. In addition, other corroborating testimony, bearing on the critical and literary aims of early Quakerism will be drawn from the writings of contemporary Friends.

Most biographers of Penn, in stressing his life as courtier, promotor of the "holy experiment in Pennsylvania," and man of religion, have touched very lightly upon his literary life, particularly his acumen in observing the trends and purposes in the literature of the Quaker group. In 1703 William Penn, in preparing this particular "Preface to the

Reader," was performing, as the minutes of the Second Day Morning Meeting indicate,[2] a service often required of members belonging to this board of censorship. No other preface of this period, designed for Quaker books, excels this one in its pointedness in clinching the literary principles which the Friends employed. No other Friend probably had so clear a conception of the psychological connection, existing between reader and writer, as William Penn; and no other Friend of his time, on account of the advantages he had received in his home, at Oxford, on the Continent, and at court, probably understood so well as he the demands of the London reading public.[3]

2

The significance of William Penn's preface, combining as it does a presentation of the ethical with the critical purposes of his associates, might equally as well have been applied to numerous other collected works. The Friends would have seen little humor in the quip with which Suckling satirized Ben Johnson in the *Session of Poets:*

And he told them plainly that he deserved the bays,
For his were called Works, the others' but Plays.

Works to the early Friends were serious productions, useful for spreading Quaker propaganda and for preserving their otherwise ephemeral tracts. The first collected *Works* of the Friends were those of George Fox the younger,[4] and of Richard Hubberthorn, both in small quartos, and published respectively in 1662 and 1663. Braithwaite says that "the practice of posthumous recognition may be said to have become established with the ample folios that enshrined the memory of Burrough in 1672, William Smith three years later, Howgill in '76, Fisher in '79, and Penington in 1681. The freshness of the titles often conceals the heavy traveling that awaits the patient reader. William Smith exudes *Balm from Gilead,* Howgill's works are *The Dawning of the Gospel Day;* Richard Samble of Cornwall is preserved to posterity in *A Handful after the Harvest Man* (1684), and Robert Barclay in *Truth Triumphant* (1692)."[5]

In this preface Penn had in mind two classes of readers, the Quaker and the non-Quaker, but for the most part his remarks are addressed to the latter. He reiterates the purposes expressed in many "notes to readers" of Quaker books —the belief that present and unborn generations might profit by the reading of the "gospel labours" of an early Publisher of Truth, and that every fragment which related to the making of Quaker history was important. Penn desired also that the life and works of John Whitehead should go down to posterity as "one of the first experimental witnesses" to the "Day Spring from on high,"—the visitation of the inner Light that had come to "so many thousands" of Friends "in this Northern Island."[6]

In the preparation of this preface Penn was speaking not only for the Morning Meeting, but indirectly for the London Yearly Meeting which had authorized the board of censorship, and hence for the entire membership. He accordingly reënforced his words by adding, "We the Friends all give one and the same testimony." He felt it necessary "to warn and caution" the non-Quaker reader lest "after perusing the book," he "might be ignorantly displeased or under any unreasonable disappointment." To aid the well-disposed or "friendly reader," who was not familiar with Quaker tracts, Penn painstakingly explained that such a person could not expect to find in the ensuing pages the satisfaction that comes from acquiring knowledge, or from sensory appeals addressed to ear or eye, or from purely intellectual stimulation.

Since this collection of John Whitehead's tracts is representative of numerous Quaker "collected works," it becomes important to examine in some detail the contents of the volume. After a cursory survey of this kind Penn's critical opinions may be enlarged upon and applied to Quaker literature in general. John Whitehead[7] (1621-1696), Penn took pains to note, had once been a Cromwellian soldier, who had been "reached" or "convinced" in prison at Scarborough as early as 1652 by William Dewsbury.[8] Unlike Fox and Nayler, few spectacular details are attached to his life. For over forty years Whitehead pursued the work of the unremunerated Quaker minister,[9] devoting most of his traveling days to Lincolnshire and neighboring territory until, as a testimony[10] preliminary to his works, relates, he "went to his grave in a Good old Age like a Shock of Corn in its Season."

3

John Whitehead's series of tracts, which found their way to the Morning Meeting in the autumn of 1703 were, as just noted, typical of scores of doctrinal and confessional writings of the Friends. In print the next year they were to fill more than three hundred quarto pages. John Whitehead, in defending Quaker "Truth," confined himself to three types of writing: epistolary, controversial, and confessional. His letters were couched in the phraseology of the New Testament epistles, and superabounded in admonitions and in encouraging words for the "tribulated flock."[11] Like their biblical prototypes, they were almost devoid of references to persons and to secular events. They resembled, furthermore, their models on account of their liberal sprinkling of marginal cross references to biblical texts. These letters he had addressed to magistrates and justices, to individuals, or on occasion endorsed them "to be read in meetings" for worship "among Friends when they are gathered to wait upon God."

A second group of tracts representing his controversial works were presented with a singular lack of rancour; in subject matter they touched on practically all the questions that aroused the ire of the Calvinists—the inner Light, the ordinances, and scriptural interpretations. A few lines, quoted from his initial statement on the separate title page of *A Manifestation of Truth,* the most important treatise included in the volume, indicate his personal and pacific attitude toward his opponents and toward controversy in general:

Writ in answer to a Book which a nameless Author has written against the Quakers . . . by John Whitehead, who hath no pleasure in stirring up Strife and Contention about things in Nature [affairs of the world]; and therefore [the author] hath laboured rather to manifest the Truth to the unbiased reader than particularly to Traduce his Adversary, desiring it [his *Manifestation of Truth*] may be instrumental to remove from them all Prejudice, that they may receive the Naked Truth, which is Christ Jesus.

The third part of his collected works treated of personal affairs in a very impersonal manner, for he consistently subordinated his own interests to those of the Quaker group. For instance, in one tract he gave a lengthy account of his trial in the summer of 1682 at the assizes in Lincoln for his refusal to take the Oath of Allegiance;[12] in a second, he employed his own "call to preach" as a point of departure for a discussion of worship and the work of the ministry;[13] and in a third, the most readable from a modern standpoint, he presented his spiritual autobiography under the title of *The Enmity between the Two Seeds.* The hostile seeds in the metaphorical appellation signify the tempting serpent of the world at odds with the inner Seed, the "spark within the clod," capable of spiritual growth. In this confession he presented with many graphic details his dissatisfaction with his early puritanical training. Looking retrospectively at this period of his youth he wrote, "I was tossed from Mountain to Hill" and found "no true rest for my soul." This state of distress lasted until he came under the teachings of William Dewsbury. Though the collected works of the Friends contain numerous religious confessions dealing with a storm and stress period, few members of the Society have painted as vividly as he the successive steps by which the Quaker convert passed from a period of religious excitement to one of mental peace.

Representative, furthermore, of both the collected works and the autobiographies of the Friends were the testimonies that preceded the writings of this early itinerant minister. In this case they numbered six. The testimony, one manifestation of the Quaker passion for records, had various uses. It could preserve biographical data, preach a sermon, serve as an obituary notice, pay tribute to "departed worth," or preface a volume. A few idiomatic Quaker expressions, drawn from these testimonies, will not only present aspects of John Whitehead's personality, but will also help to explain Penn's insistence that readers must not hope to secure merely intellectual satisfaction from the reading of this book. Thomas Thompson testified that John Whitehead was "weighty and profound in Declaration, not desiring to raise Sounds [i.e. vain and empty words] in Meeting, but to keep to the seasoned Life of Righteousness"; the Monthly Meeting at Thealby in Lincoln wrote that in his association with them he had been "a nursing father, tender and affectionate, apt to teach . . . and qualified to speak a Word in Season to every State and Condition"; and David Crosbie declared that Whitehead was "a man of such meek and quiet spirit that his life and conversation preached daily amongst whom he came."

4

Such in brief were the works and such was the man whom Penn and the Morning Meeting wished to introduce to the reading and book-buying public of 1704. Penn felt that a mystical synthesis underlay his three cautions, that the reader must not expect "the learning of the schoolmen," a display of rhetoric, or intellectual food; in other words he wanted to convey the idea that the Friends wrote with the vision "of a higher wisdom" in mind, which could only be perceived by "the spiritual senses" or faculties of the reader. His first caution in full was this:

First, then, the reader is not to expect the Learning of the Schools, unless it be of the Prophets, and of the Enlightened and Spiritual Generation of Men; and of plain, sound and practical knowledge to be felt by those that are in any measure restored to the Exercises of the Spiritual Senses . . . and then he [the reader] will not be disappointed in the perusal of the following book.

In this passage, Penn thus differentiated between two methods of obtaining knowledge, the one intellectual and the second emotional. Here Penn implied, in the first place, that the reader must not expect the type of learning in which he himself had been trained—neither *The Anatomy of Melancholy* for example, annotated with quotations from Latin and Greek writers, *The Histrio-Mastix* of Prynne, marginated with notes and with notes upon these, nor the intellectual philosophy of John Locke, nor even the scientific prose of the Royal Society to which Penn was a contributing member.[14] All such manifestations of learning the reader of a Quaker book must expect to find conspicuously absent.

In Penn's estimation a substitute of higher value could be

obtained by a thoughtful reader, that is, the learning "of the Prophets, and of the Enlightened and Spiritual Generation of Men; and of plain, sound, and practical knowledge, to be felt by those . . . [who] are restored to the Exercise of their Spiritual Senses." Penn, it is known, valued highly the knowledge that came from the classics, history, and philosophy "in their own place" as he expressed it;[15] but he felt that wisdom could be gained through reliance upon inward revelation—a knowledge that would lead to truth of conduct in life. He would have scouted "as an airy notion" or as a flagrant example of "this world's learning," the theories on which later behaviourists have worked and which were beginning to be promulgated even in his time, that ideas come from the world without and that the senses are more powerful teachers than instincts and intuitions.[16]

To differentiate between these two methods of acquiring wisdom, Penn cited the case of Moses as a specific illustration. Moses, as Penn explained, though educated in the highest intellectual circles of Egypt, could never have led the children of Israel into the promised land with the knowledge contained in the papyrus rolls of the Pharaohs, but only through spiritual communion with God. Only thus had the Hebrew prophets acquired knowledge. Dr. Rufus M. Jones has defined a prophet as "a person who is profoundedly conscious that he is a divinely selected herald, that he speaks *for* God, and is under commission to utter the will and purpose of God to his age."[17] In this sense the guiding power which made Moses the leader of the children of Israel was considered "prophetical" by Penn. As the Quaker viewed it, the "learning of the prophets" was "the movement of the spirit," the divine afflatus, poured forth upon willing instruments during the work time of the day, in retired periods of meditation, in Quaker meetings for worship, especially upon such preachers and writers as John Whitehead.

Penn furthermore insisted that knowledge gained through communion with God might be "plain, sound, and practical" when felt by those who "were restored to the Exercise" of their "spiritual senses." In essence, Penn was merely saying that the Friends desired to stress in their writings their practical mysticism rather than to please the intellect with out-of-the-way or intricate learning. This intimate knowledge, once grasped "by the spiritual senses" and obeyed, could lead the believer, in this case the reader, "into all truth requisite for men to know." References to history, philosophy, even current events, are, comparatively speaking, rare in the books of Friends before 1725, and even for a century after that. If used at all they were employed for a specific purpose— to clarify an idea or to make a special point. The reader of Quaker literature, Penn kept insisting, must, therefore, recognize the fact that Quaker books had been prepared by men who relied upon spiritual truths for inspiration, and not upon the learning of the world.

5

To some degree at least, Penn was conscious that the tone of Quaker literature was dominated by the desire for subordinating all other interests to that of extolling spiritual truths and values. Four decades earlier in 1660, Samuel Fisher had written vigorously against the type of divinity training to which he had been subjected in his youth at Oxford, at the time that Laud was urging his visitations and his "beauty of holiness." Fisher accused the "learned linguists and academical scholastic rabbis" of "scrawling and scribbling against each other about their Hebrew and Greek texts" and yet failing to penetrate to the underlying spiritual truths of the Scriptures.[18]

Using "the freedom of the prophet Elijah against the

prophets of Baal,"[19] Fisher had assailed the antiquarian researches and quibblings of the university men with their
useless impediments of learning, and extolled the Friends,
"The Children of the Light," who, because of the Light
within were rendered capable of directing the rabbis, as he
says,

not from, but to, and by, and altogether with the letter of the
Scripture, to the Light of Him in the Heart, which the letter
came in by, who is the only Light that leads thoroughly to the
Life; even His own Life, and to Himself, who is the Truth,
Way, Door, Light, and Life . . . who alone hath the Words of
eternal Life.[20]

Since the Friends felt that "the learning of the schools"
with its accompanying divinity training, brought confusion
into biblical interpretation, they feared its influences else-
where, and avoided scholarly references which seemed unnecessary and uncalled for by the text in hand.

Robert Barclay was fully as trenchant as Fisher in denouncing "the learning of the schools" whenever it conflicted with the wisdom that came from spiritual understanding. Immediately following the dedication of his *Apology for
the True Christian Divinity* to King Charles II stands an
epistle addressed "To the Friendly Reader" and written by
the author in 1675. In this letter Robert Barclay not only
stated his contempt for those who held human knowledge
superior to that derived from divine sources, but stoutly declared himself to be an "opposer and despiser" of the university trained scholars.

For as much as that, which above all things I propose to myself, is to Declare and Defend the Truth; . . . Perhaps my
method of Writing may not only seem different, but even contrary to that, which is commonly used by the Men, called Divines; for that, I confess myself to be not only no Imitator and
Admirer of the Schoolmen, but an Opposer and Despiser of them

as such; by whom I judge the Christian Religion to be far from being bettered, that it is rather destroyed.

With even greater scorn he criticized those who depended upon "outward helps," such as reliance in preaching or writing, upon the rules of grammar, rhetoric, or oratory. In writing his *Apology for the True Christian Divinity*, he moreover gloried because he was acting neither the part of the grammarian nor of the orator, but that "of the Christian" who drew his inspiration more from "his heart" than from "his head," and who deliberately chose not "to feed the wisdom . . . or vain pride" of this world but "to starve and oppose it." He wrote:

Neither have I tried to accommodate this my work to Itching Ears, who desire rather to comprehend in their Heads the sublime Notions of Truth than to embrace it in their hearts; for what I have written comes more from my heart than from my head. . . . I act not here the Grammarian or the Orator but the Christian. . . . And to make an end, what I have written, is written, not to feed the Wisdom and Knowledge, or rather vain pride of this world, but to starve and oppose it.[21]

6

Elaborate imagery and flowing diction, Penn, with his knowledge of contemporary and classical literature, knew to be almost entirely lacking in Quaker literature. He, therefore, worded his second caution to English readers thus:

Neither, Secondly, hath this Godly Author labour'd a nice or polished Stile, which men usually do, to give a Lustre to, or Varnish their Matter with, but writes as an Enlightened and Experienced Man. It being the way of God to reveal . . . his Dispensations not after the oldness of the letter but after the newness of the spirit by [men] so qualified, that they know what they teach and whereof they affirm; who do not witness by Reports only or at Second Hand, but such as have seen, tasted, felt, and handled the same Powerful Word of God, which they declare unto others. . . .

This second caution of Penn's was based on a principle similar in its origin to the assertion that the reader must not expect the learning of the schools. John Whitehead, to repeat a few words of Penn, did not write "a nice or polished Stile . . . to give a Lustre to, or Varnish" to his work, but wrote "as an Enlightened and Experienced Man." It must not be forgotten that Penn had learned to read when literary English was still influenced by the conceits of Donne, the rolling Latin periods of Milton, and the mellifluous prose-poetry of Jeremy Taylor.

In addition to his classical education Penn knew and admired the prose of Bacon, Herbert of Cherbury, Cowley,[22] Boyle, and the Cambridge Platonists. All of these authors, with many other authorities on theology, history, and science, he gladly recommended for study to his young friend, Sir John Rodes.[23] Penn in his lifetime had witnessed the changes in English literature from the euphuism of Thomas Fuller to the direct statements of Dryden, Defoe, and Swift. He knew the plainness of the Quaker's language and he wanted his readers not only to recognize but to understand the reasons why the Friends consciously avoided adornment. In as much as the Friends had abjured ornamentation in their meeting houses because they feared that anything sensuous might intervene between themselves and God, so they transferred this attitude to other affairs of life[24]—to dress, speech, and to their manner of writing.

The primitive Friends had come into contact with much of the aversion to superfluous adornment in the current puritanism of the Commonwealth. In their avoidance of ornateness of style, they not infrequently expressed a fear of using "over many words." "Overmuch speaking," or the practice of "outrunning the Spirit" in meetings for worship, was a practice much guarded against from the earliest days of the Society. John Crook, in an epistle addressed to

Friends, repainted for them the pioneer days when a common stream of religious experience had awakened them to group consciousness and to mutual support under persecution. In this letter he drew attention to the fear of the primitive Friends lest they give way to the temptation of "speaking out of season" with meaningless and "empty words." He wrote:

O what Carefulness, What Watchfulness, What circumspection, What awfulness of God . . . was upon our Spirits, lest we should speak our own Words, work our own Works, walk in our own ways, or think our own Thoughts! So diligently did we keep watching over our own Hearts . . . which caused us to learn to Bridle our Tongues, that our Words might be few and savoury, ministering grace to our hearers.[25]

Unfortunately the desire for "words weighted with power" did not effect an economy of words in writing. In this respect the Friends sinned with their contemporaries in religious controversy. The fear of "over many words" did result, however, in a conscious avoidance of inflated diction and elaborate figures of speech. Whenever the Friends resorted to metaphors, they chose them from homely life about them or from the Scriptures. Fox said once that the Ranters "had spoken themselves dry," and on another occasion declared that young John Story had "a flashy, empty notion of religion." Richard Hubberthorn, for instance, wrote, "The word was in my heart, and was as a fire or a hammer"; and Alice Hayes declared, "I am His fan in His hand," and upon another occasion that the Word was to her "a refiner with fire" and a "fuller with soap."

7

The third caution which William Penn mapped out for the readers of John Whitehead's book cannot be entirely dissociated from the first two. In endeavoring to establish the intangible psychological connection that must exist between writer and reader, he wanted the reader to feel that the written works of John Whitehead had come from the man's innermost life, including experiences as a prisoner persecuted for his beliefs, as a seeker after God agonizing through religious crises, and as husbandman and ministering Friend. Penn, it must be noted, was apparently conscious that style in its largest sense was a matter of personality, and that within the pages before the reader John Whitehead had expressed his own aspirations, as well as those of the group. According to Penn the value of the book lay seemingly in this very quality of self-expression. The reader was to put himself into such a mental attitude that voluntarily he would try to see Whitehead's point of view, and if possible come to realize vicariously the experiences of the author. Penn wrote:

Thirdly let him [the non-Quaker] read, therefore, with an inward as well as an outward Eye and Read no Faster than he feels and understands in himself, and brings things to the inward Test and Touchstone. And if he has not attained to the Experience of these Truths, he may by the Spirit's Mirrour in himself or the Glass of Righteousness see so far as to give an assent to the Truths therein Discovered. . . .

In the above passage Penn desired to show the deep habitual concern of the Friends that their writings should take hold of and move the peruser. The writer was to appeal directly to the inner forces of the reader who, Penn continued, was to "Read no Faster than" he felt and understood within himself, and could bring things to "the inward Test and Touchstone." Penn evidently considered that the last noun needed clarification, for he proceeded to explain by a series of synonyms, common to Quaker phrasing, that "this Touchstone" was "the Divine Principle in man," "the Seed and little leaven in the kingdom," "the Light of Christ within," and the "ingrafted Word."

He urged the reader to "go no faster" than he could both feel and understand in his own consciousness, and by a process of introversion apply the truth of the inner Light to his own life. Specifically he compared the results of this mental process to the case of the Samaritans, who, after they had talked with the woman at Jacob's well, and after they themselves had seen Christ, reported, "We believe . . . for we have Heard him ourselves and Know that this is INDEED the Saviour of the World."[26] Penn, with some forecast of modern psychology, was evidently anxious that before the reader should declare that the experiences, related by the writer, were false illusions, he should hold his judgment in abeyance until he could put himself into a frame of mind similar to that of the author. Penn, therefore, in this third caution was making two pleas: one indicating that the book had been written by a man far more concerned with spiritual than with temporal or secular matters, and the other begging the reader to bring to the book an unprejudiced mind in order that he might open-mindedly consider the beliefs and experiences of the author, who had, in Penn's words, "seen, tasted, touched, and handled the . . . powerful Word of God."

Penn's preface of 1704 is the most conscious expression made by a Quaker of the period in respect to the type of literature that the Friends had and purposed to produce. Particularly in urging the vicarious participation of the reader in the emotional experiences of the writer, Penn was no doubt trying to counteract the growing inroads of early eighteenth-century deism, and the antipathy expressed in Anglican centers against enthusiasm in religion.[27]

In summarizing this preface, it is manifestly clear that

Penn believed *The Written Gospel Labours of John White-head* had been designed not to extend any reader's knowledge into history, philosophy, or science, or to please the ear or eye, but to suggest a relationship whereby the reader might participate, through the medium of the printed page, with the spiritual life of the author. The main appeal was to be directed to "the inner sense," "the inner eye." While the analogy of the third point must not be pressed too far, in essence it will be found to lie close to the heart of much of the confessional literature of the Friends.[28] Penn's three previsionary cautions—do not look for "worldly" learning, adorned style, or intellectual stimulation—dominated the literary aims of the Friends for two generations, and for over a century, much of the work of their successors.[29]

Chapter VI

DISTRIBUTION OF LITERATURE

1

In the long struggle for religious toleration, the press became a strong weapon. The Friends' policy of passive resistance allowed them no other. Through the press the Friends advertised their "sufferings," voiced their protests against unjust legal discriminations, and at the risk of confiscation of property and of personal imprisonment, continued in the face of laws against "seditious printing" to write, publish, and circulate their tracts. They very early perceived that tracts could reach the minds of many who would never voluntarily come in contact with Quaker preaching. With unceasing persistency they financed and distributed their numerous publications in the three kingdoms, in European countries from Turkey to Norway, in the West Indies and the American Colonies. They sold them at the doors of Parliament,[1] in book stalls in English cities, or set out on horseback "with two dozen little books in their pockets"; women even cried them in the streets.

Sale of books, free gifts, and methodical distribution through Quarterly and Monthly Meetings were adopted as the most expedient agencies for disseminating Quaker literature. A letter, written by George Fox to Margaret Fell, unofficial secretary of the Friends in the northern counties of England, quite incidentally mentions three very typical methods employed in the circulation of tracts,[2] namely, presentation of copies, street selling, and disbursal through various Friends' meetings. After his solemn New Testament method of greeting her in the name of the Lord, he informed her that several copies of a book,[3] recently written by him, had been presented to the king, to the mayor, and to the aldermen of the Common Council in London. Next he told her that he had previously dispatched additional copies to Scotland, Ireland, Barbados, and Virginia, with instructions that they were to be distributed "to the Parliaments assembled and to their governors," where, he added with apparent satisfaction, "They sing them in the streets." In the third place he requested Margaret Fell to see that copies were ordered by the Monthly and Quarterly Meetings in the vicinity of Swarthmore, and furthermore advised her to supervise the distribution of these particular tracts to all the near-by justices, bailiffs, and mayors, remarking with his characteristically keen eye for contrasts, that they ought to "give a great light to dark people."[4]

As early as 1656, Fox interested himself in the dissemination of the printed works of the First Publishers of Truth. Many years later, in recalling the responsibilities assumed in those days by the Lancashire and Westmorland Friends, he entered the following statement in his *Journal:*

And at ye first ye north tooke 600 of every sorte of bookes that was printed & it continnued for many yeeres till ye Truth was spreade over ye nation & this was settled when we first begann to printe: & then. . . . Itt was left to ye freindes liberty for every County to sende for what they liked from all of ye nation; butt ye north att ye first boare ye charghes of all ye printinge for severall yeeres.[5]

2

Missionary literature was freely distributed abroad.[6] Even royalty received gifts of Quaker literature. Besides the English monarchs, books were presented by Thomas Story and

Robert Barclay to Peter the Great on his visit to England,[7] and by William Penn to Princess Elizabeth of the Palatinate,[8] the granddaughter of James I. At some personal risk Penn, on a missionary tour in Germany, distributed pamphlets to a rich young merchant of Bremen, and to Collegiants and Calvinist students in Groeningen.[9] Besse recorded that in Rome in 1659, when the Inquisition was a force to be reckoned with, Samuel Fisher and John Stubbs had "spread some books among the Friars."[10] In 1660 John Stubbs and Henry Fell carried an epistle, printed in Latin and English, to Prester John, supposedly "the Christian king of Ethiopia," whom they desired to visit. They only desisted from this undertaking when they found it impossible to persuade any shipmaster to carry them to this monarch's country.[11] In regard to these two men the British consul at Grand Cairo wrote to an English merchant at Leghorn, "I forgot to advise you how that the Quakers, going down to the Marine, did throw pamphlets into the Streets in Hebrew, Arabic and Latin, and if they had staid a little longer, it might have set them burning."[12] Anthony à Wood further illustrates the fearlessness of Fisher and Stubbs on this journey by stating that these Quakers "testified against the popish superstition to several cardinals, and distributed copies" of their literature[13] in Rome.

Similar evidence of the belief of the Friends in the press is apparent in the efforts of early Quaker missionaries to distribute their literature in France, Germany, Holland, and Scandinavian countries. The religious confession of William Dundas, entitled *A Few Words of Truth from the Spirit of Truth*, presents in vivid detail the author's endeavors to spread Quaker propaganda in France and also the risks that these ministering Friends incurred. From France in 1666, William Dundas sent to England for several hundred tracts. Through his generous disbursal of these, he incurred the suspicion of governmental officials. One evening, after being warned that he was under suspicion for the distribution of literature, supposed to be subversive to Catholicism, and that his premises were to be searched that night, he reported that he felt uneasy and troubled in mind. Acting upon what he felt to be divine intuition he arose, and immediately prepared to send some books "by post" into influential quarters, "to the Judge Criminal at Diep and some to the Jesuit's College there, and some to the Scottish College at Paris." Only after this behest had been fulfilled could he write, "I had rest in my spirit and my body returned to a right temper."[14] From Dieppe, however, as his confession shows, he fearlessly proceeded to Caen, where he again aroused the enmity of Calvinists and Papists by gifts of Friends' books.

In Scandinavian and Danish countries, however, Stephen Crisp and William Caton, in the distribution of Quaker tracts, met with much more hospitable treatment. In 1670 Stephen Crisp in Denmark and Sweden, and also in Holland, made several donations of books.[15] In Holland both William Caton and Stephen Crisp found a sympathetic hearing for their message; both lived there for a time, married Dutch wives, translated many Quaker books into the Dutch language,[16] and impressed the teachings of Friends upon the Dutch communities in which they worked.

While many missionaries were carrying the Quaker faith and tracts to foreign lands, other Friends saw that English-speaking countries were in nowise neglected.[17] Fox, for instance, wrote to Friends in London reminding them that since several ships were leaving immediately for Jamaica and New York, it would be well to see that Quaker books and epistles were put aboard. A manuscript letter of Richard Hubberthorn, dated 1660, addressed to George Fox, supplies additional information concerning the circulation of Quaker pamphlets.[18] He wrote "some is given forth in

Whitehall and others of them is sold in divers shops, and some of ye women Cryes them about the Streets." The latter procedure appears to have been a not uncommon occurrence.

3

Hostile sources bear witness to the energy of the Friends in the circulation of their tracts. Near the close of the century, in order to demonstrate how dangerous and distasteful the zeal of the Quakers was to religion and to orthodox Anglicans, Francis Bugg,[19] "an apostate" Friend, wrote a score of books against the people of his former adoption. Before his apostasy, from about 1659 to 1684, he had been an enthusiastic preacher and writer among the Friends. With animosity directed against the Society, in his autobiographical *The Pilgrim's Progress from Quakerism to Christianity,* he reprinted a letter dated 1693 from a Friends' Meeting for Sufferings "to shew" as he said, "their care of their own books: Nay, them very books which teach that the Scriptures are Death, Dust, Beastly Ware, Serpents Food."[20] To awaken his readers to the menace of Quakerism, as he saw it, he pictured the irrepressible zeal of the Friends in circulating their controversial tracts. With apparent regret and chagrin, he recalled "with what restless zeal myself and others used to advance Quakerism in the beginning, and how we sent our books the nation over by packhorses and otherwise"; and with evident condemnation of self he added, "I myself have given away twenty shillings worth at one meeting."[21]

In another tract, *The Quakers Yearly Meeting,* Francis Bugg declared that the Quakers published two kinds of books, one designed for their members and one for outsiders; he endeavored to alarm the public on account of the multiplicity of Friends' books and the unorthodoxy of their subject matter by writing, "Canst thou behold these pamphlets of theirs spread up and down the nation, and not be amazed at their impudence!"[22] In expressing his irritation he burst forth with this tirade:

Who hath wrote more than the Quakers? Whoever exposed the professors of Christianity more than they? Have they not this forty years, and more, laid siege against the Christian reputation of both magistrates and ministers? rendering the first in the Narratives of their trials, the Pharaohs and Nebuchadnezzars, and themselves the only Daniels of the Age?

In the growing membership of the Quaker organization and its ability to circulate propaganda in printed form, he discovered further cause for alarm. He cited the case of a widow who at her death possessed less than ten pounds in money, yet had in her keeping "more than 200 printed books and pamphlets of the Quaker writing, enough," Bugg asseverated, "to infect a Nation, their chief tendency being against magistracy and ministry, and all instituted religion."[23]

4

The Friends, in order to maintain their views and extol the Quaker way of life, occasionally resorted to wholesale distribution of tracts. In 1698, John Tomkins attended a conference, held at West Dereham, two miles from Stoke, to which Friends had been invited both to appear in person and to present to the ministers from Suffolk and Norfolk a defense of their beliefs. In a long letter, written to his friend Sir John Rodes, Tomkins gives an account of the disorderly conduct and procedure at this assembly. At one time the uproar, accompanied by "hooting, halooing, and laughter" became so great that the Friends were unable to make themselves heard. The Quaker representatives scattered openly in the assembly copies of a tract entitled *Christian Belief of*

the People called Quakers, of which they had previously ordered a thousand copies to be printed for this occasion. The
extensive distribution of these, continued Tomkins in his
letter, "had good service, for it divided the waters and the
people fell to reading them, and so way was made for
Friends to be heard again."[24] At the close of the first day's
conference, Tomkins noted that other copies of the same
pamphlet had been distributed at "the steeple house doors,"
and on the following afternoon copies of a second tract
called *Some Positions Touching Divers Weighty Truths.*[25]

5

In 1672, when the Great Pardon of Charles II gave the
Friends a temporary respite from persecutions, they grasped
the opportunity for giving publicity to their books and tracts
in a more systematic manner than had hitherto been possible.
An epistle sent out by a General Meeting of Friends, who
had been especially commissioned to manage "the public affairs of Truth throughout the nation," recommended the ex-
penditure of funds for the preparation and circulation of
Quaker books and tracts. It justified the collection of a fund
from Welsh and English Quakers for the use of itinerant
Friends abroad, advised that part of this amount be set
aside for recording and transcribing the sufferings of Friends
both in and out of England, and furthermore that Quaker
tracts "be disposed of and given away for public service to
the chief rulers and others concerned."[26] Separate meetings
were also urged to take upon themselves the responsibility
of ordering and distributing tracts and folios. In the American Colonies, "books published in England and Philadelphia
were subscribed to by Monthly Meetings and circulated
among the members.[27]

While large numbers of tracts were distributed gratis, the
Yearly and other meetings subscribed for many which were

to be sold to members and to any others who might wish to own or read them. The records of the Yearly Meeting, the Meeting for Sufferings, and of local meetings attest to systematic methods of distribution. The Yearly Meeting of 1682, for instance, advised "Every Quarterly Meeting in each county to take care weightily to consider and advise amongst themselves such way, method, place, and places, as fit to sell, publish, and dispose of books given forth in the service of Truth, and the numbers they should receive."[28] John Tomkins on another occasion informed Sir John Rodes that the Yearly Meeting of 1700 had "authorized the printing of 6,606 copies of Robert Barclay's *Apology*, which were to cost two shillings ten pence in calf leather and two shillings and seven pence in sheep," and that the meeting had also ordered the translation of fifteen hundred copies of the *Apology* into French for dispersal "into foreign parts and information of strangers."[29]

The minutes of various meetings exhibit the responsibility felt by these organizations for a methodical dispersal of Quaker literature. The Yearly Meeting of 1684 urged both Quarterly and Monthly Meetings "to correspond with the printers here [in London] for books of Truth, and take care for the spreading of serviceable books and papers."[30] In 1695 the Yearly Meeting agreed that each Quarterly Meeting should keep in a safe depository one copy of every "newly printed book," and that each Monthly Meeting should subscribe as the books came from the press for two of each sort valued "under two shillings six pence"; furthermore it particularly recommended that "where Friends have occasion for a greater number," they should send to the printers for them.[31]

Reciprocal action was in this way brought into play between the Yearly and subordinate meetings. In 1725, to cite another instance, Gilbert Mollison, a brother-in-law of Rob-

ert Barclay, wrote from London that he had forwarded to
the Quarterly Meeting at Aberdeen fifty copies of *How Sin
is Strengthened and How it May be Overcome*.[32] He requested that the Aberdeen meeting dispose of twenty copies;
the Urie, of twenty, and the Kilmuck of ten; he rather sig-
nificantly urged that those "on whom God had bestowed
much outwardly" should be encouraged to send to London
for more copies, and also for additional "books of Friends
for the spreading of Truth" in Scotland.[33]

One quotation from the manuscript minutes of the Second Day Morning Meeting gives evidence that each Quarterly Meeting was urged to handle the quota assigned to it.
On this occasion the committee was engaged in editing *The
Gospel Labours of John Whitehead*, discussed in the last
chapter. Their plea ran as follows:

12th 5 mo. 1703
A letter from the Quarterly Meeting at York, signed by Thos.
Hammond giving an account. They agreed to take off one hundred of John Whiteheads Books and Lincolnshire have also signified they will take 100 more—and there are about 150 to be
sent to the several meetings and that, not being thought sufficient
the Friends following are desired to write to the several Quarterly Meetings in Nottinghamshire, Leicestershire, Huntingdon-
shire, Northamptonshire, Buckinghamshire and Cambridgeshire,
where he [John Whitehead] hath travelled and suffered to know
what they'll take off besides their quantity.

John Tomkins
William Warren
John Field
or
any two of them

A curious one page advertising sheet, preserved in a volume of bound tracts in the Friends Reference Library in
London, throws a sidelight on the interdependence of the
Quaker metropolitan and country bookseller. It indicates,
too, that all Quaker meetings did not respond to proffered

opportunities in purchasing books. The sheet, dated "8th of 4th mo., 1682," had been sent out by a bookseller, whom Dunton designated as "thee and thou" Clark whose print shop was in George Yard in Lombard Street.[34] In this single advertising sheet Benjamin Clark offered for sale twenty-four current publications varying in price from a half penny to twelve shillings. The latter represented the cost price of the folio edition of *The Works of the Long Mournful and Sorely Distressed Isaac Penington,* published during the preceding year. Clark prefaced his inventory with a note in which he sought a greater degree of coöperation from the Quarterly and Monthly Meetings than he had previously received, as he stated, both for the sake of the press as well as for that of "Truth."

Dear Friends,
Having (through Providence) run through the work of one year, for the Printing of Friends' Books, I thought it not amiss to Publish a Catalogue of some Books I have printed for you, which Method I intend to take yearly (God willing) that any Friends as have not had those sorts, may be furnished with them, with desire to give directions which way I may send them: and others that are over-clogged may be eased by returning of them that I send, desiring that Friends would be considerate of a publick way to disperse Friends' Books to the ease of the press (which is very chargeable) and to the advantage of Truth, which is all desired by your Friend, who is ready to serve you.

BENJAMIN CLARK.[35]

6

Belief in the press was closely associated with the desire of the Friends to further the aims of the Society. At least two examples exist where educators saw fit to put before the public the writings of children that Friends, particularly young Friends, might be encouraged to right living by the examples of youthful Christians. Of these juvenile publications, one consists of a slender volume of poems written by

Jonas Lawson, the son of the educator and widely known botanist, Thomas Lawson. The lad, a boy of great promise, had died in his fifteenth year, and the father, in harmony with the increasing desire of religiously-minded people to preserve dying sayings of "worthies in the Society," believing that others might profit by an account of the boy's youth, of his pious death, and by the reading of his poems, published them in 1684 under the monitory title of *A Serious Remembrancer*.

The other example of juvenilia consists of a series of testimonies, penned by a group of school children at Waltham Abbey, to pay tribute to the life and influence of a beloved schoolmaster, John Matern. These testimonies[36] appeared with the title *An Account of a Divine Visitation and Blessing, attending the Religious Care and Exercises of Waltham Abbey School; with the Gracious Dealings of the Almighty toward some Others in their Tender Years*. This John Matern "whom the children chose to honor" was by birth a German. Although trained in Germany for the Protestant ministry, he never became fully reconciled to the teachings of Calvin. After studying the principles of the English Friends, he desired to unite with them, and later accepted a position at Waltham Abbey under its headmaster, Christopher Taylor, where he seems to have exhausted his energies in his work. In addition to the duties of usher, Matern filled the rôle of "correcteur" of books at the Friends' printing house, translated "Calvinist and Hollandish writings into High Dutch," and with the headmaster brought out *A Compendium or Abridgement of Three Languages, the Latin, Greek, and Hebrew*.[37]

The school at Waltham Abbey housed about fifty students. Among them were children of some of the leading Friends of England, such as William and Edward Penington, the children of Isaac and Mary Penington, and Margaret Rouse, a granddaughter of Margaret Fell Fox. For a year before the death of John Matern in 1679, an intense wave of religious emotion had swept over the school.[38] Both girls and boys are reported to have trembled from the intensity of their spiritual experiences, and according to the *Account of a Divine Visitation,* "some were melting into tears and lamenting for two or three hours together." Evidently John Matern had fostered an intensely emotional atmosphere in this school, had been equally beloved by his pupils and co-workers,[39] and had given himself unstintingly to his work.

Eleven contributions, written by the pupils in the Waltham Abbey school, "were thought good to be published," not, as the foreword of the tract emphasized, that the efforts of these school children should be exploited but "that the mercy . . . of our compassionate Father may be proclaimed in the ears of many; and that others who peruse them may praise the God of heaven."[40] This preface closed with the didactic and pious hope that these printed tributes might "be serviceable to children," especially young ones, and to teachers and instructors. The ages of the eleven children varied from ten to sixteen years. It is of course impossible to ascertain how much this juvenile copy was revised for the press. The diction sounds overly mature; in scriptural phrasing and general tone, it very closely resembles the language used in adult Quaker testimonies. One of these, short enough to be quoted in entirety, is the handiwork of the twelve year old step-granddaughter of George Fox. It throws light both on early Quaker education and upon the widespread belief in the press as a factor in the moral and spiritual training of youth. The letter itself represents a commingling of imitativeness and childish ingenuousness.

I have this to say for my dear teacher, John Matern. He was one that lived in the fear of the Lord, and when he lay upon his deathbed, he glorified the Lord, and made sweet melody in his soul; we had a blessed meeting, and the presence of the Lord was amongst us. Oh! he was a blessed man, indeed; . . . in his lifetime it was his greatest joy to see his scholars grow in the fear of the Lord, and if he saw the enemy prevail over any he would with grief of heart admonish them to have a care lest the enemy should prevail again. He also was greatly exercised if any of his scholars did not mind their business and their learning to the outward and would encourage them that did. Assuredly he preached righteousness in his life and conversation. He hath made his calling sure, and now is at rest, for he hath left a good savour behind him and the remembrance is blessed. He is gone to the Lord, and is at peace forever and evermore.[41]

The Friends, it is clear then, looked upon the press as a legitimate means for projecting throughout the world the social and religious challenge of Quakerism, and for strengthening the ties of relationship within the church.

CHAPTER VII

THE LITERATURE OF "SUFFERINGS"

1

The Society very early saw the value of keeping the sufferings of its membership directly before the eyes of the public. The leaders perceived that their *acta martyrum* could serve as testimony against legal abuses, eulogize Quaker saints, further the spreading of propaganda, and act as a "remembrancer" for future readers of Quaker history. "Sufferings" was a term employed by the Friends to indicate any infringement upon property rights, or loss of health or life incurred through adherence to their beliefs and practices. Records of "sufferings for the sake of conscience" include "the taking of an iron pot from a poor man" in New England;[1] the confiscation of quantities of sugar owned by Friends in the West Indies; imprisonments, lasting from a few hours to twenty years; and sickness, banishment, or death resulting from injury and from penal confinement.

Minutes of Friends' meetings, journals, protests, formal and informal letters, and numerous manuscript records present ample evidence of the habitual care taken by the Friends to preserve and print accounts of their sufferings. The Yearly Meeting in London assigned the censoring of Quaker publications to the Second Day Morning Meeting, and the supervision of printing to the Meeting for Sufferings.[2] The journals, particularly those of George Fox,[3] Thomas Ellwood,[4] and John Banks,[5] furnish invaluable sociological data in regard to unsanitary conditions—the filth and overcrowding—in seventeenth-century prisons. George White-head, John Gratton, and Richard Davies picture vividly the distress[6] of Friends upon seeing their household and shop goods carted away in loads for refusal to pay tithes, and upon beholding their relatives and friends thrown into prison for worshiping in conventicles. Nonconformists were at the mercy of informers, who received a large share of the fine imposed upon dissenters who persisted in violating the Conventicle Act,[7] which forbade more than four, or according to some accounts five, persons to gather for worship where a religious service was conducted without the use of the English prayer-book.

Manuscript and printed petitions were used to bring the sufferings of the Friends to the notice of royalty and of the public. Among many documents *The Humble Petition to the King of above a Thousand Prisoners, commonly called Quakers* of 1682 directed attention to the increasing number of imprisonments. It stated that "Jailes were filled without regard to Sex, Age, or Conditions" so that health and life were impaired; that "innocent and industrious families were left destitute" and that "the Violence and Woful Spoil" of the informers would cause "many to shut up their shops and leave their trades and Farms."[8] Whiting gives the number of 10,778 Friends who suffered imprisonment during the years 1660-1680. One hundred ninety-eight were transported over seas.[9] Besse lists three hundred thirty-eight Friends who died in prison from results of confinement. A recent investigation raises this last number in England and Wales to at least four hundred fifty.[10]

2

Since deprivation and imprisonment bulked very large in the lives of practically all of the "ministering" Friends as well as of others in their constituency, the subject of suffering found expression first in tracts, then in letters of protest, and a generation later in memoirs. The constant and methodical recording of sufferings was based on the clearly defined objective of acquainting the public first with the sufferings of the group, and secondly with the body of beliefs that made the Friends willing for the sake of conscience to endure religious persecution. Added to these was an additional wish to assure whatever government was in power that the Friends held no ill will against it, but were only seeking freedom of speech and of the press that they might worship and preach as their consciences dictated. With civic and political affairs they concerned themselves as little as possible.

A reading of the "sufferings tracts" clearly indicates the dovetailing of individual with group interests, for uniformly wherever a writer declared his own innocency before the law, he asserted that he was making his persecution and unfair treatment public for the sake of the group of which he was a part; and if he proclaimed the sufferings imposed upon the group, he identified himself with the group. As early as 1656 *The Wounds of an Enemie in the House of a Friend*, an eighty-page tract, was issued by Thomas Salthouse and Miles Halhead to protest against illegal procedure and to clear the writers from several charges, among the latter, conspiracy against the government, vagrancy, and blasphemy.[11] Thirty-three italicized words in the long title asserted the desire of the authors to vindicate themselves in the eyes of the tract-buying public. They stoutly maintained that the pamphlet was "Published for the Clearing of their Innocency from the cloud of transgression, of which they are supposed to be highly guilty, by Reason of their Silent Abiding such long and cruel sufferings."[12]

A preface to a "sufferings tract," whose title begins with *A Brief Relation of Some Part of the Sufferings,* shows that Irish Friends utilized the press for proclaiming their innocency and also their loyalty to a government that refused to tolerate their beliefs or their demands for liberty in worship. The preface began:

To the end, Reader, that thou mayst be informed of the manner of our Sufferings . . . we have caused to be printed some part of what we have suffered these eleven years, that thou mayst see, how, where, and for what (sometimes without and contrary to the Law and sometimes under color of the Law) much Havoc has been made of our Goods, which we here put to public view in a plain way and manner, for we are a plain people.[13]

3

Some leaders were conscious of the fact that the Friends were making religious history. George Fox and Ellis Hookes had early seen the importance of collecting records of suffering in order to keep the reputation of the Society clear from current condemnation and from future criticism. The Friends Reference Library in London has preserved intact forty-four folios of manuscript records detailing the persecutions suffered by the early Friends.[14] The collectors evidently had in mind the preparation of a thesaurus upon which future historians might draw. It was not until 1753, however, that Besse's monumental *Collection of the Sufferings of the People Called Quakers, for the Testimony of a Good Conscience, from the Time of their first being distinguished by that Name to the Time of the Act . . . of Toleration . . . in the Year 1689* was published. Neither Besse nor any subsequent Quaker historian has exhausted these quarries. In 1726, a quarter of a century before Besse's two folio volumes appeared, James Dickinson perceived that on account of the persecutions which they had endured, the Friends had already achieved a recognized place in the history of religious toleration. In that year, while attending a quarterly meeting at York, he wrote in his *Journal*, "I laid

before Friends the necessity there was, to take Care to preserve the Accounts of Friends Sufferings . . . that those
accounts might be serviceable to future generations."[15]

Later in the same year he again reiterated this plea before various meetings in Cumberland, and at the Half Year
Meeting in Dublin. After the Dublin conference he noted,
"The Meeting took it under Consideration, and became zealously concerned that Care might be taken for preserving the
Records of Friends Suffering for the Benefit of future Ages
that they might know how the Lord raised up a People, who
were no People, to bear Testimony to his Name and Truth
upon the Earth, not only to believe, but also to suffer for
it."[16]

Much earlier in Quaker history, Edward Burrough, a prisoner, who knew at first hand the filth and vileness of London penal dungeons,[17] wrote an open letter to the Men's
Meetings just before his death in Newgate in 1662. In it
he suggested that these meetings make themselves responsible for preserving all the sufferings to which Friends had
been subjected. At this time, when the Society was little
more than a decade old, he advised that data should be "pru-
dently recorded, plainly, fully, and amply," definitely expressing the hope that such facts would prove to "be of service to this age, and for all ages to come."[18] More than
sixty years elapsed between Burrough's letter and Dickinson's plea, but the undertaking, though frequently brought
to the attention of the Society,[19] was never carried to completion until 1753.

Joseph Besse's *A Collection of the Sufferings of the People Called Quakers* is an exhaustive compilation of "sufferings" literature. Though not published until 1753, its factual
material belongs largely to the lifetime of the pioneer
generation from 1650 to 1689, and its compilation in meth-

odical form to the 1689 to 1725 period. Besse, it should be noted, had published abstracts of sufferings in three separate quartos between 1733 and 1738. In his two folios he systematically lists the sufferings of Friends under geographical headings, such as the American Colonies, the West Indies, England, Holland, the Mediterranean countries, and Asia. Altogether his collection is a vast depository of letters, documents, proclamations, and petitions, which at first hand present panoramically vivid pictures of religious intolerance in the second half of the seventeenth century. The persecution of the Friends naturally called forth much printed literature. More than ten per cent of the total output of seventeenth-century Quaker tracts is directly connected with the subject of persecutions of the Friends of the first generation. Smith's *Descriptive Catalogue of Friends' Books* lists two hundred and twenty-four sufferings tracts and books published before 1689.[20]

The memoirs of the Friends attest to the high value they placed upon the actual data of persecution. A curious letter, written by Luke Howard, the Dover shoemaker, and preserved in his journal, indicates how permeated even the humble leaders of the Friends were with the idea of preserving records of sufferings. This letter was dated from Dover prison "the 4th of the month called February 1689." A certain Thomas Stratford at Dover, it seems, had attempted to break down a wall so that his coach could pass through a Quaker burial ground. The shoemaker,[21] believing that his neighbor would not desire that posterity should know of his "foul and dark night work" after "he was dead and gone," penned the following words as a friendly but pointed warning: "We may in love tell thee that we give to London an account of all we do suffer, of all kinds, once a quarter, to be kept on record for ages to come to have a view of, when we are dead and gone." It may be noted here that Luke

THE LITERATURE OF SUFFERINGS

Howard's letter was effective, or, at least, that the projected road was not built.

4

During the Commonwealth and after the Restoration, printing for Friends became a hazardous undertaking, often entailing fines and imprisonment as well as the confiscation of both press and printed matter. Consequences were particularly severe after L'Estrange was appointed official licenser in 1662,[22] for the publications of all the sectaries were then considered seditious. At the accession of Charles II the fanatical uprising of the Fifth Monarchy people, a sect which hoped to establish a spiritual kingdom of the "Saints," brought the Quakers with their half-understood principles under close governmental observation. Under the guidance of Clarendon, the new Stuart régime looked with suspicion upon the Friends. As previously stated, it viewed with disfavor the refusal of the Quakers to take the Oath of Abjuration,[23] to accede to the payment of tithes and ecclesiastical demands,[24] and later to take the Oaths of Supremacy and Allegiance,[25] to grant titles to officials, and under the Conventicle Acts of 1664 and 1670 to give up their meetings.[26]

Since the writings of dissenters usually failed to receive the official *imprimatur* of the licenser, any printing in defiance of law was accompanied by risk. For that reason many of the Quaker publications appear without the name or place of the printer or bookseller, though many tracts boldly carried both. Occasionally it was necessary to have one part of a folio set up by one printer and a second or third part by another. The result of this subterfuge is evident in the numbering of the pages, where the reader suddenly discovers that page 115 follows 178; the catch word, however, at the bottom of the page is usually accurate. Immediately after the Restoration, the difficulty of securing publishers for tracts is indicated by the following notice taken from "The Table of Books," preceding the *Works* of Richard Hubberthorn, printed in 1662. A note accompanying this table contains an editorial apology for errata and a request for consideration from the reader: "It is desired that what faults thou findst that have escaped the press, in the ensuing treatise, to correct with thy pen; where thou canst not, friendly pass it by."

Another editor in this same year inserted[27] a similar note in William Smith's *Balm from Gilead*. With small regard for pronominal antecedents, his statement ran:

Reader, it is desired that thee wouldest observe that the year of the Lord must be the principle directions to find out the particular Books mentioned in the Table. The number of the folio is set down, and it may be some help, but they could not follow in order because the book was printed in several places, by reason of the difficulty of getting books printed. There may be some errors escaped the press; which if thou find, thou art desired carefully to correct them.[28]

Distributors of Quaker publications, even in the early 1650's, were often faced with difficulties. In 1654, seven Quakers complained to Cromwell that they had been confined in a common jail room for twenty-four weeks, writing, "Wee for Conscience Sake now lye, for noe Cause at all: but owning sume books." After stating that these books had been written by Friends and publicly sold, they closed their petition with a pledge of loyalty, destined to have frequent repetition before the Restoration, "All of vs haue been Alwaies faithful to our vtmost to the Commonwealth."[29]

Two years later General Monck[30] sent word to Secretary Thurloe that an alarming amount of literature was streaming into Scotland through the proselyting endeavors of the sectaries. "You see by the enclosed letters and books what pains these Quakers take to get Proselytes. . . . I have ordered the commanding officer to secure him [Alexander

Parker] and George Fox, and an officer to look after the books, so many that the carriage from here [Leith] to New-castle came to 14/. In Hartford, Thomas Harris, accord-ing to an old document, was imprisoned for setting up a paper against a priest.[31] For the year 1662 Besse entered this report: "Henry Boreman died a prisoner [in Newgate] on the 17th of October, having been committed for selling religious Books; he left a wife with three children then liv-ing, and with child with the fourth."[32]

Printers and booksellers knew with certainty the risks which they were undertaking, but "for the sake of Truth" and conscience, they fearlessly assumed them. Robert Wil-son, a bookseller, about to send a consignment of tracts to Ireland, begged the agent at Bristol to use his care and dili-gence in sending the books across the channel. He said that he himself had been very often "plundred by ye Rulers of my goods" who burned his books both "at home and abroad." He closed his plea by stating reasons for his anxi-ous care, "It being a thing of concern this day to truth, as well as my owne perticuler."[33] The shop of Andrew Sowle (1628-1695), a veteran publisher of Friends' books, was re-peatedly searched and his printing presses broken into pieces.[34] The story is told that on one occasion at least, in-stead of hindering officials in their searches, Andrew Sowle "set meat and drink before them according to the command (Rom. xii. 19, 20), 'to feed even your enemies.'" With the firm seventeenth-century belief in "providential punish-ments" the writer of the biographical testimony of Andrew Sowle completed this account by adding that Sowle's "good so overcame their evil that some of them departed under a concern; but one of the chiefs, who was filled with malice against Truth, survived not long after, but died in a miserable condition."[35]

Immediately after the Restoration, it was even less safe

than it had been under Cromwell to traffic in Friends' books. In Winchester, in 1660, an officer of the law, H. Benets by name, reported the seizure of Quaker literature, and furthermore supplied his superior with the reassuring information that the person of Ambrose Rigge,[36] a Quaker preacher, was in prison, "whom," he continued, "we doe detaine as a pernicious fellow," and from whom we have "taken a bundle of books." Braithwaite gives a long list of printers who suffered imprisonment during the Restoration period for handling "the seditious books" of the Friends.[37] A list of forty-four dispersers of Quaker literature also appears in the State Papers for the years 1664 and 1665.[38]

Through the press during their years of most rapid growth, the Friends utilized every means available for the accomplishment of their purposes. They endured revilings, imprisonment, tedious journeys, and confiscation of books and presses. Undismayed they continued to produce controversial and more literary material in abundance. As the membership of the Society increased, and as a unified organization evolved, by slow degrees the leaders, under the direction of the Yearly Meeting, turned their attention to the supervision of publications. This censorship, in connection with the growing conservatism of the Society, was fraught, as the next chapter will show, with both beneficial and harmful results for the literature of the Friends.

Chapter VIII

QUAKER CENSORSHIP

1

Censorship of Quaker literature was the natural outcome of the missionary and ethical aims of the Friends. Under the direction of the Yearly Meeting, the Second Day Morning Meeting undertook, in 1672, the duty of censoring all manuscripts published under the name of the Society.[1] The members of the board assumed two responsibilities: they were to formulate replies to adverse criticism brought upon their group, and they were to pass upon the diction and rhetoric of the manuscripts submitted to them. In a less direct manner they fostered the spirit of conservatism and of group solidarity already at work and constantly increasing among the Friends. Through this committee the Society became better able to secure unanimity of expression and to forestall printing injurious to its interests. In so far as the Morning Meeting checked fanatical tendencies, held the diction up to higher standards, and helped authors to clarify the points at issue, it was beneficial; in so far, however, as this board stressed merely the interests of the group, it tended to hasten the day of eighteenth-century exclusiveness and of barrenness in literary productivity.

Certain Friends early saw that the integrity of the Society could easily be endangered through the unrestricted use of the press. They, therefore, sought means for checking what they termed "unwise printing." In the tense atmosphere of the Protectorate and of the decade following, when the vision of Quakerism was drawing men and women of varied religious backgrounds into the Quaker group, it was inevitable that many tracts should be put into circulation which could not at that time or later be agreeable to the thinking of the entire body of Friends. Although these later Friends held unwaveringly to the ideals of primitive Quakerism, they chose to proclaim the doctrine of the inner Light in a more conservative fashion and in a less spectacular manner.

The Morning Meeting desired to free the Quaker group from charges of fanaticism which, with justice in many cases, had been brought against it. This body became cautious about circulating records of visions, prophecies, lamentations, healings, and fasts. The age of prose and reason was at hand, especially in religion where deism, an intellectualized approach to religion, quite in opposition to the Quaker theory of spiritual experience, was making itself felt. These new leaders faced conditions exactly the reverse of those which had confronted the First Publishers of the 1650's.

2

The censorship of Quaker publication had at first been semi-official. During the Commonwealth many manuscripts had been submitted to George Fox for approval; but on account of the increasing membership of the Society, the distribution of writers over wider areas, and the frequent imprisonment of the leaders, no definite plan for review of Quaker books came into force. After the Great Pardon of 1672, the Yearly Meeting appointed ten Friends "to see that books were carefully corrected and that no new book or new edition of an old one should be printed without" an order from this committee.[2] The establishment of the Morning Meeting set in operation two things of marked influence upon the subsequent history of the Society—a system of censorship and the Friends Reference Library.

Several of the best educated of the spiritual leaders, most of them London Friends, composed the first board. At its opening meeting it laid the foundations of what is today probably the most complete, if far from the largest, of the church libraries in England by approving the substance of the following resolutions:[3] First, that two books of every kind written by Friends in the past should be procured, and kept together; second, that in the future every bookseller should bring into this depository two copies of current publications dealing with Quakerism; and third, that copies of all books "that had been written against Truth from the beginning"[4] should be assembled at headquarters. In addition, it was decided that without delay any book adverse to the principles of the Friends should be brought before the board that answers might "be dispatched with all convenient speed."

From 1672 to 1901, when the duties of the Morning Meeting were merged with the work of other committees, the minutes of the Second Day Morning Meeting have been preserved in the Friends Reference Library in London—a monument to the passion of the Friends for recording all details pertaining to their history, organization, and religious experiences. These minutes indicate that the censors, before bestowing the official *imprimatur* of the Society, conscientiously read, discussed, and examined the manuscripts submitted to them; and in editorial capacity gave suggestions either for revising or for amending them, or expressed disapproval or unequivocal rejection.[5]

3

Though the influence of the Morning Meeting was undoubtedly far-reaching, care must be exercised in attributing the changes in Quaker literature after 1672, and particularly after 1689, entirely to the work of this board. The evaluation of influence is rendered difficult for several reasons. The problem would be greatly simplified if more manuscripts, just as they came into the hands of the committee were extant so that comparison could be made with the printed works. Fortunately a few such manuscripts exist. Of these the most important for this purpose are the documents[6] from which, at the request of the Morning Meeting, Thomas Ellwood compiled the *Journal of George Fox*. (Ellwood's excisions and their significance will be discussed later in this chapter.) To determine the extent of the Morning Meeting's influence upon the style of Quaker writers also presents difficulties, because the simplification noted in the writing of the Friends in respect to word choice and sentence structure accords with tendencies also observable in contemporary writers in the last half of the age of Dryden and of the Queen Anne period.

In spite of these difficulties there yet remains much outward evidence in the detailed minutes of the Morning Meeting, and much internal evidence in the changed style and subject matter of Quaker literature to justify the attribution of considerable influence to this conscientious board of censors. Certain changes in style are noticeable. By the beginning of the eighteenth century, the old fantastic titles, such as *A Handful after the Harvest-Man* and *A Wren in the Burning Bush, Waving the Wings of Contraction to the Congregated Clean Fowls in the Ark of God* entirely disappear in favor of such carefully considered and officially approved nomenclatures as *The Collected Gospel Labours of*

John Whitehead, Persecution Exposed in Memoirs of John Whiting, and *The Christian Progress of George Whitehead.* By 1725 a certain piquancy of style due to the picturesque and homely phrasing, characteristic of the earliest Quaker writers, is lost. Such colloquial turns as "my place of outward being," "the cumbers of delight," "I did not know my bit and bridle," "airy spirits" and "frothy nature" when applied to frivolous persons, become less frequent. On the other hand, however, certain idiomatic phrases descriptive of the inner life are retained with great constancy, such as "concern," "conviction," "a weight was upon me," and "I was moved of the Lord."

A greater degree of accuracy supplants, comparatively speaking, the former complexity of style. Part of the credit should be attributed, without doubt, to the active interests of the Morning Meeting. The minutes give testimony of repeated suggestions for alteration or revision, and of absolute rejection of manuscripts where the material was chaotic or the statements confused. One illustration from these records will show the Meeting's care for the editorial duties it assumed. In 1675, Samuel Watson submitted a tract entitled *An Heavenly Visitation.* After deliberation the Meeting reported that it was not "satisfied with ye maner & ye stile of ye discourse between Jehovah & his immortal birth," and felt that it would not "clear matters to peoples understanding, but [would] beget double questions and disputes in their minds." For this reason the secretary recorded, "Friends think it not safe to be printed" and therefore "it is laid by for G[eorge] W[hitehead] and R[ichard] R[ichardson]"[7] to survey.

Of great frequency are the Morning Meeting entries which suggest alterations involving correctness, curtailment, or additions. Even *A Serious Remembrancer* of the school master,

Thomas Lawson, received two notations: first, that the manuscript should be corrected before printing, and second, that some of the allusions should be omitted because the Meeting did not consider them "weighty and pertinent";[8] even the scholarly Robert Barclay's translation of his own *Catechism* into Latin was assigned to a member of the Morning Meeting, the learned schoolmaster, Richard Richardson, with the injunction that the latter should "compare the Lattine with the English and if it be true, to print it."[9]

4

Improvement in texture and style was, however, in the minds of this censoring board only incidental to the prime motive of furthering the interests of Quakerism. These men and their successors, among the latter many of the best informed of the Quaker ministers and elders, Stephen Crisp, George Whitehead, Richard Richardson, William Penn, and Thomas Ellwood, assumed responsibility for the literature that was designed for circulation. If one judges from the number of Quaker books printed and the minutes of the Morning Meeting, it is clear that a half day a week would not suffice for accomplishing the work delegated to them, and that many a midnight candle must have been burned as the wearied elder perused the crabbed writing of these seventeenth-century devotees.[10] The minutes often record that two men who were to report to the committee as a whole at a subsequent time would be assigned to one production.[11] Thomas Ellwood did practically all the work of revision and collation for Fox's *Journal.* The minutes, however, show that most frequently the committee met as a body to pass on the manuscripts submitted to it.

The deep responsibility felt by the Second Day Morning Meeting for the morale of the Society as well as for its reputation among "the world's people" is chronicled many times in these minutes. One example is of more than ordinary interest since the original copy on which the minutes are based has been preserved and can be compared with the records of the meeting. The manuscript, epistolary in nature, is without title and consists of eight small pages, six of which are crowded with fine handwriting. The seventh contains the endorsement and the last is left blank. This epistle was submitted to the Morning Meeting in 1678 by Sebastian Ellythorp who saw much to reprove in the behavior of parents among the Friends. In content and tone it resembled many submitted to the board of censors.

Sebastian Ellythorp, it is quite clear from the manuscript, believed that the younger generation of Friends was departing from the ways of "plain people."[12] With circumspection he saw that the fault lay not so much with the young people as it did with their guardians. He especially directed Quaker parents to inform and correct their offspring, and he severely criticized them because they allowed their children and servants "to leave their houses or employment" to partake of things that "were pleasing to youthful nature" at Christmas, Easter, or May Day—such things as "riotous eating, drinking, revelling, playing at cards or other secret or open gaming, crouding, shouting, and sporting."

When Ellythorp's missive had been read in "full assembly," "the sense of the Meeting" was clearly against sanctioning publication. The committee decided after deliberation that the epistle would have only a limited appeal and, in a public manner, would expose certain shortcomings of Friends; yet this board, composed as it was of conscientious men, felt that Ellythorp had spoken against certain evils within the group—evils which should not be overlooked— and therefore granted the author permission to circulate among the men's and women's meetings manuscript copies of his letter. The secretary in reviewing the discussion completed his minutes for the day with these words: "Let this epistle be sent to these meetings that they may take care to reform such things that are amiss among them, that their [the Friends'] weakness and nakedness may not be expressed in print to the whole world."[13]

Almost as soon as the Morning Meeting was established, it began to show a disinclination to stamp its approval upon writings of highly mystical and prophetical nature. Apparently the mysticism involved in following the inner Light seemed to them a simple matter; philosophical mysticism, appealing, to use Barclay's phrase, "more to the head than the heart," filled them with apprehension. A long entry in the Morning Meeting minutes for 1678 shows a reluctance to countenance attempts to rationalize mystic experience. Ralph Fretwell, before his "convincement" a judge of the court of common pleas in Barbados,[14] submitted in 1678, a paper dealing with the teachings of Jacob Boehme. In this case members of the Morning Meeting deemed the article to be neither "suitable nor safe" for publication because they considered the Behmenists "a mixture of Light and Darkness."[15] This change of view in the spokesmen of the Society is especially significant at this period because two decades earlier William Bayly, Solomon Eccles, and other Friends not only felt themselves indebted to Jacob Boehme but advocated his mystical teachings.[16]

5

The Morning Meeting, if one judges by the minutes, was a long-suffering and superconscientious body of men. On the whole it seems to have been firm and consistent in its decisions, and to have met some difficult situations with considerable tact and patience. The name of Judith Bowlbie appears frequently on the pages of these vellum bound records. Her predilection for prophetic style and denunciation seems to have cost the Morning Meeting much time and some perturbation. The first paper submitted by her in 1686 was treated with characteristic Quaker caution. The minutes state that a paper written by Judith Bowlbie concerning *Impending Judgment* had been read, and laid by "till she be further enquired of."[17] The results of the inquiry evidently were not favorable, for a second paper entitled *A Warning and Lamentation over England*,[18] a Jeremiad entreating England to repent in sackcloth and ashes, received a more drastic minute. It ran thus, "A paper of Judith Bulby read called a Lament, etc., which Friends see it not safe to print, as it is at present, nor at any time without some alterations or amendments."[19]

Fourteen months later an entry indicates that Judith Bowlbie was even yet endeavoring to convince the Morning Meeting that her spirit of prophecy was an inward revelation, and that consequently her effusion should find expression in print. She did, however, follow certain suggestions given her by the Morning Meeting and amended her document; but even so her paper still failed to please. The Meeting, evidently feeling that the spirit of the group was sounder than "the private spirit" of Judith Bowlbie, continued to maintain with firmness that her *Lament* "was not mete to print," but conceded that she "might be permitted officially to circulate it in manuscript."

In her desire that this *Lament* should be heeded by the public, Judith Bowlbie must have been as persistent as the old Hebrew prophets, for three years later the minutes contain a copy of a letter sent to Judith, signed by eight members of the Morning Meeting, beginning "Our love in the blessed Truth salutes thee." It continues, "This is to let yee know that we have read the paper thou left with us to be read and printed if we thought fit." This editorial staff po-

litely, patiently, and painstakingly stated its reasons for with-
holding its *imprimatur,* explaining, first that her statements
were inaccurate; and second, that in the time of peace they
considered it unwise to print further attacks against magistrates. They, however, again granted her one concession, that
of circulating copies of a small section entitled *Following
the Lamb,* but made it very clear that even this privilege
could not be granted until they themselves had made "some
little alterations."[20] One wonders what Judith felt about her
rejection slip.

Frances Donson, evidently of a denunciatory type of mind,
sent from Virginia to the Morning Meeting in London a
paper which she entitled *To Ye Lying.* This manuscript
fared worse than those of Judith Bowlbie, for with finality
her condemnation of lying was thus minuted: "It is the
mind of the meeting that it is not fitt to be delivered, and
Friends, finding no sattisfaction in it, desire her to be still
and quiet."[21]

The growing conservatism of the Friends in permitting
the publication of incidents savoring of enthusiasm or of
fanaticism is demonstrated by the excisions of Thomas Ellwood in his collating and editing of the various manuscripts
which made up the *Journal of George Fox.* This work had
been delegated to him by the Morning Meeting, of which
he was a member. The Ellwood edition remained the stand-
ard life of Fox until 1891. The journal in its entirety was
never published until Dr. Norman Penney edited it in 1911
for the Cambridge Press.[22] In the introduction, Mr. T. Edmund Harvey notes the omission of "James Nayler's being
under a fast fourteen days, Richard Hubberthorne's great
fast," . . . "Solomon Eccles's fasting for seven days on
the voyage to America," and "Fox's 'Sounding the Day of
the Lord' alone on Pendle Hill, and on another occasion
of his lying out on the fields all night."[23] Other omissions

include references to healing, to "providential punishments," to visions and to premonitions. Mr. Harvey's careful analysis shows very definitely the interest of the Morning Meeting in preparing this important Quaker document for the press, and its desire to eliminate details which partook of the supernatural or of fanaticism.

6

Opponents of the Quakers found much to criticize in the efforts of the Morning Meeting to control through the press its didactic, theological, and propagandist measures. Among the hostile critics was William Rogers of Bristol, once an energetic, but later "an apostate" Friend. In his *Christian-Quaker Distinguished from the Apostate and Innovator* he castigated his former allies for cabining and confining the Spirit. As a separatist from the main Quaker group headed by Fox, he called himself a Christian Quaker.[24] This group of "apostates" carried almost to the limit enjoined by the Ranters the belief that nothing should be allowed to hamper the working of the Spirit. Rogers reasoned that the Morning Meeting was not giving writers in the Quaker group liberty to write as "the Spirit moved" them. He denied scriptural precedent for the establishment of such a censoring board;[25] yet he clearly stated that he had no objection whatsoever to the Society's efforts toward curbing scandalous printing among its own constituency. His chief objection lay in the power of this committee to exercise the final decision in respect to suitability of printing, especially in its ranking of the power assigned it by the Yearly Meeting above "the divine moving" that arose in individual hearts.[26] Judith Bowlbie's case, just reviewed, in its plea for divine inspiration in composition, would represent a case in keeping with his argument.

Rogers's tractate did not go unanswered. Thomas Ell-

wood, one of the men attacked, replied with *An Antidote
. . . Versus the Christian Quaker,* which contained a public
statement of the avowed purposes of the Second Day Morning Meeting. Ellwood admitted the correctness of Rogers's
surmise concerning scriptural silence for the establishment
of a censorial board for Quaker publications by admitting,
not without a touch of sardonic humor, that the art of printing—"the means we now have of spreading and defending
Truth among the world of Books"[27]—had not been invented
till centuries after the writing of the New Testament. In a
serious vein Ellwood argued for the censorial work of the
Morning Meeting by declaring that the work demanded, not
"a private spirit," but "the exercise of the Spirit of Truth
and a *sound judgment,* in examining and weighing such
Treatises as were intended to be published for the service of
Truth."[28] In itself, Ellwood's statement is indicative of the
interplay of individual minds with the Quaker group mind.
This, as has been suggested, was the distinguishing point of
difference between the Quakers on one side and the Ranters
and Christian Quakers on the other.

On the whole the Second Day Morning Meeting exercised
its powers judiciously. The secretary in his minutes made
very clear "the sense of the meeting" when either absolute
rejection or approval was agreed upon. While the members
exercised considerable influence in regard to accuracy and
style, they were over and above all concerned with attaining
literature that would further the interests of the Friends in
their campaign for making life a spiritual matter, and for
denying calumnies written in opposition to them.

Quaker literature ultimately suffered in their hands. The
influence of the Morning Meeting was such that it strengthened, to borrow a psychological term, the "mental set" of
the Society in the direction of exclusiveness. The members

of the committee stamped their approval upon Quaker history, biography, and autobiography, upon doctrinal writings and upon controversy. Penn voiced the opinions of the Morning Meeting when in 1704 he requested the readers of Friends' books not to hope for "the learning of the schools," or for "lustre" of style, but entreated them to read with the "inward eye" for spiritual and not for intellectual enlightenment.

The Morning Meeting little realized the effects of such a policy upon the future of the Society and upon its literature. It was, however, logically following out certain tendencies inherent in Quakerism. As we have seen, the chief desideratum of the Friends was mental and spiritual peace, the harmonizing of the human with the divine will, which they found in their mystic idea of the pervasiveness of God. They feared that experience of divinity would be lost through contacts with the world, and that reliance upon reason and intellect would inhibit receptiveness to inner Guidance. As long as the Society possessed leaders who combined mental culture with spiritual leadership, its literature was not appreciably affected. The direful results became apparent in the eighteenth century only after the earlier writers had passed away and almost no leaders with literary and wide cultural backgrounds were prepared to take their places.

CHAPTER IX

VENTURES IN HISTORY AND BIOGRAPHY

The Friends assayed almost every form of writing current between 1650 and 1725. The community of experiences, physical, emotional, and mental, shared by the entire membership, as previously noted, fostered a literature definitely intended to serve the needs of the corporate Society. The Friends, however, included more in their practical program than controversial and didactic writings; they branched out into history, essays, and verse, and discovered in the newly opened field of autobiography an opportunity for the expression of self. Before 1725 they had published over eighty religious confessions and journals, a number probably greater than all the non-Quaker autobiographies printed in England during the preceding seventy-five years.

Their puritanical bias disinclined them toward drama and *vers de société*. They were too much in earnest to indulge in satire, but all other literary forms in use from Cromwell's day to that of George I, they made their own. They saw in history and biography a method for preserving records of the progress of the Society; in essays, meditations, and aphorisms a chance for the exposition of their beliefs; in poetry an opportunity for elegiac verse, for paraphrasing the Scriptures, and for depicting emotion; and in their confessions and autobiographies the most ideal plan available for interpreting the Quaker idea of practical mysticism through the revelation of the inner Light in individual experience.

1

History and biography enabled the Friends to present Quaker beliefs and to teach conduct in life, as well as to record the main facts in Quaker history and in the lives of their martyrs and preachers. Except for William Caton's abridgment of the *Ecclesiastical History* of Eusebius Pamphilus and Ellis Hookes's *The Spirit of the Martyrs Revived,* they confined themselves to chronicling their own past and to the retelling of biblical narratives. The formal writing of history was, comparatively speaking, a late development with the Friends. The first generation had been too much occupied in maintaining the integrity of the group to do more than collect materials on which later historians worked. The writers of the second generation turned this material into annals recording the growth, persecutions, and beliefs of the Quaker sect.

The two important early histories of the Society were published by William Penn in 1694, and by the Dutch Quaker, William Sewel in 1722.[1] Penn's history *The Rise and Progress of the People Called Quakers* in its original form, prefaced the first folio edition of *The Journal of George Fox.* In this introduction Penn touched very lightly on the factual side of the Society's annals, but in doctrinal fashion concentrated upon the faith and practices of the Friends. The character portrayal of the founder of Quakerism stands out as the most striking passage in Penn's history if one judges this preface as a human document. Penn pictured George Fox as "an incessant labourer," "a new and heavenly minded man" who excelled in prayer, "a divine and a naturalist," and "an original" man "being no man's copy."[2] Later in the year 1694, this introduction, with

the title by which it has since been known, was published as
a separate book. The fact that before 1838 it had been reprinted twelve times in England, four in America, and translated into Welsh, Danish, French, and German, attests its
popularity with the Friends.

By far the most important of the Quaker histories *The
Rise, Increase, and Progress of the People Called Quakers*
was the work of William Sewel, the son of Judith Zinspen-
ninck-Sewel. She herself had composed a book of proverbs,
and as a minister had exerted considerable influence among
the early Quaker converts in Amsterdam. No book written
by or for Friends, with the exception of *The Journal of
George Fox,* is so well known as this history. Frequently reprinted, it was widely read by Friends throughout the eighteenth century. In the early nineteenth it was brought to the
attention of a wider reading public by Charles Lamb, whose
associations with his Quaker friends, Charles Lloyd and Ber-
nard Barton, enabled him to catch the spirit of primitive
Quakerism underlying Sewel's account. For this reason his
eulogy will bear quoting here:

If you are not acquainted with it, I would recommend to you,
above all church-narratives, to read Sewel's *History of the
Quakers.* It is in folio, and is the abstract of the journals of Fox
and the primitive Friends. . . . Here is nothing to stagger you,
nothing to make you mistrust, no suspicion of alloy, no drop or
dreg of the worldly or ambitious spirit. . . . You will read here
the true story of that much injured, ridiculed man . . . James
Naylor: what dreadful sufferings, with what patience he endured even to the boring through of his tongue with red-hot
irons, without a murmur; and with what strength of mind, when
the delusion that he had fallen into, which they stigmatized for
blasphemy, had given way to clearer thoughts, he could renounce his error, in a strain of the beautifullest humility, yet
keep his first grounds and be a Quaker still![3]

In addition to the strong human element which Lamb perceived, these volumes of Sewel's *History* contain an immense compilation of first-hand historical material, such as legal documents, verbatim accounts of trials, petitions, epistles, and proclamations. The ample index and numerous citations of authorities represent a conscientious effort to present a painstaking record of the main facts of Quaker history. The pages contain graphic pictures of Friends' being carted to prisons, sometimes with spinning wheels in hand; of missionary journeys into Wales and the Colonies; of conventicles broken up by informers; of meeting houses torn down, and of Quakers on plague-ridden ships in the Thames in 1665, waiting for the decree of banishment to be put into effect. For these reasons the laborious researches of Sewel have become a treasure for all subsequent Quaker historians.[4]

Mention should also be made of *The General History of the Quakers* by Gerard Croese, a non-Friend. This book was first published in Latin in 1696, and in the following year translated into German and English. When news of the approaching publication reached London, the Quaker leaders became alarmed over certain statements contained in it hostile to the Society. They prevailed upon John Dunton,[5] the English publisher, to grant them permission to add an appendix to the book. Working in conjunction with the Morning Meeting, Joseph Wyeth, William Crouch, and Thomas Ellwood prepared a forty page addition, bristling with replies to all of Croese's arguments and assertions deemed by them as "unmete for Truth."[6] Besides the original material of the Latin text, the English edition appeared with a letter of George Keith's, a defense of the Friends, and a statement of Quaker principles, which had recently been drawn up in Philadelphia.

2

Thomas Ellwood, a prolific contributor to Quaker literature, interested himself in preparing an elaborate biblical history. He designed this book largely, though not wholly, for younger readers. The main title of his work *Sacred History* indicates the character of the treatise, and the subtitle *The Historical Parts of the Holy Scriptures of the Old Testament; Gathered out from the other Parts thereof, and Digested . . . with respect to Order of Time and Place* suggests the plan of the author. Four years later he included in a second part the historical sections of the New Testament. These were combined into one edition in 1720, and reprinted four times within the century. As indicated by his titles and by his three prefaces, he arranged the narrative episodes of the Bible as far as possible in their chronological order. By the omission of genealogical tables and of records of war, he hoped to simplify the study of biblical history. In treatment he not infrequently paraphrased the scriptural account, taking the privilege "to skip to and fro, from book to book, chapter to chapter, and verse to verse, forwards and backwards."[7] He made three unequal divisions of the Old Testament, for the length of the third equals that of the other two. Part one carries the narrative to the death of Moses; part two to the last combat of Saul, and part three to the return of the Hebrews from their second Babylonian captivity.[8]

In his efforts to be accurate in the concrete as well as the abstract, Thomas Ellwood, like Sewel, is true to his Quaker training, for he scrupulously acknowledged his indebtedness to his sources. The following example from his second preface illustrates Ellwood's conscientious respect for authority:

The helps I have had in compiling this history, have been chiefly the Criticks and Craddock's *Harmony of the Four Evangelists* with his *Apostolical History.* Out of either of which I have sometimes made bold to borrow here or there a quotation; yet not often, if ever, without owning to whom I am indebted.[9]

Frequently in the body of *Sacred History*[10] he referred to his source material; at other times he indicated a philological interest[11] in tracing the root meaning of a word back to its use in an older language, or made it clear that he had employed different versions of the Bible in order to ascertain the exact shade of meaning which he believed the original author had in mind.[12]

Ellwood's slow-moving pedestrian style lacks vividness of detail, for also true to Quaker principles, he made no attempt to use rhetorical embellishment or to display his knowledge. The sentence structure is, however, free from complexity. Whatever grace of style *Sacred History* possesses has resulted from the author's familiarity with the imagery of its scriptural basis. A seventeenth-century atmosphere, observable in word choice and in background, frequently creeps in. Ellwood, for instance, while describing the stoning of Stephen, apparently had in mind the breaking up of Quaker conventicles which, as a youth, he had witnessed in Buckinghamshire.[13] He thus envelops the incident with an English setting:

For that confident and forward youth, Saul . . . thrusting himself boldly into this mischievous work, made havoc of the church, not only molesting them in public meetings, but even following them home, and entering into every house, haled out both men and women, and committed them to prison.[14]

Ellwood had no intention of glossing over his didactic purpose. He hoped that the reading of his *Sacred History* might not deter anyone from further study of the Scriptures, but on the other hand, he saw no reason why it should not spur students on to engage in a comparative study of the Scriptures, and thus lead "to a greater reverence and admiration of the Lord." He, furthermore, entertained the pious hope that his book might prove a worthy substitute for the reading of the "lewd novels and lascivious poems" on which people were "misspending" their time. He deplored the current taste for "romances and vice-prompting plays," and wished that his history might "at the same time both please and instruct." "I hoped," he wrote,

I would do no unacceptable service, at least to some, in presenting them with this *Sacred History* so digested as might both invite their attention, and recompense their pains in reading, with the double advantage of godly instruction and virtuous pleasure.[15]

3

Biography, like history, presented opportunities for portraying the aspirations and characteristics of Quaker worthies as well as for picturing the social background of Quakerism. The Friends employed two types of biography, the testimony and the biography proper. The former has already been defined as a short sketch which paid tribute to the character of a deceased Friend, and one which, generally in prefatory capacity,[16] combined eulogy and elegy with biographical matter. Of these there is nothing finer in Quaker literature than Penn's character sketch of George Fox recently mentioned, and the elegiac dithyramb of Francis Howgill, where, in the language of David's lament for Jonathan,[17] he mourned for Edward Burrough, "dead before his prime" in Newgate Prison. Burrough, in Howgill's estimation, was "a man of peace, who loved it" and one whose "strength was bended after God."

Before the respective imprisonments which shortened their lives, Francis Howgill and Edward Burrough had journeyed together and had endured persecution in Ireland and England. In his testimony Howgill likened their friendship to that of David and Jonathan. In his expression he has caught both the rhythm and the phrasing of the King James Version:

I am distressed for thee my brother! Very pleasant hast thou been to me, and my love to me was wonderful, passing the love of woman. O thou! whose bow was never turned back, neither sword empty from the blood of the slain, from the slaughter of the mighty; who made nations and multitudes to shake with the Word of Life in thy mouth . . . and to the Seed of God brought forth, thy words dropped like oil, and thy lips like the honeycomb. . . . Shall I not say, as David said of Saul and Jonathan . . . 'The beauty of Israel is slain in high places.' Even so wast thou stifled in nasty holes and prisons, and many more that were precious in the eyes of the Lord. . . .[18]

4

With but few exceptions, the biographies portray only the lives of Friends. Ellis Hookes, who modeled his *Spirit of the Martyrs Revived* upon the plan of John Foxe's martyrology, did review the lives of the Christians who were persecuted for their beliefs, and at least one small collection of lives of the apostles, published by Friends, is extant. Most writers devoted their attention to depicting the life history of Quaker men and women. Richard Hawkins, for example, wrote the life of his uncle Gilbert Latye;[19] Thomas Aldam, an account of his father, "an early publisher and sufferer for Truth";[20] and Daniel Roberts, of his father, John Roberts of Cirencester, a Gloucestershire farmer.[21] Many of these biographies were little more than extensions of the testimony, and quite frequently were composed by members of the bereaved family.[22] Wives and husbands contributed many of these testimonies.[23] John Richardson wrote an account in which he paid high tribute to his second wife Anne, who assumed all family cares that he might follow the unremunerated calling of a "public" Friend.[24] The best written

and most vivid of these accounts were left in epistolary form
by Mary Penington. They contain vignettes of seventeenth-
century life both without and within Quaker circles, among
them graphic pictures of her two husbands, the young puritan, William Springett and the Quaker mystic, Isaac Penington.[25]

Among the biographies proper,[26] the lives of Gilbert Latye
and John Roberts succeed best in picturing the Quaker way
of life. Richard Hawkins presents an unforgetable picture of
his uncle, Gilbert Latye, an early convert, who relinquished
a profitable living as a London tailor because he refused to
deck "the apparel of persons of considerable rank" at court
with a "superfluity of lace and ribbons."[27] *The Life of John
Roberts* of Cirencester, on account of its effervescing humor,
often not far distant from pathos, offers good reading today. When it was reëdited in the nineteenth century under
the title *A Quaker of ye Olden Time,* Oliver Wendell
Holmes pronounced every word of it to be "golden." Daniel
Roberts makes it very clear that his father possessed a quality which we now associate with Abraham Lincoln, for by
means of well chosen anecdotes John Roberts in his arguments with bishops, apparitors, and justices, was able to
drive home his points, frequently to the discomfiture of ecclesiastical representatives.[28]

The early Friends saw that ethical lessons could be taught
by biography as well as by paraphrasing the Scriptures.
Three quaint biographies of Peter, Paul, and Andrew, with
a brief mention of thirteen other apostles, fill out the last
forty-four pages of William Caton's abridgment of *The
Ecclesiastical History of Eusebius Pamphilus.* Quite likely
these lives were used as padding, for the initial title-page is
silent concerning them. The introductory "General Epistle
for Young Schoolars and Little Children," written by Caton,

and a didactic poem by Gershon Boate entitled "A Father's Advice to his Child or A Maiden's Best Adorning," indicate that the compilation had been designed for young Friends.[29]

The writer of these apostolic biographies remains anonymous. At the close of the four-page life of Paul occurs a description of the apostle's person, in which the unknown writer combines the prevalent seventeenth-century stylistic delight in punning with Quaker caution for accuracy of expression. The last phrase shows the writer's belief in the preponderating power of the spiritual over the material, for he maintains that despite the low stature of the apostle, the spirit of Paul rose to visions.

He [Paul] was a man said to be of low stature, and somewhat stooping, his complection fair, his countenance grave, his head small; his Eyes carried a kind of beauty and sweetness in them; that he was low [he] himself plainly indicates, when he tells they were wont to say of him, that his bodily person was weak, and his speech contemptable, [sic.] in which he is stiled by Chrysostom a man three cubits high (or a little more than four foot high), and yet tall enough to reach heaven.

5

On the borderland between history and biography two important books need mention here. One, Joseph Besse's *A Collection of the Sufferings of the People Called Quakers,* has already been discussed.[30] The second was compiled by John Whiting, an indefatigable searcher among Quaker documents, who published the first bibliography of Friends' books in 1708 and the first biographical dictionary of the Quakers in 1715. The latter *Persecution Expos'd in some Memoirs relating to the Sufferings of John Whiting and many others called QUAKERS . . . with Memoirs of Many EMINENT FRIENDS deceased . . . till the Year of Release 1689* contains fifty-four sketches of prominent early

Friends. Like Clarendon in his *History of the Rebellion,* Whiting made himself both a participator in events and a reporter of them.

The book shows considerable research and for the period is unusually well indexed. Dates appear at the top of every page; division titles are clearly indicated, and the margins are crowded with place names and supplementary data. The biographical entries, though interspersed with other material, follow one another in chronological order. Whiting, employing idiomatic Quaker phrasing, begins each history somewhat monotonously with such expressions as "About this time 1684 our dear friend Lawrence Steel, of Bristol, died though not in prison,"[31] or with "I shall conclude the year 1685 with the Death of another faithful servant of God, and none in the least in Travels and sufferings, viz., Robert Widders of Kellet in Lancashire,"[32] or with "Two days later died that Ancient Suffering servant of God, and minister of Jesus Christ, William Dewsbury, of whom though I have mentioned somewhat in the beginning of this Treatise in relation to his imprisonment in Warwick, yet I cannot but give some further account of him, being so Eminent in his Day. . . ." After such introductions of obituary nature, Whiting proceeds with the historical details of birth, occupation, religious conversion, the adoption of Quaker habits of life, travels, and, as the title of the book indicates, with heavy strokes he etches in the "sufferings" of these fifty-four "eminent men and women." He sometimes completes the sketch with a list of the written works[33] and not infrequently concludes with the dying sayings of the deceased,[34] a highly approved custom of the time.

Whiting distinctly sought accuracy of statement. If he were unable to furnish and vouch for the data he needed, he inserted a matter-of-fact remark to that effect, as "Roger Longworth and James Harrison, both of Bolton in the moors

in Lancashire [died 1678]; and both great Travelers at
Home and Abroad in the Service of Truth. . . . I knew
them both, but cannot say much for want of memoirs."[35] Almost "cradled and rocked in conventicles,"[36] trained from
infancy that his "aye" should be "aye" and his "nay," "nay,"
John Whiting was deeply concerned that future times should
have a truthful account of his day.[37]

The forty-four volumes of manuscript "sufferings accounts," previously noted, the manuscript records of *The
First Publishers of Truth,* the scrupulous preservation of
minutes of the Morning Meeting, the Meeting for Sufferings, and the Yearly Meeting,[38] as well as numerous collections of epistles,[39] attest the high value which the Friends
placed upon permanent records. The historical value of their
biographies and histories is for this reason enhanced by the
documentary evidence behind them. In the hands of the
Friends, history and biography were felt to be instruments
for explaining the spiritual and practical values of the
Quaker way of life, and for leaving records of the Society
and of its leaders.

CHAPTER X

QUAKER ESSAYS

The Friends found the essay particularly adaptable for explaining Quaker points of view. In expository manner, this seventeenth-century innovation supplemented their more vehement controversial tracts. Until after the Act of Toleration of 1689, the Quaker genius had been too much occupied in crusading for the interests of the Society to concern itself with such literary themes as "On Great Places," "On Vulgar Errors," or with critical discussions dealing with the superiority of blank verse over the heroic couplet. Even after 1689 it is rare to find in Quaker writings anything that can be identified strictly as an essay in the *belles lettres* sense of the word. In this chapter, therefore, the term essay will be used to cover several miscellaneous types of expository writing in which the Friends engaged, such as pleas for peace and for emigration to colonies, as well as essays of reflective, prophetic, and travel nature.

1

The Friends marched in the vanguard of the movement for international peace.[1] Among the earliest English writers to make distinctive literary contributions to the movement for peace, William Penn and John Bellers hold foremost rank. In 1693 William Penn, after a period of forced retirement from court, composed and published an *Essay toward the Present and Future Peace of Europe,* in which he advocated a world court to settle questions of boundaries and of disputes. His plan was an extensive one, for he desired to include the Muscovite and the Turk in a general diet of Europe in order to establish international rules of justice.[2] Peace, he maintained, could and must be found in justice and not in force of arms. Two Latin phrases, which form the principal heading of this essay, *Beati Pacifici* and *Cedant Arma Togæ*, interpret his thesis[3] for both individual and international efforts to secure peace.

Twenty years later in 1710, John Bellers carried Penn's proposals for world peace even farther by suggesting in *Some Reasons for an European State*, an "annual guarantee and an annual congress, senate, dyet, and Parliament to settle bounds and rights of princes and states." John Bellers, a member of the Royal Society and known today as the father of sociology,[4] looking forward to the advancement of the social sciences, wrote numerous essays of philanthropic nature. He saw clearly the relationship between economics and living conditions in England, and through his essays frequently endeavored to draw attention to constructive measures for aiding the poor, who were suffering on account of maladjusted economic and political situations.[5] George Fox, who objected to Thomas Fuller's ridicule[6] of his *Battle-door* and the plain language of the Friends, would have agreed heartily with Fuller's aphoristic statement that negroes were images of God carved in ebony.[7] The care and education of slaves interested Fox deeply,[8] as it has successive generations of Friends. John Woolman exemplified the Quaker stand against slavery in the eighteenth century, and John Greenleaf Whittier in the next.

2

A class of essays, known as "plantation tracts," belongs distinctively to the literature of the last half of the seven-

teenth century.[9] They were designed to encourage emigration to America. Some of these tracts were written by
planters themselves, and others by promoters of colonization schemes in England. The Friends, desiring to demonstrate the practicability of their "holy experiment" in Pennsylvania and the Jerseys, had their share in such essays. To
urge Englishmen to participate in this attempt, Thomas
Budd,[10] William Penn, and William Loddington, among
others, enlisted in colony "planting." Thomas Budd wrote
the most complete of these essays *Good Order Established in
Pennsilvania and New Jersey* (1685). Budd believed that
the distressing conditions of the poor might be relieved by
emigration from England to the Colonies. He therefore described with attractive details the woods and fields of Pennsylvania, the natural resources of the land, the possibilities
for various trades and industries, and envisioned a fast approaching day when in addition to religious freedom, colonists could expect to find a sound banking system for their
financial undertakings,[11] and good schools[12] for their children.

Though William Penn spent but two years in America,
he gave great thought to the experiment which he was pro-
moting. For the furthering of his plans, in 1682 he sent to
London to the Committee of The Free Society of Traders
of Pennsylvania an account similar to Thomas Budd's,
but briefer.[13] Its long title *A General Description of the said
Province, its Soil, Air, Water, Seasons, and Produce, both
Natural and Artificial, and the Good Encrease thereof with
an Account of the Natives or Aborigines* anticipates the
contents, which with succinctness he treated under thirty-
three heads. Several relate to his observations upon and his
faith in the Indians. In this epistolary essay he detailed the
Indian mode of life, marriage customs, training of children, and expatiated on his theory of the origin of the In-

dians, which, in concurrence with popular belief, he ascribed to the ten lost tribes of Israel. In the eleventh section he gave his impressions of the spoken language of the Indians thus:

> The language is lofty, yet narrow, but like the Hebrew; in signification full, like shorthand in writing; one word serveth in the place of three . . . I must say that I know not a language spoken in Europe that hath words of more sweetness or greatness in accent and emphasis than theirs. For instance, Octocockon, Rancocas, Oricton, Shak, Marian, Poquesien, all which are names of places, and have grandeur in them.[14]

Throughout this letter Penn's favorable description of the native Indians of Pennsylvania shows his unwavering Quaker belief in the essential dignity and brotherhood of man.[15]

The long title of William Loddington's eighteen page essay *Plantation Work, the work of this Generation, Written in True Love to all such as are Weightily inclined to Transplant Themselves and Families to any of the English Plantations,*[16] is suggestive of the writer's purpose. Loddington[17] in 1682 addressed his plea particularly to emigrants who were thinking of joining Penn who had recently sailed for Pennsylvania. This Quaker schoolmaster built his entire tract upon probable arguments which prospective colonists, "weightily inclined" toward settling in America, might bring up. To forestall doubts and questioning, he first pointed out that neither the ocean voyage nor the building of homes in a new land could present insurmountable difficulties. If any struggled against the belief that it was either wrong or unpatriotic to drain England of good tenantry, Loddington had an answer ready. He assured such persons that "the Lord would raise up others to take their places." In further support of this plea, he cited as scriptural proof the cases of Abraham, Moses, and Noah, who by "oft transplanting themselves" to new and distant regions, had felt and answered divine calls of similar nature.

By insisting that colonization was "the work of this generation," not of the passing one, he made short work of the argument that affection for relatives would retard emigration. He emphatically denied the current rumors that "America was a place of unsettled brains, wandering minds, which were void of solidity and gravity," as well as reports that settlers would not be able to secure permanent titles to their lands. In style Loddington writes with compactness, employs Quaker idioms, cites Scripture freely, and what is unusual but in perfect keeping with his calling of schoolmaster, quotes from literary sources—on this occasion from Bacon's essay "A little Model for Plantations." Loddington agreed heartily with Thomas Budd and William Penn in urging that all "colonists weightily inclined" should set their faces westward and without scruples and without fears proceed with resolution.

3

Essays in which a meditative strain is present are abundant in the writings of the Friends before 1725. That such should be the case is to be expected of a group given to introspective probing and to searching the heart for "the seed of the act." Isaac Penington's ample folio contains many[18] essays in which, as a mystic, he treats the theme of the inner Light. In *Balm from Gilead*, William Smith meditates on topics varying from the worldliness of bearbaiting to the immanence of divine love. In 1683 John Crook penned his *Sick-Bed Meditations;* in these he speaks little of himself but dwells almost constantly upon the prison sufferings which his associates were undergoing for "the sake of conscience." A note of optimism creeps into these meditations, for he consoles himself with the belief that from the persecutions of the Friends "a better people will be raised up" who in the future will be able to "reap with joy" and cause "the earth to be filled with the knowledge of the Glory of the Lord."[19] Alexander Jaffray, the Scotch laird of Aberdeen, after his conversion to Quakerism, filled many pages of his *Diary* with reflections upon Christian living and upon the condition of his own soul. William Shewen pondered at length upon the "precious results" that had come to him through the discovery that the Friends "were partakers of the same wisdom and revelation in and with which John wrote his book of *Revelations.*"[20]

Meditations sometimes resulted from a period of leisure enforced upon the Friends. A wintry voyage from England to Virginia in 1699[21] gave Thomas Chalkley an opportunity of glorifying God in fifty-six brief reveries, which he later published as *Fruits of Divine Meditations at Sea.*[22] Imprisonment very often bore fruit in meditations penned in both prose and verse. William Thompson, a schoolmaster at Nottingham, versified his reflections upon human life and upon God.[23] William Bennitt wrote *Some Prison Meditations of an Humble Heart*[24] and Thomas Taylor *Some Prison Meditations . . . a Free-Gift Sermon.*[25] During his imprisonment in Derby in 1680, John Gratton, for the benefit of "his wife, children, Friends, and all mankind," put into the form of a didatic poem his conviction that "stone walls do not a prison make."[26] Approximating the popular heroic couplet in one of these musings, he thus explained that the secret source of Quaker fortitude under persecution lay in the Friends' consciousness of the presence of Divinity within:

> Yea, let me tell thee, man, who e'er thou art,
> We have a certain earnest in our heart,
> Of the inheritance that is above
> The reach of man, the fame we prize and love,
> Which we call Light, Grace, or Spirit of Life,

That leads us out of Trouble, Care and Strife
And teacheth us to worship God aright

.   .   .   .

Mind Truth, God loves it in the inward parts,
Which God hath plac'd to bear rule in our hearts,
For 'tis the Lamb that takes the sin away,
In them that hear his voice and Him obey.[27]

The meditations of the Friends for the most part centered about the inner harmony which allegiance to the inner Light had brought to them.

4

Meditations readily fall under the general heading of essays, but the prophetical writings of the Friends defy definite cataloguing and for this reason will be treated as extensions of the essay. The majority belong to the early period when zealous enthusiasm often merged into fanaticism. In general the prophetical literature of the Friends consisted of laments[28] over the state of Christendom, of warnings[29] against corrupt administrators of law, and sometimes of visions of the near or distant future.[30] The use made of prophetic writings, especially during the Commonwealth, by the Quakers can be traced to individualistic interpretation of the Bible, to the unrest of the times, and to a pronounced feeling among the more ecstatic of the primitive Friends that they were the remnant, chosen by God, for rediscovering and preserving a spiritual religion. In their study of the Old Testament they had found that the prophets from Isaiah to Malachi had bewailed the sins of Israel. The Friends, following scriptural models, and borrowing phrases from the major and minor prophets, bewailed the state of England.

Many Friends of the second generation disapproved of these tendencies, and because they believed these laments to emanate from fanatically inclined representatives of their group, they strove to check them through the Morning Meeting. Excerpts from a tract named *An Alarm to All Flesh,* and issued by Edward Billing a few months after Charles II came to the throne, will illustrate the nature of these prophetic outbursts, both as to their intensity and the desire of their authors to extol Quakerism. This ten page prophecy opened with a crescendo of denunciations, with which Edward Billing assailed the inhabitants of the earth and besought mankind to repent. As he proceeded his tone gradually became milder, until he brought his diatribe to a quiet close by describing the prophetic mission of the Friends in this world. With a strong undercurrent of emotion, and with a profuse sprinking of capital letters and italics, he thus began his *Alarm to All Flesh: with an Invitation to the True Seeker:*

HOWLE, HOWLE, SHRIEKE, YELL AND ROAR, ye Lustful, Cursing, Swearing, Drunken, Lewd, Superstitious, *Earthly Inhabitants* of the Whole Earth; BOW, BOW, ye most surley Trees, and lofty Oaks, ye tall Cedars, and low Shrubs, *Cry out aloud:* HEAR, HEAR, ye proud Waves, and boisterous Seas, also LISTEN, ye uncircumcised, stiff-necked, and mad raging Bubbles, who even hate to be reformed.

In the name of the Lord God of Gods, and King of Kings, HEAR, HEAR; REPENT, REPENT, forthwith REPENT, for . . . ye shall feel the Irresistible and Mighty hand of the Almighty Lord God of Heaven and Earth, . . .[31]

In the latter half of this lament in preparation for his closing assertion, Billing reassured his readers by explaining that the foregoing had been "transcribed by the hand of me, *Edward Billing,* who neither hates nor fears any man, but is a lover of all men in the Lord." With a gentleness which contrasted sharply with his opening denunciations he ended the tract by proclaiming the mission of "the despised and scorned Quakers." He represents the Creator speaking of them in the very words with which Zephaniah had delivered his prophetic message to the people of Jerusalem:

Then I will turn to the people a pure language, that they may call upon the name of the Lord, to serve Him with one consent: I will also leave in the midst of thee an afflicted and poor people and they shall trust in the Name of the Lord. The remnant of Israel shall do no iniquity, nor speak lyes; neither shall a deceitful tongue be found in their Mouth; for they shall feed, and lye down, and none shall make them afraid . . . and I will get them a praise and fame in every land where they have been put to shame.[32]

Prophetic literature was employed by the early Friends, partly as a medium for voicing protest, partly for freeing individual consciences from personal responsibility toward their generation, and partly for declaring faith in the high mission to which Friends believed they had been called.

CHAPTER XI

SUNDRY VENTURES—VERSE AND ALLEGORY

1

In consideration of the distrustful attitude of the Friends toward "the learning of the world," and of their fondness for unadorned prose, Quaker verse between 1650 and 1725 is surprisingly plentiful, and reaches fairly high levels.

The Friends found many uses and many places for poetical effusions. Verses appear at the end of prefaces such as Burrough's introduction to *The Great Mistery of the Great Whore,* and Penn's envoy to *The Truth Exalted in the Works of John Burnyeat;* and often at the close of Samuel Fisher's controversial articles.[1] Hookes employed an envoy to complete his preface to the *Spirit of the Martyrs Revived.* Numerous verse broadsides[2] from Quaker pens also found their way to bookstalls, some mildly satirical,[3] others pietistic[4] or elegiac[5] in nature. Hymns and religious meditations in verse were occasionally wedged in between controversial and autobiographical essays when previously printed tracts were republished in collected *Works.* In 1659 Thomas Stubbs wrote in free verse "A Declaration of Life and Power in me"; Samuel Fisher in 1660, "A Lamentation over Lost Souls"; Thomas Taylor wrote hymns and biblical paraphrases; Robert West, "A Song of the Lord"; William Smith, "The Shepherd's Care over his Flock," and numerous other hymns; and Humphrey Smith, "Lines of Secret

Inward Melody and Praise to the Lord." These few examples are representative of many.

The composition of at least eight small volumes of verse belongs to this period. Six of these, as the following table indicates, were printed:

1661	Perrot, John	*A Sea of the Seed's Sufferings through Which Runs a River of Rich Rejoicing*
1679	Sixmith, William	*Some Fruits brought forth through a Tender Branch*
1684	Antrobus, Benjamin	*Some Buds and Blossoms of Piety*
1702	Mollineux, Mary	*Fruits of Retirement: or, Miscellaneous Poems, Moral and Divine*
1722	Bockett, Richard, Jr.	*Fruits of Early Piety*
n.d.	Ellwood, Thomas	*A Collection of Poems on Various Subjects*[6]
MSS	Martin Mason[7]	
MSS	John Kelsall[8]	

To these volumes of miscellaneous verse must be added *A Serious Remembrancer,* containing the juvenilia of the fourteen year old son of Thomas Lawson, and *The Davideis* (1712) of Thomas Ellwood, a long epic poem in five books, written in the heroic couplet popularized by Ellwood's contemporaries, Dryden and Pope.

A fascimile copy of a manuscript in The Friends Reference Library, annotated by H. T. Wake, presents evidence that in the early days of Quakerism poems were circulated in manuscript, as were the contemporary lyrics of the Cavalier and later court poets, and the *Satires* of Samuel Butler. This document contains four poems, copied by Thomas Carleton[9] in 1665, when he was a prisoner at Carlisle. The first poem, from which the manuscript takes its name, was written by John Raunce of High Wycombe. As a broadside, bearing the title "A Few Words to All People,"[10] it found its way into print and prophesied a coming devastation of London by fire and plague. The second bears a prison endorsement, "Willyam Smith, Worcester Gaole, ye 26 of ye 2 month, 1661," and is entitled "A Joyful Sound of the Lamb's Day."[11] The third poem, "Ye Mountains and Ye Hills," was written by John Swinton, the Scotch co-laborer and co-sufferer of Alexander Jaffray at Aberdeen.

The last of the four came from the pen of Edward Burrough. Only one other poem[12] by this early Publisher of Truth has come to light. The poem, which Burrough named *Love*, completes the Raunce manuscript. It is here quoted in full to illustrate the type of Quaker verse that was then in circulation, and to illumine a side of Edward Burrough which is not readily perceived in his folio of collected controversial tracts *The Memorable Works of a Son of Thunder and Consolation*. The poem paraphrases from a Quaker point of view the thirteenth chapter of Second Corinthians.[13]

LOVE

Love is a vertue that endures forever
A linke of matchless Jewels none can sever;
Had I the tongue of men and angels too—
If love were wanting [what] good could I do?
Love far surmounts all earthly Diadems
Though decked with pearls,
With rubies, and with Jemes.
Love is the life of all things under the sun;
Love must the laurell weare, when all is done;
Love's eye is tender; love doth gently draw
The mind to God without a penall Law;
Love thinks no evill, love never did invent
Fines, premunire, gaoles, nor banishment,
For innocents. Love hath no spleene, nor gall;
Love's like the royall sun, love shines on all.

Two other manuscript poems will have to close this very brief survey of the poetry of the early Quaker group. Like their essays in prose, their verses represent the manifest interest that their authors had in following the general trend of late seventeenth and early eighteenth-century literature. *Vers de société* and drama, as was pointed out before, are lacking, as is also the sweeping satire of Butler or the more personal type of Dryden and Pope. The first of these poems without title shows traces of Miltonic phrasing, especially of "Il Penseroso." Its author, Martin Mason, contributed prolifically to Quaker literature between the years 1655 and 1665.[14]

> Hence vaine delights! Be gone, you empty joyes
> That circumvent the Wise and Earthly Toyes.
> Insnare not me, nor temptingly beguile,
> Thy Golden baite shall not my soul defile
> Doe I not knoe the end of Worldly Mirth —
> An Enemie to the immortil Birth?
> There is a secret joy unknown to thee
> Surmounts as farr all thy felicitie
> As does the Sun in its Meridian light
> Exceed the darksome and obscurest night.
> Then, transitory mirth, court me noe more,
> Thy worthless shadow I shall not adore,
> The spring of Wisdome let me live upon
> That will abide when empty joyes are gone.
> False World, adieu. Pure Wisdom, guide my minde
> That Joy which is Celestial I may finde.[15]
>
> M:M:

The manuscript diaries and poems of the Welsh schoolmaster, John Kelsall of Dolobran, cast interesting sidelights on the attitude of the Friends in the early eighteenth century toward verse and verse writing. Kelsall admits that when he felt some scruples in regard to poetizing his thoughts, he quieted his conscience by saying that it could not be wrong to compose verses because he then would be checking inner guidance; and since both "facility and freedom" and "an inclination" in that direction had been vouchsafed him, he felt that he "could not be easie to let such comfortable thoughts and meditations pass without taking notice of them."[16] Poetical inspiration, he thought, came to him from God. The following poem, in the heroic couplet of Dryden, shows some familiarity with the phraseology of Milton, to whose poetry John Kelsall respectfully refers in his diary. The last couplet expresses Quaker belief in the mystic unity of man and God.

> Oh! thou Almighty, whose majestic Sway
> The Earth and Seas, the Fire and Air obey,
> By whose Right Hand and providential care
> All things exist and still upholden are.—
> Thou didst not men unactive wights create
> But gave Them Talents to improve their State.
> Which Sanctifyed by thy Truth and Word
> Should to thy Honour, and their Good Accord.
>
> Bless my Essays, and truly guide my heart
> When it in flowing members shall impart
> Such raptured Thoughts, and such inspired things
> As from Dimmest meditations springs;
> Let not my muse n'ere exercise her Flame
> Wherein thy Praise is not her chiefest Aim,
> Profaneness sha'n't, or levity defile
> My Chaster Laye, or vitiate my Style—
>
> Let not my Fancy wander to mis-use
> That understanding which thou shalt infuse
> Nor 'ere my thoughts so far divided be
> But they may meet again and enter still in Thee.[17]

2

Romance and allegory held but a small place in the approximately three thousand Quaker publications antedating 1725. The early Friends would no doubt have repudiated the allegation that they indulged in the writing of romance. If, however, a recent critic's distinction is correct, that the romanticist approaches and develops his theme by the method of deduction and the realist by induction,[18] the Friends, even though they would have denied the fact, did write romance. In the supreme belief that Providence would direct the individual in the minutest details of life, the early Friends took as a sweeping deduction "God is over all," and set forth to carry over land and sea the message they believed to be God-given. Their treatment of their voyaging in leaky seventeenth-century boats, their traveling by "packhorse on the down," their stonings, beatings, escapes from pirates and from the inquisition, prove this fact. The pages of Sewel, of *New England Judged,* of *This Short Relation . . . of Katherine Evans and Sarah Chevers,* and the *Account of the Travels . . . of Barbara Blaugdone* add their share of contributory evidence.

For these writers God moved "in a mysterious way," and through their mystic approach to divinity, they saw in nature and man "the providences of God." Almost every page of Robert Fowler's narrative of the voyage of the *Woodhouse* across the Atlantic in 1657, and Jonathan Dickenson's *God's Protecting Providence* glows with the belief of these travelers that "God's hand in the cloud, in the wave, and in the wind" was over all. The latter account narrates the adventures of twenty-nine passengers who were shipwrecked in "the Gulph of Florida" in 1696. In the face of tremendous hardships they made their way by land to the Carolinas. "The little sucking child" in their company probably owed its life to occasional nursing by Indian mothers. One passage in its acceptance of the sweeping enunciation "God is over all" will illustrate the nature of *God's Protecting Providence.* At one time before losing its small boat, the company had taken to sea to escape hostile Indians when a theatening storm made it advisable to seek land. "It pleased God," Jonathan Dickenson wrote, "to order it so, that we went on shore, as though there had been a Lane made through the breakers, and [we] were carried to the top of the bank."[19] Not few were these romances of missionary adventure with belief invincible which early Friends, scorning the connotation of the word romance, denoted as "travels" and "sufferings" in the ministry.

3

Symbolism with the Friends has never been a highly developed trait. In the early days allegorical subjects abounded, such as the title of the religious experience of Thomas Green, *A Declaration to the World, of my Travel and Journey out of Aegypt into Canaan through the Wilderness and through the Red Sea, from under Pharaoh, and* [who] *now hath a Sure Habitation in the Lord where Rest and Peace are Known* (1659), or the prophetic warning of Christopher Taylor to the rulers of England (1655), called *The Whirl-Wind of the Lord gone Forth as a fiery flying Roule.* Although a strain of allegory, relying for its phraseology on the Scriptures and for its interpretation on both current[20] and biblical[21] ideas concerning dreams and visions, runs through much of their literature, the early Friends produced but one allegory. Under the metaphorical title of *A Short History of a Long Travel from Babylon to Bethel,* it represents the spiritual autobiography of a seventeenth-century man of religion, Stephen Crisp. Quaker autobiographies,[22] letters,[23] and collected works[24] also contain many allusions to dreams, openings, and visions, which were symbolically interpreted. The Friends, however, did not deliberately choose to cultivate allegory as a form of presenting spiritual truth through the medium of fiction. This statement seems to be substantiated by the fact that the only outstanding allegory of this period,

the work of Stephen Crisp, though written just before his
death in 1691, was excluded from his collected works in 1694
and not published until 1711.[25]

Stephen Crisp's *A Short History of a Long Travel from
Babylon to Bethel,* very obviously based upon Bunyan's *Pilgrim's Progress,* is today one of the most interesting of the
early Quaker contributions to literature. It consists of a
brief account of the search of the Quaker Christian for
his chief desideratum in life—spiritual peace. This allegory
may be looked upon as the metaphorical counterpart of over
eighty Quaker religious confessions. In its particular ap-
plications Crisp's *A Short History of a Long Travel from
Babylon to Bethel* stands in the same autobiographical relationship to *The Memorable Account of the Christian Experiences* of Stephen Crisp, as *The Pilgrim's Progress* does
to Bunyan's *Grace Abounding to the Chief of Sinners.* Bunyan with greater genius pictured the endeavor of the human
soul in such a way that his portrayal approximated the universal experience of Christians. With much vividness Stephen Crisp, working in a narrower field, emphasized one approach only, the Quaker's way to spiritual peace.

The inner Light, the center of this allegory, becomes under
the pen of Stephen Crisp, a gleam which at first the way-
farer saw dimly; and because he perceived it vaguely it
led him over mountains with steep declivities,[26] past snakes
and scorpions,[27] and sometimes, like an *ignis fatuus,* enticed
him into "swamps and quagmires"; but always as he
"minded" or concentrated upon the Light, he found that it
flooded a narrow path that led him safely across and at last
to the "house of the Lord," Bethel, where he found spiritual
peace. This haven was not, however, a celestial city such as
Christian and Hopeful reached, where rest and praise
dominated, but a new life where Stephen Crisp found a plan

of active participation in Christian work divinely mapped out for him.[28] While reminiscently recalling in this allegory the waverings of this Light, Crisp, quite incidentally, introduced his own gropings among the Anglicans and the Baptists, where he found that the former with all their "learning from books," and the latter with "their river of immersion," only complicated his problem. The Light, present though but dimly perceived in his childhood, as the allegory indicates, only brought him to peace with himself, nature and God, when he had surrendered selflessly to its leadings.

4

Two other ventures of the Friends elude all ordinary types of classification, for they are truly curiosities of literature. Neither the *Battle-Door* of George Fox or *A Musick-Lector* of the eccentric Solomon Eccles, however, can be passed over without mention because they represent distinctive efforts to advertise two social tenets of the Friends—the use of the "plain" language and the aversion to music.

In his *Battle-Door for Teachers and Professors to Learn Singular and Plural*, George Fox, the unschooled Quaker leader, undertook the task of persuading divinity and university scholars that they were wrong in using the second person pronoun in the plural in addressing one person. The term battle-door refers to the rude substitute for a slate used at that time by English schoolboys. Fox, in his *Battle-Door* stressed not only the democratic use of the second person singular, but with the help of two university trained men, John Stubbs and Benjamin Furly, attempted to prove through reference to historical grammar and through comparative literature that he was right in his contention that *thou* not *you* was the correct form. To do this, the collaborators prepared elaborate paradigms of the declension of the

personal pronoun in the ancient tongues, such as the Babylonian and the Philistine, and in Romance, Teutonic, and
Slavic languages—thirty-five in all.

At the close, Fox's assistants added a second part, in which
certain reforms for the instruction of youths were advocated. From textbooks in common use Stubbs and Furly
had selected salacious passages which they thought "tended
to lasciviousness." Pleading that more moral examples from
the classics[29] could be employed for illustrating grammatical
and rhetorical principles, they offered their cullings of objectionable illustrations as "a rod and switch for the school-
masters" of England.

In addition to *The Battle-Door* another tract, *A Musick-
Lector,* written by the fanatical Solomon Eccles, also stands
in a class by itself. In a curious manner it brings together
three literary forms, not usually associated together—the
essay, the Socratic dialogue, and the religious confession of
an author. *A Musick-Lector* was designed to show that all
music which interferes with communion between the soul
of man and God is wrong.[30] The author presented his
arguments through a symposium, made up of three speakers.
One is a musician, a master of the art, "zealous for the
church of England"; the second, a Baptist; and the third is
a Quaker, Eccles himself. By means of dialogue, the author
makes it evident that the Anglican considers music to be
"the gift of God," that the Baptist thinks it a "decent and
harmless practice," and that the Quaker approves only "of
the music that pleaseth God." Through the use of query
and answer, Solomon Eccles graphically detailed to these
men of differing religious persuasions the personal struggles that had led him to renounce his profession and means
of supporting his family. He told them that once he had
been a music master in London, but after accepting Quaker
principles he had actually burned his musical instruments on

Tower Hill. At the end of this symposium the author allows the Quaker to achieve a victory for the correctness of his view of inner direction, for he convinces the Anglican that the latter's pursuit of music had "unwittingly become his idol."[31] In a final analysis Eccles's colloquy of *A Musick-Lector* stands out as a sermon on the inner Light upon the text, "Thou shalt have no other gods before me."

The Friends ventured into many fields of literature—essay, prophecy, allegory, and poetry. In none did they reach great heights, yet for the most part they seldom fell below a fairly high level of expression. Ellwood in his introduction to *Davideis* in 1712 expressed the Quaker attitude toward plainness of style in writing. "I don't affect," he wrote,

the title of poet . . . I am content to walk in the middle way; where the safest walking is, and where I shall be sure to find virtue: than which I desire no better walking. . . . I write for common readers; in a style familiar, and easie to be understood by such.

In suggesting the strength and weakness of the Friends' literary attainments, Thomas Ellwood in these words passed judgment upon himself and upon the Friends of his generation. Unity of strength lay in the basic ideal of democracy of life and in adherence to biblical models, while weakness resided in the Friends' willingness to be content with literary masters whom they could imitate and equal, and not with those who could urge them on to higher attainments.

CHAPTER XII

SERMONS, PROVERBS, AND ADVICES

1

The Friends did not design their sermons for publication. According to their belief, a sermon represented the outpouring of the Spirit upon worshipers who delivered in extemporaneous manner the message vouchsafed to them. Though their sermon literature was oral, it exerted an inestimably great influence over their written and spoken language; for this reason sermons figure importantly in Quaker literature. The didactic writings of the Friends, including maxims, proverbs, and advices, consequently are closely associated with their sermons. These reach their culmination in Penn's religious conduct book *No Cross, No Crown.*

Preaching has left a marked impression upon the subject matter of their journals,[1] and has helped to preserve much of the terminology which soon became idiomatic with the Friends.[2] Many of these terms had originally been the common property of contemporary religious bodies.[3] In thousands of meetings from Scotland to the West Indies, such phraseology as "concern," "conviction," "to the outward," "the motions of the Light within," "the leadings of the spirit," "carnal reasonings," "reasonings of the flesh," "hireling priests," "experimental knowledge," and "the day of the Lord's visitation to us," must have been repeatedly sounded in meetings for worship, and have indelibly impressed the minds of early Quaker scribes.

The number of extant printed sermons actually delivered by Friends during the first seven decades of Quaker history will scarcely total sixty. At first glance this number seems very small. In an age when the pulpit wielded more power than the press, when between 1660 and 1669 Pepys in his *Diary* chronicled his own attendance at church three hundred and twenty-five times,[4] and when volumes and volumes of sermons, from Donne at one end of the century to Calamy at the close, were being published, the Friends have left but a minimum of printed sermon literature. This apparent anomaly corresponds exactly, however, with the Friends' idea of worship.

Since in the thinking of Friends a Quaker sermon sprang from divine prompting, any forethought as to what should be spoken in meeting was considered a dependence upon "outward aids," either upon memory, or upon intellect, or upon books. A strong feeling likewise existed against the recording of sermons as props or supports for future addresses; yet many Friends felt no compunctions[5] against recording in their journals, a brief digest of the individual sermon "opening" that had been accorded them in a morning or afternoon meeting.

One such entry appears in the autobiography of Samuel Bownas. Very early in the eighteenth century, while traveling as an itinerant or "public" Friend in Pennsylvania, Bownas felt that he had reason to be grateful to Providence for the inspiration that came to him in meeting after meeting. At the same time, however, he was oppressed by a fear lest he should succumb to the temptation of ascribing this success in preaching to his own ability and to his own mental resources. After reviewing his recent endeavors, he conscientiously confided to his diary his constant fear that in his own thoughts he might be robbing God of the power that belonged to Him, writing:

I went to Darby, and had a small meeting, and so to Philadelphia, and had a brave meeting, insomuch that I was filled with admiration at so uncommon a supply of doctrine every day, which gave me cause to be more and more humble, and when some Friends would speak in favor of such an opportunity or branch of doctrine, it would give me a shock, lest by any of these unwary commendations, I should take to myself that honor which was due to the Father of spirits, and so fall into robbery unawares.[6]

Reliance upon any other source except divine inspiration was scrupulously guarded against. Soon after the event just recorded, Bownas gave a brief résumé of a particular sermon that he had preached on inward revelation, in which he enumerated the types of "outward helps" that a Quaker. preacher should avoid. For this reason the following entry defines in negative fashion the attributes that a Quaker sermon should not possess.

At this meeting [a quarterly meeting] at Bristol I was divinely opened with fresh matter, setting forth the service of the spiritual ministry, which was free from all contrivance and forecast of the creature [the human will], in preparing itself either with former openings, or beautiful collection of texts, or sayings from books or writings, all which gatherings would bring death, and could be no other in the best and more favorable construction, though well looked on by some, than the ministry of the letter, under the pretense of the ministry of the spirit, which is a deception of the highest nature.[7]

These quotations clearly indicate that Quaker preachers in their delivery of sermons were expected to avoid all devices that would draw the attention of the auditor from spiritual matters to "worldly learning," or to rhetorical or oratorical devices.

2

Since the sermon was looked upon as a spontaneous, God-given utterance, a strong prejudice existed against taking

sermons down in shorthand and against printing them lest
speakers should depend upon these and not upon future out-
pourings of the Spirit. The few that have come down to us
are illuminating on account of their similarity to other forms
of expression used by the Friends and on account of the
identity of motives apparent in both their oral and written
literature. All the extant sermons of this period seem to be
pirated copies, first taken down by people outside the Society
and printed.[8] Sewel, upon inserting in his *History of the
Quakers* a sermon on "Regeneration," delivered by William
Dewsbury shortly before the latter's death in 1688, took
occasion[9] to shift responsibility and to disarm criticism by
informing his readers that he had found the sermon already
in print.[10]

Thirty-two sermons of Stephen Crisp (1621-1692) of
Colchester were pirated as the foreword announces, by "an
unknown admirer in another sect" and printed for Nathaniel Crouch, a non-Quaker bookseller in London. Stephen
Crisp had acquired a reputation as an itinerant missionary
in Holland, where many of his books had been translated
into the Dutch language.[11] This admirer of the Friends,
who may very well have been Crouch himself,[12] made several preliminary assertions in his foreword. He alleged that
he was too modest to allow his name to appear in print;
that he had intense admiration for the Quakers; and that
on his own initiative since he possessed "the art of short
writing, he had taken down many of their sermons and
prayers from the mouths of divers of their preachers."
Furthermore, he guaranteed that he had not altered the sense
in any way, though he did acknowledge the supplying of
titles, but these he insisted were uniformly "agreeable to
the subject matter treated therein."

Crouch did not print all of the thirty-two sermons at one
time. The edition of 1693 contained only seven. It seems

that he had a shrewd eye for business, for during the year
1693-94 he brought out three separate editions of these sermons, the last one containing twelve, and later on he pushed
three subsequent editions through the press. By 1823 Crisp's
sermons had been reprinted or reëdited fifteen times. It is
apparent also that these sermons were in demand among the
Friends, for before 1707 the Quaker booksellers, Mary
Hinde[13] and J. Sowle,[14] brought out three editions, presumably for circulation among members of the Society.

3

Two collections of miscellaneous sermons, bearing the
rather sombre titles of *Concurrence and Unanimity* (1694)
and *The Harmony of Divine and Heavenly Doctrines*
(1696),[15] had considerable circulation among the Quakers
and were frequently reprinted. Crouch, who doubtless remembered the demand for the sermons of Stephen Crisp,
again became responsible for publishing these.[16] Mentioning
the earlier edition in his new foreword, Crouch expressed
regret that Crisp's sermons had not met with the approval
of "all the chief Leaders and Teachers of the People called
Quakers"; and for that reason he felt "obliged in Truth
and Justice to make some of them public . . . to demonstrate
the concurrence and unanimity" of the Friends. The person
whom he designated in this prefatory note as "the reporter"
had selected sermons from representative preachers, such as
Robert Barclay, George Whitehead, Charles Marshall, and
William Penn.[17]

Like much of the didactic literature of the Friends, these
sermons on examination prove to be gospel exhortations,
and also like many other sermons of the century, were devoid of incident and of illustrative material.[18] At the end of
each appears a long prayer printed in italics. Out of the fif-

teen sermons in *Concurrence and Unanimity* only one can
be classed as an occasional address. This one William Penn
preached at the burial of Rebecca Travers,[19] who had died in
her eightieth year. Her home in London had been for years
a hospitable gathering place for itinerant "public" Friends.
All Quaker sermons, even those delivered at weddings and
funerals, were inspired by the Voice within. In paying
tribute to Rebecca Travers, Penn quoted freely from the
Scriptures, and as an exhortation for the group assembled
recalled the part that this mother in "Quaker Israel" had
played in the history of the Society. He spoke with direct
simplicity:

Our deceased Friend received Truth in the early days, the Days
of the Dawning of God's Power in this land in this City. The
Remembrance of it was sweet to her Soul; let us remember the
Love of God, and the Power and the Glory of the Name of the
Everlasting God that shined then, that we may be encouraged to
keep together as a peculiar people, to the Praise of Him that
hath called us out of Darkness into Marvelous Light.[20]

The inhibitions placed on the preparation and recording
of sermons found release and were sublimated into other
literary types. The epistles exchanged by early Friends regularly began with expressions and turns of thought which,
to any one outside the Quaker fold, would be termed a
sermon.[21] Except for name the epistles[22] sent by the First
Publishers to various meetings, and those[23] issued later
by the Yearly Meeting served the purpose of written sermons of homiletic and hortatory nature. As in the extempore
addresses delivered in assemblies, the authors frequently
claimed divine pressure for their composition.[24] In addition whole sections of the collected works[25] and journals,
as well as many controversial tracts[26] are sermons in content and intent. In a certain sense also the Quaker interest
in records[27]—records of membership, of the First Pub-

lishers, and of sufferings—furnished a compensation for permanent commemoration, which other nonconformist bodies were leaving to posterity in their formal addresses.

4

The sermons listened to twice on the first day of the week and upon the morning of the fourth day have left their literary traces in epistolary and advisory literature. If printed sermons were absent, a compensatory abundance of didactic literature, consisting largely of "advices" and of aphorisms, abounded. "Advices" dealing with abstract and concrete phases of the conduct of life are conspicuously present in both formal and informal epistles. Before departing for Philadelphia in 1682, William Penn addressed to his children a farewell letter overflowing with advice on education, conduct, and worship—a letter to which more than a century later the critic, Jeffrey, referred as "touching and venerable in its affectionateness and patriarchal simplicity." Jeffrey furthermore maintained that Penn's wise sayings possessed "a far richer and more pathetic sweetness than the epigrams and apothegms of modern times."[28] In 1700, nearly twenty years after this letter of admonition, Penn wrote a much longer series of advices similar in nature, which he also dedicated to his children. They were published as the *Fruits of a Father's Love*. Many Friends, in letters similar to Penn's, adopted this popular habit of assembling the wisdom[29] which experiences of life had brought them. Of these the most beautiful Quaker epistle came from Appleby Gaol in Westmorland, where Francis Howgill spent the last few years of his life as a sufferer "for conscience' sake." There he wrote for his daughter Abigail an epistolary legacy in which he urged her to maintain consistently the Quaker way of life. Through the lines of this testament throb a father's anxiety and love, calmed by his unbounded belief in the inner Light to protect and guide his child through the problems of her life.[30]

To this should be added Richard Claridge's letter, designed for the moral and spiritual welfare of his daughters, John Crook's *Advice to my Children and Grandchildren*,[31] and Thomas Gwin's *The Will and Testament*. Under the caption of "Universal Love," one section of *Balm from Gilead* teems with advise. Its author, William Smith, for instance, begged parents not to teach their children "to bow and scrape," for such actions, the author maintained— not without some assumption of the knowledge of Divine Mind—neither met with God's approval nor showed "good breeding, nor good manners."[32] In another chapter William Smith gave liberal directions and specific advice to "masters and dames of families," and in still another to "servants in their places."[33] Aged people were not forgotten, and neither were those who lived a single life.[34]

5

The Friends, from their study of the book of *Proverbs* and perhaps more from their puritanical outlook upon life, acquired a great fondness for "wisdom" literature. Many maxims and apothegms are found in their collected works, in broadside sheets, and in their manuscript commonplace books. Thirty-five proverbs fill two folio pages of William Smith's *Balm from Gilead*.[35] Two broadsides in the Friends Reference Library contain the maxims of Richard Greenway and David Barclay, the latter the father of the Quaker apologist. The first of these, without date, place, or name of printer, is headed *A Present from the Owners of the Ship Leeds-Industry to her Sailors, Being Meditations of R[ichard] G[reenway] at Sea*. In all, it embraces twenty-six brief meditations, as suited however, to the needs of landsmen as to seamen. David Barclay's broadside presents twenty-three aphorisms in the form of advice to servants. The eighth, to take specific instances, reads, "Rise early; for it is difficult to recover lost time," and the thirteenth, "Be not what is called an eye-servant, appearing diligent in sight, but neglectful out of it."

The proverbs of the Dutch Quakeress Judith Zins-Penninck Sewel,[36] the mother of the historian, William Sewel, were translated from the Dutch in 1663 by her brother-in-law, William Caton. These show a close following of the biblical proverbs, as "He that casteth care upon the Lord, he is holpen in his time,"[37] and "He that loveth wisdom, learns the fear of the Lord; and he that follows after, obtains it."[38] Martin Mason left among his manuscripts a number of verses in which he essayed various types of epigrams then popular in current literature. One of these, except for the fact that the Friends eschewed memorials in stone as "of no service to the deceased," might have graced a seventeenth-century Quaker gravestone:[39]

> Whoever tryes this World as I have done,
> Shall surely finde, before his glasse be run
> The Earth's a Trouble and the World a Snare,
> Let Sion's Offspring of the World beware.

Two very different ones are concerned with the subject of health:

> Let health and wealth contribute what they can,
> 'Tis a good conscience makes a happy man.

The second shows the conceitist's devotion to "word embroidery":

> Youth, tyme improve; and tyme of health use well,
> For many Tyme ofttimes youth and health abuse.[40]

The highest literary level reached by any Friend of this period in aphoristic writing is found in William Penn's *Some*

Fruits of Solitude in Reflections and Maxims Relating to the Conduct of Human Life. Thoughtful as a child, and so thought-provoking at Oxford in the early days of the Restoration as to become a *persona non grata* to the authorities,[41] Penn strengthened his natural tendencies toward reflection by the early adoption of the Quaker's contemplative habit of mind. In several writings he recommended to young persons the practice of early addicting one's self to solitary meditation, and of making this a lifelong process.[42] His *Some Fruits of Solitude* represents the accumulation of years of observation and reflection upon life, as student, traveler, minister, courtier, and founder of a colony. His adages range from rules of conversation to personal cautions, and from the advantages of country life to "the obligation of great men to God."[43] Dry humor, an understanding of humanity, and sound practical wisdom characterize these epigrammatic utterances. Space will allow for only a few examples out of his eight hundred and fifty-five proverbial maxims. These will partially portray the range of his interests and the pithiness of his expression:

The want of due consideration is the cause of all unhappiness that man brings on himself.[44]

Friends are true twins in soul; they sympathize in everything, and have the same love and aversion.[45]

Let the people think they govern, and they will be governed.[46]

Five things are requisite to a good officer: ability, clean hands, dispatch, patience, and impartiality.[47]

6

Next in literary merit to his *Some Fruits of Solitude* stands Penn's *No Cross, No Crown*, a book designed primarily to explain Quakerism to the "world's people" and to keep before Friends the ideals of the Quaker sect. The book belongs to a *genre* which owed its development largely to the seventeenth century. *No Cross, No Crown* should be read in connection with Jeremy Taylor's *Holy Living* and *Holy Dying* and Richard Baxter's *Saints' Everlasting Rest,* all of which might be termed religious conduct books. In many respects their authors have expanded the designs of the early courtesy books which aimed at the training of a gentleman. These writers of religious handbooks wished to lay down rules for the making of a Christian.[48] Of these, Penn's *No Cross, No Crown* is the least broad in outlook. The same theme—man's pilgrimage on earth, his strivings for spiritual satisfaction, and his hopes of immortality, when fictionized and treated allegorically in Bunyan's *Pilgrim's Progress*—appeals with few reservations to Catholics and Protestants. Of the others, *Rules for Holy Living* and *Holy Dying* are more tolerant and less dogmatic in their purpose than *The Saints' Everlasting Rest.* By Penn's emphasis upon the Quaker methods[49] for obtaining the crown —that is, perpetual harmony with the designs of God—he curtailed the very values he had in mind, of imbuing non-Quaker readers with a desire to quicken spirituality in their own lives.[50] In the face of the prevailing sectarianism of his day, he would have been reluctant to accept a modern view, attributed to the Hindu, Ramah Krishna, that if God is infinite, the approaches to Him must be infinite also.

Two considerations are worthy of note in *No Cross, No Crown.* In comparing this Quaker classic with the religious conduct books of his contemporaries, Jeremy Taylor and Richard Baxter, the fact first becomes immediately evident that William Penn throws heavier stress than the other two on actual living in the world, and less upon "the saints' everlasting rest." Though he does not disregard a future life with rewards for good and evil, he seldom appeals to fear or celestial happiness as motives for conduct. The method of inculcating piety in *No Cross, No Crown* differs in the second place from that of *The Saints' Everlasting Rest* and of *Holy Living* and *Holy Dying*. Baxter employs the plan of an extended sermon; Taylor, in *Holy Living*, that of a religious essay and in *Holy Dying*, that of a rhapsody, undertoned with deep personal emotion.

Penn, on the contrary, in order to bring home to his readers "the deadly sins" of pride, avarice, and luxury,[51] employed in many chapters the ubiquitous seventeenth-century character sketch. In sermonizing upon the evils inherent in luxury, Penn made a strong plea for plain living, plain speech, and plain entertainments.[52] He very obviously used the character sketch as a practical and educational device. Penn found life too serious and too engrossing for him to inject into his personifications the elements of satire so dominant in the earlier characters of Hall and Overbury, and in those of his contemporary, Samuel Butler. As usual with his Quaker contemporaries, Penn does not "varnish or gloss" over the purpose he had in mind. In its broadest aspects, Baxter in his *Call to the Unconverted* and later William Law in *A Serious Call to a Devout and Holy Life* had the same purpose in view. *No Cross, No Crown* was primarily a direct appeal to readers to turn from the pleasures of the world to contemplative and virtuous living. "Christ's Cross is Christ's way to Christ's Crown" is Penn's text throughout.

No Cross, No Crown was first written in 1668, in the Tower of London where Penn was confined, charged by the Bishop of London with blasphemously endeavoring to elevate the Holy Spirit above the other members of the Trinity. The volume was re-issued in 1682, much enlarged with an addendum of a hundred and fifty pages. In this new section, in his effort to prove the value of virtuous living or the "good life," he gave the results of his searches through the writings of antiquity,[53] the church fathers,[54] and of modern writers[55]—Raleigh, Donne, Grotius, Selden, and Cowley.

In his search through the works of such men as Machiavelli, Montaigne, and Donne, whom he also quotes, he must, however, have encountered instances which would have contradicted his main thesis, but these he allows to pass without mention.

Stylistically speaking, when Penn holds himself down to sententious expression, he is at his best in *No Cross, No Crown*. Often he achieves pithiness, as when he says: "A proud person makes an ill child, servant, and subject; he contemns his parents, master and prince; he will not be a subject,"[56] or "The covetous man is a monster in nature; . . . an enemy to the state; a disease to the body politic"; or when he writes aphoristically,[57] "Great is their peace, who know a limit to their ambitious minds,"[58] or "Poverty wants some, luxury many, avarice all things,"[59] or "Clothes that were given to cover shame, now want a covering to hide their shameful excess."[60] *No Cross, No Crown* may be looked upon as a religious conduct book which permitted outsiders to examine the Quaker faith and practices, and which urged upon the members of the Religious Society of Friends the deep responsibility of exemplifying practical Christianity in their own lives.

Though controversy was the natural defense to which the Friends were forced to resort for the preservation and promulgation of their beliefs, they ventured into many fields of literature, but in doing so they uniformly employed them to further the interests of the group. History and essays, biography and verse, added their share to this one end. Above all, the journals and confessions through expression of self, gave the Friends, as the final chapters will show, their supreme chance for exemplifying the Quaker idea of practical Christianity.

CHAPTER XIII

THE QUAKER AND THE "WORLD'S" JOURNALS

The autobiographies and the religious confessions of the early Friends contain the most complete revelation to be found in their writings of the Quaker attempt to make religion both practical and spiritual. In addition to out-numbering the journals of "the world's people" which found their way into print, the Friends injected into their autobiographies a marked degree of introspection, and so composed their life histories that they served the double purpose of unfolding the experiences of the writers and of the group they represented.

In her *Religious Confessions and Confessants*, Mrs. Burr has called attention to the amount of introversion to be found in Quaker journals.[1] It is only recently that the Friends have been recognized as pioneers in the field of English subjective autobiography. These journals deserve a prominent place in any discussion of Quaker literature, since they reveal through first-hand information the inner springs of action which gave an individual cast to the Quaker group and its writings. This chapter will attempt to differentiate the Quaker from the non-Quaker contemporary autobiography, while the succeeding chapters will trace the evolution of the *genre*, describe its contents, and consider its confessional and introspective phases.

1

The first steps in defining the Quaker journal are to describe its most characteristic features, and then to differen

tiate it clearly from contemporaneous autobiography. Such
an effort involves a knowledge of the numbers produced,
and of the motives, style, and subject matter. The Quaker
journal may be defined as an account, written at first hand,
of the personal and religious life of one who became so identified with the Quaker group after he had once surrendered
himself to its teachings, that his memoirs expressed the
aims and beliefs of the Society. In other words, the Quaker
autobiographer was a Friend first, and an individual penning
his memoirs second. This definition refers particularly to
the typical Quaker journal, of which more than twenty-five
were actually in print before 1725, and to more than twenty
others written by Friends whose youth and maturity belong
to the period under study.[2]

Besides the complete journals, nearly fifty Quakers of
this period have left personal records of varying nature,
such as the two reminiscent epistles, previously mentioned,
which Mary Penington wrote for her daughter, Gulielma
Penn, and for her grandson, Springett Penn. Other fragmentary personal accounts relate to experiences encountered
on "gospel journeys," such as Robert Fowler's voyage in
1657—to aid the Quaker martyrs in Boston—in the good ship
Woodhouse, which sailed across the Atlantic "without regard to latitude or longitude," guided solely by the hand
of divine Providence.[3] The journey was carried on, as
Robert Fowler with infinite belief in God's "protecting
Providence" said, "by the Lord like as he did Noah's Ark,
wherein he shut a few righteous persons, and landed them
safe, even as at the Hill Ararat." Many Quaker confessants chose not merely to write, but to print, records of their
difficulties in orientating themselves to the acceptance of
Quaker dress, speech, and social customs. Practically every
narrative contains a detailed account of the spiritual struggle involved in the surrender of individual will to the lead-

ings of the inner Light, and of the resultant peace which followed.[4] Such religious confessions became the *raison d'être* for forty separate tracts written by the first generation of Friends, and held the most prominent position in an equal number of complete autobiographies composed by the second.

"Ministering" or "public" Friends wrote practically all the Quaker journals. In large measure this fact accounts for the unity of tone, of style, and also for the identification of personal and life interests with those shared by the group. "Public Friends" acted as the chief cementing forces in unifying meetings of Friends scattered throughout the English speaking world. Frequently they preached in gatherings held in private homes;[5] they sometimes held forth five hours at a time in meetings for worship;[6] by personal contact they knew what Friends were accomplishing in London and in distant communities;[7] they visited the imprisoned or they themselves suffered in dungeons; they counseled those who were undergoing religious crises,[8] and disputed with Baptist, Presbyterian, and Deist.[9] The "public" Friend was thus newscarrier, unofficial emissary, religious disputant, preacher, and spiritual adviser. With these interests always to the foreground, it follows logically that the ministerial journals should become the depositories of all facts, emotions, and experiences that pertained to individuals who had the welfare of the Quaker group at heart.

The Christian Progress of George Whitehead presents exceptionally well the dual interest of a Quaker author writing his memoirs in terms of the history of the Society.[10] This voluminous autobiography depicts a seventy years' devotion to the spiritual ministry and executive work of the Friends. As a youth of eighteen, Whitehead began active work by preaching Quakerism in Norwich, but spent the greater part of his life in and about London, where at one time he pleaded for Friends at the bar of the House of Commons, and where in 1672 he was instrumental in obtaining the Great Pardon, which released nearly five hundred Quakers[11] from the prisons of England and Wales. In 1708, in behalf of the Yearly Meeting, he assured Queen Anne of the Society's grateful acknowledgment of her support; and at the age of seventy-three he bespoke the thanks of the Friends and tendered their pledge of loyalty to both King George I and the Crown Prince.[12] His journal, a representative one, subordinates all other interests to his religious training, his acceptance of Quaker principles, and his part in the work and organization of the Quaker movement.

The dual characteristic of the writer's motives, merging with those of the group, is the distinctive quality of Quaker memoir writing. Practically all of the sects that arose during the Commonwealth—for example, the Ranters, Fifth Monarchists, and Muggletonians—produced literature[13] similar to that of the Friends in its prophetic, scriptural, and controversial aspects.[14] Though in the first decades of Quaker history several important separations occurred,[15] yet in the main the Society presented a solid front to the world. The journals, more than any other form of Quaker literature display an unusual type of "unanimity and concurrence" in affairs that concerned the individual and the corporate whole. This dual spirit, as previously noted, aided largely in saving early Quakerism from Ranterism. Men and women who "felt the call" to go to distant meetings or to foreign lands regularly presented their plans[16] to their own Monthly Meeting for confirmation, and at a subsequent time elders were appointed by each meeting to see that ministers in their extemporaneous sermons "did not outrun the Spirit." In this way, by the individual's voluntarily subordinating himself to the group, early tendencies toward fanaticism were held in check.

2

Three noteworthy characteristics sharply differentiated the journals of the Friends from the memoirs of "the world's people." In the first place, the Friends had clearly in mind the idea of early publication at or soon after the death of the writer; in the second, they adopted such a uniformity of style and subject matter that their journals present a conspicuous lack of variety; and in the third place, the writers achieved a skill, remarkable at that time, for expressing inward states of mind and of analyzing springs of action. Except in sporadic cases before the nineteenth century such introversion was an extremely rare quality in English autobiography.[17]

These lines of demarcation become worthy of note when the fact is considered that between 1650 and 1725 over forty Quaker memoirs, with homogeneous qualities, were either completed or in the process of being written, while outside the Quaker group practically no autobiographies bore marks of a pronounced community aim in style or in content. Although the Elizabethan age produced little that can be termed autobiographical, the seventeenth century supplied an exceedingly rich contribution of diaries and memoirs, varying from the chivalric account of Herbert of Cherbury, and the euphuistic and romantic pages of Sir Kenelm Digby of the early part of the century, to Count Hamilton's racy delineations of the court of Charles II in the *Memoires de la Vie du Comte de Gramont,* and to the domestic records of Lady Warwick, of Lady Fanshaw, and of Margaret of Newcastle. Among the able diarists Sir Symonds D'Ewes, John Evelyn, and Samuel Pepys rank high; and outstanding in religious autobiography tower Bunyan's *Grace Abounding to the Chief of Sinners* and the *Reliquae Baxterianae.*

In emphasizing the group qualities apparent in Quaker

autobiographies, a possible reservation should be made of a small group of Scotch Covenanters whose spiritual diaries show some similarities as to thought and language, but which present practically no evidences of collusion with other writers in their group.[18] The Quaker contribution, therefore, with twenty-six published autobiographies and twenty others now known to have been under way, and with a total of more than four score fragmentary ones with homogeneous elements, presents a decided contrast to the general run of seventeenth and early eighteenth-century memoir writings.[19]

The definite belief that memoirs should be published for the benefit of posterity soon became traditional with the Friends. To this custom the Yearly and the Morning Meetings added encouragement. Quite the contrary condition existed in the larger literary world without the Society. Though many "secret histories" were written, only a very few were made public. With the exception of the autobiographies of Richard Baxter and John Bunyan,[20] both deeply religious in character, not one of the non-Quaker journals mentioned above was published before the middle of the eighteenth century, and most of them not until the nineteenth.[21] On the other hand, nearly all of the early Quaker confessions were in print before the death of the authors, and the typical or complete journals within a comparatively short time after the decease of the author. That these journals were written with a view toward definite publication is clear from an examination of their prefaces and introductions[22]—where ethical and didactic aims appear almost as set formulas—and becomes even more evident from an examination of the following tables.

In the order of publication in separate columns these three tables list the first forty-seven Quaker autobiographers, their chronological dates, and the year of the publication of their complete journals. The term "complete" implies a survey which reviews not merely the period of conversion, or an account of a gospel journey, but one which, regardless of length, chronicles the main events in the life of a man or woman. The religious confessions, since they involve features characteristically their own, are omitted from these tables and will be listed in a later chapter.[23] The first table presents the names of twenty-six Friends whose journals were in print by 1725; the second includes fourteen Quakers whose autobiographies were published after 1725 but whose youth, maturity, and missionary work belong to the 1650-1725 period; the third gives the names of seven Quakers whose life work belonged to this period, but whose memoirs escaped early publication. The first bibliography at the close of the book has attempted to include all the early literary material that can be recognized as strictly autobiographical.

A study of the following tables reveals several facts. In Table I the average length of time that elapsed between the date of the author's death and the date of publication was less than three years. In averaging, the name of William Caton has been omitted because Caton's journal, on account of licensing enactments, could not "safely be printed" until 1689, twenty-four years after its author's death in 1665. Table II shows a longer interval elapsing between the death date and date of printing, in this case five years; but even this disparity adds confirmation to a definite plan for publication when comparison is made with the publication of non-Quaker memoirs and diaries.

The third list, representing less than a sixth of the complete records, indicates more differences. No reasons for the deferred publication of the lives of Deborah Bell, Joseph Pike, and Patrick Livingstone, which follow closely the beaten trail of the typical journal, can be asserted. The fact that Henry Lampe, a German by heritage and education, later a merchant in Lancashire, and William Stout, ironmonger of Lancaster, were not itinerant Friends, may account for the long deferred publication of their autobiographies. Alexander Jaffray's death in 1673, when the

TABLE I
JOURNALS PUBLISHED BETWEEN 1689 AND 1725

	Name	Dates	Date of Publication
1	Caton, William	1636-1665	1689
2	Halhead, Miles	1614-1689 (?)	1690
3	Burnyeat, John	1631-1690	1691
4	Vokins, Joan	-1690	1691
5	Fox, George	1624-1690/1	1694
6	Crisp, Stephen	1628-1692	1694
7	Hebden, Roger	1620-1695	1700
8	Marshall, Charles	1637-1698	1704
9	Howard, Luke	1621-1699	1704
10	Crook, John	1617-1699	1706
11	Thompson, Thomas	1632-1704	1708
12	Peters, John	1646-1708	1709
13	Rigge, Ambrose	1635-1704/5	1710
14	Davies, Richard	1635-1707	1710
15	Sansom, Oliver	1636-1710	1710
16	Taylor, John	1637-1708	1710
17	Stirredge, Elizabeth	1634-1706	1711
18	Banks, John	1638-1710	1712
19	Crouch, William	1630-1710	1712
20	Ellwood, Thomas	1639-1713	1714
21	Edmundson, William	1627-1712	1715
22	Whiting, John	1656-1722	1715
23	Gratton, John	1641-1711/12	1720
24	Hayes, Alice	1657-1720	1723
25	Osborne, Elias	1643-1720	1723
26	Whitehead, George	1636-1723	1725[24]

heaviest stream of persecution for the Quakers in Scotland was under way, as well as the distance of his home in Aberdeen from the Yearly Meeting headquarters in London,[25] easily accounts for the absence of his name from the earlier lists.[26]

In comparison with the majority of Quaker memoirs, several in the last group present a vividness of touch, with gleams of humor, pathos, or mystic fire, for which one often searches long in reading Quaker accounts that run truer to type. The marked variations from the norm in this third group, however, make one regret that more journals were not preserved for later publication, and make one apprehensive that editors and censors have excised a heavy toll for

TABLE II

JOURNALS OF FRIENDS WHOSE LIFE WORK LAY
IN THE 1650-1725 PERIOD

	Name	Dates	Date of Publication
1	Story, Christopher	1648-1720	1726
2	Raylton, Thomas	1671-1723	1728
3	Wilson, Thomas	1654-1725	1728
4	Barcroft, John	1664-1723	1730
5	Dickinson, James	1658/9-1741	1745
6	Story, Thomas	1662-1742	1747
7	Chalkley, Thomas	1675-1741	1749
8	Bewley, George	1684-1749	1750
9	Fothergill, John	1676-1744	1753
10	Holme, Benjamin	1682-1749	1754
11	Bownas, Samuel	1680-1753	1756
12	Bangs, Benjamin	1652-1741	1757
13	Richardson, John	1667-1753	1757
14	Hall, David	1683-1756	1758

investigators interested in other lines than that of the history of one sect.

The average reader would willingly give up copies of letters of protest, pages of epistles, and enumeration of journeys, if only Ellwood had spared him more glimpses of Milton, or if John Croker had divulged the details of his sea adventures and of his life in Labrador, in 1687, where he was shipwrecked.[27] A modern reader rejoices in the sprinkling of local color—which later editors have not deleted—

such as the difficulties of continental travel which the improvident Henry Lampe[28] related, or the danger from highway robbers which William Stout faced when he made his annual journey from Lancashire to London for supplies. The reader again wishes that more journals had escaped official censorship[29] when he peruses the meditations upon domestic[30] and civic events[31] of the Cromwellian period as they appear in the long unpublished *Diary of Alexander Jaffray,* and when he turns over the manuscript octavo volumes

TABLE III
JOURNALS THAT ESCAPED IMMEDIATE PUBLICATION

	Name	Dates	Date of Publication
1	Bell, Deborah	1664-1738	1762
2	Jaffray, Alexander	1614-1673	1833
3	Pike, Joseph	1657-1729	1837
4	Croker, John	1673-1727	1839
5	Livingstone, Patrick	1634-1694	1847
6	Stout, William	1665-1753	1851
7	Lampe, Henry	1660-1711	1895
8	Kelsall, John	1683-1745	MSS

of the early eighteenth-century Welsh schoolmaster, John Kelsall of Dolobran.

Without doubt the expectation of immediate publication tended to standardize the autobiographies of the Friends. Naturally a man who knows that the history of his life is to be published while he is yet alive, or soon after his death, will be very cautious about his excisions and inclusions.

CHAPTER XIV

QUAKER JOURNALS AND QUAKER LIFE
PRE-QUAKER EXPERIENCES AND
MARRIAGE

The journals of the Friends graphically portray the
Quaker experiment of making Christianity practical, and
living sacramental. In a larger way they represent common
humanity, in this case English men and women, facing life
problems when conditions in the political and religious
world were in a state of flux. This fact makes these self-
reviews valuable to students of psychology, sociology, and
literature. "A record of personality," as a recent critic has
said, "is more enduring than a record of fact."[1] These eighty
and more Quaker writers who have left confessions and
more complete records were primarily concerned with the
interests of the Quaker sect; for this reason the quality of
universality in them is necessarily curtailed. Their specific
value lies in their contribution to the motivating forces of
nonconformity. Between the years 1650 and 1725 no other
series of first-hand records reveals, as fully as these Quaker
journals do, the struggles of religious groups to secure liberty to worship as they pleased, and more particularly to
evolve for themselves a type of religion that would bring
them spiritual satisfaction.

1

The Quaker journalist, as previously noted, subordinated
his major interests in life to those of the group, and wrote

his autobiography with a reading public in view. The pattern he established varied but little in respect to order and life interests. With but few exceptions he began his account with a statement of purpose which in time became almost a formula. For instance, Alice Hayes wrote on her opening page, "It hath been in my heart for many years to leave behind me a brief relation concerning the way and manner of the Lord's dealing with me from my youth up to this day."[2] As a rule the autobiographer passed cursorily over questions of ancestry and social standing;[3] he seldom failed to portray graphically the period of his conversion and acceptance of Quaker beliefs;[4] frequently he related in detail his hesitancy to deliver his first Quaker message in a meeting of worship, included his call to the ministry,[5] his missionary journeys, and the general progress of the Quaker movement. About the warp of these chief events he wove the other autobiographical details, such as his family relationships, his sufferings, his correspondence, and his adjustments to Quaker practices and customs.

The Life of John Gratton, published in 1720, in its conformity to the Quaker pattern exhibits all the features of the typical Quaker journal from 1690 to 1725, and for a century after that. This particular memoir has been selected for illustration because the purely typical qualities in it are more clearly differentiated than they are in the better known *Journal of George Fox*. The latter, in relation to the entire *genre* of Quaker journals, towers far above the others in its conversational tone, in its revelations of pathological states, of spiritual strength, of the power of leadership and of self-analysis. In all these respects Fox's *Journal* transcends the typical Quaker journal. John Gratton was the "Apostle of Quakerism to a 'poor, unworthy and despised people, scattered amongst the rock mountains and dark valleys of the High Peak country' in Derbyshire."[6] Gratton's life was typi-

cal of many religiously minded people who were left stranded
in the flotsam and jetsam of the Commonwealth. Many of
these turned to the new sects; some became Quakers. Gratton affiliated with the Friends only after deeply considering
for years Quaker beliefs and practices in relation to those of
the Anglicans, Presbyterians, and of the puritan sects; but
after "conviction" to their principles, he devoted the last
forty years of his life to the Quaker ministry.

Seventeenth-century titles, often running to inordinate
length, frequently served as miniature prefaces. The fifty
words of the full title of John Gratton's autobiography give
a condensed forecast in idiomatic phrasing of the subject
matter of the volume. The wording, as it appears on his title
page, is quoted in full.

A

Journal

of the Life

of

That Ancient Servant of Christ

JOHN GRATTON:

Giving an Account of his Exercises when Young

And how he came to the Knowledge

Of the Truth and was thereby

Raised up to preach the Gospel;

As also his

Labours, Travels, and Sufferings for the Same

Four of the stereotyped Quaker expressions in this title
give an anticipatory summary of the contents of this autobiography, as well as that of two score others. "Exercises
when young" uniformly referred to the period of religious
conversion, occurring most frequently in childhood or adolescence but sometimes later. "Knowledge of the Truth"
meant primarily Quaker Truth; "labours and travels" in
the ministry signified the activities of the unremunerated
itinerating preacher in home or foreign missionary work;

"sufferings for the same" acquired the signification of persecutions which upholders of Quakerism, particularly its spokesmen, had to face.

At the very outset, following an approved Quaker custom, John Gratton declared that he felt himself to be under divine compulsion to write the review of his life and expressed the pious hope that the account of his efforts might be of service to others:

It hath often been in my heart, and lain long on my mind to write a short account to leave behind me of the Lord's gracious dealings with me . . . to the end that my children and others, who may see these lines, may be encouraged to trust in the living God, and to cast their care upon him.[7]

Like many of his fellow-workers, he stressed his earliest recollections of interest in religion by recalling memories of a serious childhood, when "visitations from the Lord" came to him while he was a little lad tending his father's sheep.[8] He records also several mystical invasions occurring in early youth, noting that at the age of eleven he had been warned through divine intimation that boyhood games, such as cards, shooting at targets, and the ringing of bells, were vain sports.[9] It will be remembered that these same temptations, suggestive of his puritanical environment, afflicted the conscience of his then youthful contemporary, John Bunyan.[10] Five or six years later a third religious wave swept over him, forcing him to question, as thousands about him were doing, all forms of religion. He tried reading books and listening to sermons preached by Anglicans, Presbyterians, and Independents.[11] He discoursed with "believers and professors" when and wherever he could, but this constant questioning brought him little comfort.

At times experiences of mystical nature seemed to impinge upon his consciousness. He described one visitation powerful enough to alter not only his emotional state but

also his physical appearance.[12] He felt that a spiritual revelation had been momentarily vouchsafed to him, and that his
long searching had received its reward in spiritual peace.
Upon reflection, however, he recalled that numerous ministers, to whom he had listened, had taken pains to warn
young people against dangers lurking in religious ecstasy and
visions. With this thought, his perplexities returned. For six
years thereafter he tried to wrest the truth from different
religious leaders, such as the Anabaptists and Muggletonians; finally, after running the gamut of Presbyterian, Epis-
copalian, Baptist, and minor sects, he abandoned church attendance.

At the close of this period when nearly thirty years of
age, another mystical experience swept over him during corn
harvest, and as he phrased it, "opened my understanding to
see"[13] that it "was the Lord's spirit only" which could instruct him. In recalling these restless years with their heights
and depths of experience, a period in which he was in contact with the puritanism of the 1650's and 1660's, he wrote
that from his earliest childhood he had always been somewhat but not fully conscious of a divine power operative
within him,[14] whose significance only became clear to him
through Quaker interpretation. In concluding the story of
his search for spiritual peace, he mentioned a distinct mystic invasion in which he declared the Lord made it known
to him "that the people called Quakers were his people beyond all other people."[15]

This final experience had the effect of synthesizing elements in his mind which had hitherto been in conflict. He
wrote, "I was in my inward man full of the power and the
presence of Almighty God . . . and I saw that it was the
Lord's Holy Spirit that appeared in me; and I believed and
could do no otherwise." A little later in 1671, when the Second Conventicle Act was playing havoc with the Friends and

other Dissenters, John Gratton allied himself whole-heartedly "with the despised people called Quakers." From this time on he secured a peace of mind that carried him with equanimity through twenty years of service, which was interrupted by distraints and imprisonments, and through another twenty of a more quiet ministry.

His life was a busy one in which family cares, trade interests, and the work of a "public" Friend kept him occupied. As a "gospeller" he journeyed into Ireland and Wales. During most of his ministerial life he traveled and preached in all the middle counties,[16] discussed theological points with "professors," preached in London in 1674 and 1678, and endured imprisonment at Derby.[17] While in jail he wrote to Friends at large, sent letters to his wife and children—some of which he incorporated into his journal—and composed some "Prison Meditations" in verse[18] and a long prose treatise *The Prisoners Vindication*. With the exception that John Gratton's "spiritual travail" lasted longer than usual, this very brief résumé represents the main skeleton of the pre-Quaker religious life presented in the typical Quaker journal. This cursory review of Gratton's autobiography, however, has not been able to suggest the glimpses which his account gives of rural England in the late seventeenth century, nor has it been able to present the sincerity of the journalist or the sacrifices that his step into Quakerism entailed upon himself and upon his family. Since the final chapters will deal with confessional phases of Quaker life, only the social aspects of the journals will now receive consideration.

2

Practically all the Quaker journalists passed over genealogical matters or family ties without mentioning them, unless these facts had some direct bearing upon Quakerism.

Margaret Fox[19] and John Croker,[20] who were of gentle birth, referred to their ancestry, the former incidentally. The latter mentioned the maiden name of his mother but considered it of maximum importance to enlarge upon the persecutions which had occurred in his family, particularly that of the simultaneous confinement of his father in the jail at Exeter, and his mother at Plymouth "for conscience' sake."[21] Among John Whiting's earliest recollections was the consignment of himself and his sister Mary to the care of an aunt while his parents suffered imprisonment for attending conventicles.[22] Thomas Ellwood, because he belonged to the landed gentry and had more social contacts than most of the Quaker memorandists, devoted space to a vivid picturing of his home life, his early education, his conflicts with his father, and associations with his neighbors, particularly with Isaac and Mary Penington,[23] in whose home he first saw Quaker teachings exemplified.

3

The journals of the early Friends contain comparatively few references to death. This fact is somewhat surprising in the writings of a seriously minded people living in an age obsessed with the idea of charnel houses, elegiac verse, and funeral sermons. Even in the testimonies, preceding the *Works* and autobiographies, little space is allotted to personal grief, and much emphasis is laid on the Christian activities of the deceased.[24] George Fox wrote simply and sincerely concerning his mother's death, the news of which reached him during his imprisonment at Worcester in 1673.

Since my imprisonment I had understood that my mother, an ancient woman in Leicestershire, desired earnestly to see me before she died: and when she heard that I was stopt, it strake her to the heart and killed her. . . . I did in verity love her as ever one could a mother, and when I had read the letter of her death sudden travail came upon me, and when my spirit had got through I saw her in the resurrection and my father in the flesh also.[25]

Infant mortality was looked upon by these ministerial writers as something that in the course of nature might be expected, or as something providential and for that reason not to be unduly mourned over. Alexander Jaffray records the death of nine children that his first wife bore him in twelve years, and of five out of the eight children which his second marriage brought him. Thomas Chalkley buried eleven out of his twelve children. In 1723, after the death of the tenth, he wrote with apparent resignation to the decree of God:

It was some exercise to me to bury my children one after the other, but . . . reflection a little mitigated my sorrow . . . yet it was safer and better for them, and they more out of danger, to be taken away in their infancy and innocence . . . which consideration tended to settle and quiet my mind in my sorrow-ful exercise.[26]

In *A Book of some of the Sufferings and Passages of Myles Halhead* the autobiographer introduced several details concerning the death of a thoughtful child whom his wife had idolized. Before its death the mother had strenu-ously opposed her husband's wish to enter the Quaker minis-try and to absent himself at intervals from home. Only after the child had been taken away, Miles Halhead relates, was she forced to realize that the child's death was punishment for her previous reluctance, and then only was "she made willing to release" him freely.[27]

4

If the Quaker journalist is chary with genealogical details such as ancestry and reference to brothers and sisters, he seldom omits the subject of his marriage. These accounts of the choice of a partner for life indicate, perhaps more than any other one thing, that ideally life to the Quaker was sacramental. In the choice of a companion, religion and life were not separated. His parents were given to him, his children came to him "providentially," but in a special way with divine help, he chose his wife. An entire chapter could be devoted to these religious courtships, the accounts of which vary in length from a few lines to many pages.[28] Modern psychologists lay seige to many Quaker beliefs on the basis of the subconscious mind, but they can scarcely doubt that these writers were absolutely sincere in ascribing their leadings to the inner Light. George Fox, at the age of forty-five, just before an arduous trip to the West Indies and American Colonies, married Margaret Fell, ten years his senior. His journal contained this brief record concerning his state of mind: "I had seen from the Lord for a considerable time before that I should take Margaret Fell to be my wife. And when I first mentioned it to her, she felt the answer of life from God thereto." With Quaker caution, and not fully satisfied that the inward prompting was God-given, and not a response to his own human desire, he wrote that he allowed "the matter to rest" for some time until she came to Bristol, where he then was. Not long after, his journal included this entry, "It opened in me from the Lord that the thing should be accomplished."[29]

Richard Davies, the Welsh Quaker, explained in his journal that he covenanted with the Lord for a wife. In 1659 at the age of twenty-four, temporarily settled in London as a hat maker, he became deeply distressed when thoughts of his spiritually barren country surged through his mind; neither was he able to shut out the conviction that he was under divine obligation to return and carry to his own people in Wales the Quaker message that had comforted him in the metropolis. Night after night until his friends began to comment upon his physical appearance, he struggled against this imperative call. The loneliness of working in an unsympathetic religious community appalled him. Over the conflict between duty and desire, he became despondent and ill. As his journal shows, he frequently argued the situation with the Spirit within, explained to the Lord his reluctance to go back to Wales, informed Him of the handicaps that would beset him in missionary work there, and pleaded his own incapacity. After one such conflict, he thus analyzed his mental state:

In this my disobedience, I continued until I lost his presence, and he smote me with trouble within, and pain in my bones, that I could not work nor labour. . . . My pain of body increased upon me, till at last I was forced to bow to the will of the great God; . . . He showed me clearly, *that I was to go to my own country.*

In this agony "upon his bed of sorrows," he covenanted with the Lord, begged for a sign, declaring that he would be willing to go if the Lord would release him from his pain, and if He would also direct him to a suitable wife for the kind of life a "ministering" Friend would have to endure in Wales. He continued:

When I had made a covenant with the Lord to go, immediately my pain was removed, and I had peace and quietness of mind. . . . I was alone, like a pelican in the wilderness, or a sparrow on a housetop. The Lord still commanded me to go, shewing me that he would provide a help-meet for me.

His memorandum shows that in surrendering his will to the will of God he believed he could safely leave the working out of the details to the Lord. If youth, propinquity, or affinity entered into his important choice of a wife, Richard Davies was unconscious of these forces. He prayed to the Lord that "she might be of His choosing," for he explained that it had not yet been " made manifest to him where she was or who she was." He thus extended his narrative:

So the Lord gave me a little time, and he alone provided a help-meet for me. . . . One time as I was in Horsleydown Meeting in Southwark, I heard a woman Friend open her mouth by way of testimony. . . . It came to me from the Lord, that that woman was to be my wife, and to go with me to the country.[30]

Again the customary and deliberate caution, which kept the Quaker from too hurriedly accepting inward prompting, manifested itself. Even though he was apparently attracted to her, he made no hasty move. Perhaps he was shy in love, but later events showed that in other problems of life he unflinchingly shouldered the responsibilities of carrying out Quaker practices in spite of conventicle acts and of informers, and that he and his wife endured imprisonment in Wales under most distressing circumstances.[31] He wrote further:

After meeting, I drew somewhat near to her, but spake nothing, nor took any acquaintance with her, nor did I know when or where I should see her again. . . . In time the Lord brought us acquainted one with the other, and she confessed that she had some sight of the same thing that I had seen concerning her. So after sometime, we parted . . . and I told her that if the Lord did order her to be my wife, she must come with me to a strange country where there were no Friends, but what God in time might call and gather to Himself. Upon a little consideration, she said, if the Lord should order it so, she must go with her husband though it were to the wilderness.[32]

After this his courtship did not proceed with absolute smoothness. At the close of the Protectorate, Wales, in the estimation of Londoners, was a barbarous country. Once when Richard Davies went to call upon her, he found that a well-wishing friend had vividly drawn the difficulties of making a home there. In all probability, Davies himself had not misrepresented the obstacles that the wife of a missionary from "a despised sect" would meet in a hostile land known to be "briery and brambly." Davies soon discovered that this friend "had begot doubts and reasonings in her mind," and that "she was in a poor condition of mind." After some deliberation the three resolved to leave the decision to the Lord, and entered into prayer, after which she rose from her knees declaring, as Davies reported the matter, "That in the name and power of the Lord she consented to be my wife, and to go along with me, whither the Lord should order us." And to these words, he had solemnly rejoined, "In the fear of the Lord, I receive thee as a gift of God to me." Not much later, according to Quaker precedent, the matter was carried to the Snail Meeting in Tower Street, London, for approval. Davies ended the record of his religious courtship with these words, "In the afternoon, . . . being the 26th of the fourth month, 1659, in the presence of God, and that assembly, we took each other for man and wife."[33] Very soon both were teaching, preaching, and suffering for Quakerism in Wales.

CHAPTER XV

QUAKER JOURNALS AND QUAKER LIFE CUSTOMS AND LETTERS

1

The Quaker memorandist of this early period, whether he came to the Society from another religious organization or was a "birthright Friend," uniformly gives space to the difficulties that he personally met in accepting the badge of Quakerism—that is, the abandonment of "the world's" social standards and the acceptance of plain speech, dress, and habits. The typical journal records one or more of these "tests." The hardship was keener for Friends like William Penn, Thomas Story, Isaac and Mary Penington, and Thomas Ellwood, who came from higher social circles.

Richard Davies found it worthy of recording that upon his return from London his father, an Anglican, turned his back upon his son, and refused to give him the usual parental blessing when young Richard refused to kneel before him. His mother, however, hurried forward to take her son's face between her hands, scanning it eagerly to see if the current rumor were true that her son had become distracted.[1] When earlier than this Richard Davies had addressed the wife of his employer in London with the disrespectful second person pronoun in the singular, he reported, "She took a stick and gave me such a blow upon my bare head, that made it swell and sore for a long time; she was so disturbed," he added, "that she swore she would kill me, though she should be hanged for me."[2]

The refusal to remove the hat before the administrators of the law and the interpretation of this act as contempt of court found repeated expression in the journals. "A plainly garbed Quaker with mild obstinancy," keeping his hat on his head before the bar of justice, frequently provoked irritation and anger in the presiding officer. The memorandist in a very human manner, and often not without a touch of egotism, seemed to delight in depicting "his own imperturbability as a foil against the rage and exasperation of the judge." Not infrequently the Quaker prisoner had occasion to glory in his superior knowledge of law,[3] which enabled him to state his case correctly or to turn the laughter of the court-room against his prosecutors. One example from Fox's account of the Quaker invasion of Cornwall will illustrate these points.

At Launceston in 1656, George Fox and several of his associates had been imprisoned for nine weeks. Out of curiosity, people came from miles around to see the Quakers, and somewhat maliciously informed them that they would find it necessary to "bow the knee" and "doff" the hat at the coming Assizes. These critics fully expected, Fox wrote, that "we would be hanged." On the day of the trial, while not only the court room but its doors and windows were crowded with spectators, a Welshman, Judge Glynne, then a Chief Justice of England, presided. According to George Fox, the prisoners "stood a pretty while" with their hats on after they had been conducted into court. Before Fox spoke, they were twice ordered to remove their hats, the second time in the name of the court.

George Fox's reply to this command was a double interrogation, the first question indicating his knowledge of the Bible, the second of common law:

Where did ever any magistrate, king, or judge, from Moses to Daniel, command any to put off their hats, when they came before them in their Courts, either amongst the Jews, the people of God, or amongst the heathen? and if the law of England doth command any such thing, shew me that law either written or printed.

This Socratic interrogation may have surprised the judge; at any rate it angered him. "Required before an English court, and a perfectly composed questioner, to cite on the spur of the moment both the authority of Scripture and of English law" no doubt caused him to feel uncomfortable.[4] He replied: "I do not carry my law books on my back."

The interrogator persisted: "But tell me where it is printed in any statute book that I may read it."

Without replying to the question, the judge shouted, "Take him away, prevaricator. I'll ferk [punish or injure] him."

The prisoners were remanded to jail, but almost immediately were resummoned by the discomfited judge, who on second thought had decided to hurl back at them a scriptural question. "Come," said he, "where had they hats from Moses to Daniel? come answer me. I have you fast now." Fox, the spokesman, if he knew no other books, had minutely examined the Bible on this score. Without hesitation, he replied,

Thou mayst read in the third of Daniel that the three children were cast into the fiery furnace by Nebuchadnezzar's command, with their coats, their hose, and their hats on.

Fox's closing comment indicates that he thought highly of his superior knowledge, for he wrote, "This plain instance stopped them; so that not having anything else to say to the point, he [Judge Glynne] cried again, 'Take them away, jailer'."[5] One wonders, however, which of the two had the ultimate advantage, for Fox and his companions were kept under guard from March 25 to September 13, 1656, and for thirteen days incarcerated in Doomsdale prison, one of the filthiest dungeons that English penal institutions of the time afforded.[6]

2

The Quaker journalist frequently included obstacles which he had to meet, such as the dissuasives of "religious professors," relatives, and friends, contempt from belligerent enemies, and from non-Quaker schoolmates. George Fox early discovered that the suggested substitutes for his religious despondency, such as marriage, the army, psalm singing, and bleeding were unavailing; Francis Howgill found the arguments of the Independents and Anabaptists illogical, contradictory to Scripture, and confusing;[7] Thomas Carleton took occasion to note that his wife charged him with audacity, puerility, and illiteracy when he attempted to argue for Quaker tenets with Lewis West, a divine of the Church of England, who, as Carleton's wife declared, had been "brought up at his book and school from childhood."[8]

Thomas Chalkley vividly recalled that as dressed in Quaker garb he went two miles through the suburbs of London to Richard Scoryer's school, he was subjected to beatings and stonings on account of "his badge of plainness which his parents put upon him." He added that the boys hooted at him, crying out that " 'Twas no more sin to kill me than to kill a dog."[9] Daniel Roberts related that soon after his father abandoned the Anglican form of service, the latter felt it incumbent "to go to the public worship house" in Cirencester to testify against timeworn liturgical ceremonies. On arrival he found the "priest" in the midst of his sermon. With his hat upon his head John Roberts stood in silence before the clergyman, who became so discomfited that he was unable to proceed with his discourse. According to the son's account, the elder Roberts was forcibly removed from the audience room and debarred from reëntry. As he was returning home, a man, apparently an outraged parishioner, hurled a stone and gave him a hard blow on his back, declaiming, "There, take that for Jesus Christ's sake." Without looking to see who the assailant was, John Roberts remarked, as he passed quietly on his way, "So I do."[10]

3

Sufferings of Friends naturally fill many pages of these journals.[11] Any one of a number of charges might clap a Friend into a cell where walls were covered with hoarfrost or into a fetid, over-crowded prison. George Fox's *Journal,* as A. Neave Brayshaw has shown, reveals the fact that Fox spent seven years in English jails, under as many charges—for interrupting a preacher,[12] for blasphemy,[13] for refusing to bear arms,[14] for not abstaining from attending Friends' meetings, for disturbing the peace,[15] for refusing the Oath of Supremacy and Allegiance,[16] and for suspicion of plotting against Charles II.[17]

Tithes, oaths, and conventicles spelled sufferings for the Friends. Over the right to distinguish between man-made laws and God-made laws, the Quaker autobiographer grew voluble. Principle was ingrained in him. In general, the early Friend gloried in his conscience, accepted the confinement as a time for meditation, religious agitation, or for writing,[18] and waited for heaven to avenge the persecutor.

Once in a while a note of bitterness crept in to the recital of events. Oliver Sansom, after recording numerous "persecutions" which "Priest Anderton" had "visited upon him," broke out with righteous indignation in his journal: "The wickedness of this priest was so great that I was willing to hope there were but few worse in the nation; for he was not only greedy but exceedingly envious." This particular outburst followed the enumeration of a half-dozen cases of distraints in which, during Sansom's imprisonment in Reading Gaol, officers had exceeded their powers. One case will suffice for illustration: Richard Smith [the bailiff] "rushing suddenly in, searched my house, . . . and drove away my cows and sheep, amounting in all to the value of thirty pounds or thereabouts though the single value for which the priest sued was six pounds and eight shillings."[19]

Scarcely a journal fails to recount the imprisonment of self, members of family, or friends. The sociologist can scarcely find better personal records of the English penal institutions of the seventeenth century than are disclosed by the journals of John Banks,[20] Thomas Ellwood,[21] George Whitehead, and George Fox.[22] Under the best of circumstances, the prisoner "for conscience' sake" was separated from his family, and kept from carrying on his business— "his affairs as to the outward," he expressed it; under the worst of conditions, he experienced clammy cold, fetid smoke, vermin, and filth.[23] The prisoner saw men and women, young children, prostitutes, and hardened offenders crowded into loathsome holes.[24] George Whitehead and George Rofe were beaten until "blood gushed" from their mouths;[25] the former reports that a jailer had cried out that he could not be hanged for injuring them because there was no law that would forbid his killing a Quaker.[26] Clothing, bedding, and food were sometimes removed, and the cell left entirely bare. Often no sanitary conveniences were provided.

George Fox wrote thus of the conditions of his prison life at Scarborough during the winter of 1665:

I was forced to lay out a matter of fifty shillings to stop out the rain and keep the room from smoking so much. When I had been at that charge, and made the room somewhat tolerable, they removed me to a worse room, where I had neither chimney nor fire-hearth. This being to the sea-side and lying much open, the wind drove in the rain forcibly, so that the water came over my bed, and ran about the room, that I was fain to skim it up with a platter. And when my clothes were wet, I had no fire to dry them; so that my body was numbed with cold, and my fingers swelled, that one was grown as big as two. . . . Besides they would suffer few Friends to come to me, and . . . I was forced for the first quarter to hire one of the world to bring me necessaries.[27]

The ministering Friend, interested in the progress of the Society, did not miss the opportunity of recording doctrinal questions and disputes over theological questions.[28] These, often retarding the narrative, sometimes drag on to inordinate length. No question concerning the beliefs of the fundamentalists or of the re-actionaries of the time, such as predestination versus universal salvation, or infant or adult baptism versus the baptism of the spirit, was omitted by these memorandists.

4

If mere abundance is any proof, any one turning over the pages of these calf-bound memoirs, profusely sprinkled with italics, capital letters, and occasional black print, will be forced to believe that the impulse toward expression found ample release in letter writing. Commonplace books must have been employed, for often the reply is placed side by side with the writer's epistle. The Swarthmore collection of manuscripts contains numerous letters sent by the earliest public Friends to Margaret Fell (later Fox). All sorts of conditions inspired letters. George Whitehead, troubled by the imprisonment of Friends confined in jail, and in ships upon the Thames during the Plague Year, wrote letters of encouragement to the prisoners.[29] George Fox's epistles, totalling four hundred and twenty, addressed "unto Gentile and unto Jew" fill two good sized volumes.[30]

Typical of the Quaker journals is the inclusion of sermon-like letters addressed to friends, relatives, and also to meetings. Like their New Testament prototypes, these missives begin with a formal salutation couched in apostolic language which suggests the religious unity of both writer and recipient. Ann Banks, for instance, in 1675 used more than half the space of her letter to her imprisoned husband for a sermonized salutation, reminiscent no doubt of prayers to which she had repeatedly listened in Quaker meetings for worship. The prose itself suggests familiarity with the cadences of the King James Version:

My dear and well-beloved Husband, unto whom my Love reacheth, though separated in body for a season, according to the good pleasure of the Lord, in a measure of that which changes not do I dearly Salute thee, who art near and dear to me, in that which God has made us sensible of, to wit, his blessed Truth, which brought us to a knowledge of himself and each other; in which Truth, that is our life, our Unity, our Fellowship stands; . . . and now though asunder, Glory endless be to the worthy Name of our God forever.

After this "greeting in the spirit of the Lord" she very briefly informed him that his father, children, and servants were well, and then added—no one will ever know with what personal sacrifice—"We are content to give thee up to do service for the Lord, being satisfied it is in answer to His requiring thee to be separated from us." Not until many decades later did the Friends depart from the type of letter that combined an invocation of divine blessing upon the recipient, and a sermonizing purpose, with the practical import of the letter.[31]

5

Domestic relations, in so far as they touch the progress of Quakerism, are often given important mention in the Quaker journals. This is especially true if coöperation between husband and wife was particularly lacking or conspicuous. The absence from home of the huband and father, even in the seventeenth century, when the wives of the middle classes uniformly contributed to the support of the family,[32] brought hardship upon the family by curtailing the income and bringing added responsibility upon the wife and mother. Miles Halhead, turning to Quakerism in 1652, became an itinerant minister the following year. He entered in his memorandum that his connection with the new sect of Quakers was displeasing to his wife who often lamented, " I would to God that I had married a Drunkard. I might have found him in an Alehouse; but now I cannot tell where to find my husband."[33] A year later, however, after her own "conviction," Halhead noted with great satisfaction that she "had given him up freely" to follow any "openings" that might come to him.

Both testimonies and journals indicate the resignation with which these unremunerated itinerants accepted their calls abroad and the hardship entailed upon them and their families. William Dewsbury, already a prisoner and destined to spend in all twenty years in English jails, writing to Margaret Fell in 1661 said, "In the life of my God, I have given them [the members of his family] up, with my own life as He may call for it, a free sacrifice; in His will; it is offered up for him to do what is good in his eyes."[34] Thomas Wilson, at the close of his autobiography, expressed the pious hope that during his absences in the West Indies, the Colonies, and in Ireland his wife might be recompensed with peace of mind if with nothing else. He wrote, "My dear wife, being a woman that truly fears God, hath fully given me up to answer the requiring of truth and I hope she will have a share in that reward and peace of which the Lord hath given me the earnest."[35] With equal resignation in her testimony concerning her husband, Mary Wilson referred to her side of the situation in this way, "It was often afflicting to me to think of being left behind, but what shall I say? the Lord hath done it. He hath given and he hath taken away."[36]

Even more tellingly the wife of William Wilson wrote of her sympathetic willingness to aid her husband in his ministerial work:

A living testimony I have to give concerning my dear husband. . . . All is but a reasonable sacrifice for the Lord . . . and this I can truly say, and that to my great comfort, that when the Lord was pleased to call him from me on Truth's Account, whether in England or Scotland, I was never a hindrance; but was willing to give him up to the service. . . . I have often bidden him to take no care for anything he left behind, but have said, "Perform thy journey as thou seest the Lord make thy way." . . . That is my great comfort though I be left behind him in this world.[37]

Letters, written in prison, give evidence that the authors were humanly concerned with thoughts of their homes and various callings. While in prison at Dover John Lilburne, a turbulent spirit in the days when Cromwell was moving toward his ascendency, was converted to Quaker beliefs.[38] Soon after this, Lilburne wrote to his wife that he wished that "she and his sweet lambs" might be present with him to understand the great peace that he had recently attained. He regretted that she "was so straitly put to it for money," but entreated her earnestly "not to cumber herself in her toilings and journeyings" for his "outward liberty," but asked her "to sit down" and if she could possibly arrange it, withdraw from people for a week so that "with much seriousness and deliberation" she might read the works of Nayler and Dewsbury which he was sending her.[39]

Another letter, badly spelled and in a cramped hand, written from the prison at Lincoln, presents a different type of interest in affairs at home:

Dear and loving wife my dear love Remembered unto the and all my children and I desire the to bear my Sepration from the patently and I doute not but the Lord w[h]om I commit my-selfe unto will bring us together againe I desire the to let the ewes of the marsh that are near lambing be goten of [off] and put them into the six acers and gete Thomas Elegde to look [blotted] them of the marsh and gett John Finch to turne some hey for the hoges when they want and put the maire into the six acers.

from thy loving husband.

RICHARD HUTCHINSON

lincolne castle
Feb 4th 1680
Direction—These for my loving wif Anne Hutchinson at her house in Gedney.[40]

Space does not permit even enumeration of the travels in the ministry—the narratives of intrepid missionaries imbued with zeal of carrying their message to the three kingdoms and the known world. Some of these stories have recently been retold by Mabel Brailsford in *Quaker Women* and by Mary Agnes Best in *Rebel Saints*. Barbara Blaugdone, for instance, tells of dangers from storms on shipboard, William Edmundson of desperados in Ireland, William Stout of highway robbers. John Burnyeat recalls disputes in New England, George Fox, lonely trips in journeying from distant settlement to distant settlement, from the Carolinas to New England, and Thomas Chalkley of missionary visits to the West Indies.

Though in somewhat stereotyped form and language, these journals of early ministerial Friends review the milestones of the Quaker life, yet in the very repetition of religious crises, persecutions, and travels in the ministry, they remain the most vivid portrayals of the Society's aims for spiritualizing life, and for the personal expression of efforts to adapt Quakerism to the problems of life.

CHAPTER XVI

THE LANGUAGE OF THE JOURNALS

1

As the Friends settled down to eighteenth-century conservatism, they by degrees adopted a type for their journals which became almost inflexible. Outside the Quaker group, autobiographers, penning their "secret memoirs," were writing with individuality, tempered by environment and cultural interests. The Friends, however, drew their subject matter from their dominant interests, and their phrasing and their vocabulary from the English of the middle classes and from the Bible.

The style of the journals corresponds exactly with the tenets laid down by William Penn in his preface to *The Written Gospel Labours of John Whitehead.* Learned allusions, references to reading, and contemporary events are all negligible qualities, while the current artificialities of balance and elaborate figures were avoided "that the vain mind" might not be distracted from content to veneer. Even the occurrences of life a little out of the ordinary, which the average autobiographer would eagerly seize upon for his memoirs, the Quaker handles with extreme caution; moreover, he is apt to exclude all such episodes, unless they illustrate some aspect of Quaker faith or practice, or formed, as Stephen Crisp allegorically put it, a part of the individual's "pilgrim's progress from Babylon to Bethel." If a secular event is introduced, it usually explains a point common to the beliefs of the group. Robert Fowler, in order to elaborate upon the providences of God, described his escape from privateers in 1657;[1] Thomas Lurting, for the same reason, narrated his own reformation from "fighting sailor" to "peaceable Christian;"[2] and Thomas Ellwood, to inform the public concerning the filth and unsanitary conditions of English prisons, enlarged on his own confinement in the Bridewell and other prisons.[3]

If current events bore on the spread of Quakerism, the journalist conscientiously inserted references to them. Thomas Story recorded a visit that he and Gilbert Mollison paid to Peter the Great, when the Czar of Muscovy was in England. They did not arrange the interview to discuss ship building, but to invite the royal guest to attend a meeting for worship and to present him with Quaker literature.[4] It is of interest to note that he accepted both. To show the ebb and flow of Quakerism, Fox reported several conferences which he had with Cromwell.[5] Though a logical response to the interests of the ministerial authors, the effort to stress only subjects connected with Quaker history, thought, and experience, resulted in a degree of monotony, clearly observable when several journals are read in close succession.

Plainness of literary style was a desideratum with the early Quaker memorandists. Distinct qualities of phrasing, patent in all early Quaker writing and choice of subject matter, form a second line of demarcation between the autobiographies of the Friends and those "of the world." Many turns of expression which constantly recur in Quaker memoirs had already found a firm place in the language habits of the group, and for many decades continued to appear in their journals.

Some of these idioms indicate an effort to express in everyday English the more or less mystical experiences and attitudes of mind common to the Friends. Several, for illustration, can be drawn from *The Journal of George Fox,* such as "I saw that none could speak to my condition. . . ."[6] "I felt a stop in my spirit. . . ."[7] "Then I was moved of the Lord to go in his power. . . ."[8] "Being clear of the place, I passed on."[9] Dr. Knight has pointed out that keen sense perceptions influenced Fox's literary style. Many expressions[10] which she mentions seem to prove this assertion, as for instance, "an abundance of thick cloddy earth of hypocrisy and falseness. . . ."[11] "There did a pure fire appear in me. . . ."[12] "All creation gave another smell unto me than before. . . ."[13] "The earth and air, methought, smelt of the corruption of the nation."[14] With a sixth sense, possibly a combination of the others, Fox wrote thus of his last glimpse of the Protector, "I saw a waft of death go before him."[15]

A certain picturesqueness of phrasing running as an undercurrent in many journals can be traced to two sources: an imagery resulting from familiarity with old Testament writers, and an addiction to colloquialisms.[16] Fox's *Journal* shows many such variations. By likening a publican to one who "bows down his head for a day like the bull rush,"[17] he fell back upon the language of Isaiah to express his scorn of one who fasted merely to seem holy, and upon the words of Malachi to describe the spiritually cleansing power of one of his own early visions—"Then I saw how He sate as a refiner's fire and as fuller's soap."[18] Homely expressions constantly re-appear. Fox wrote that he went to hear a "priest" and "found him like an empty hollow cask"; and again, "He was so full of evil air that he could not speak; but blubbered and stammered."[19] In similar manner, on different occasions he wrote that Cromwell's soldiers "walked up and down in their dumps being pitifully blanked and down;"[20] again, "It brought the Truth above all bad walkers and talkers,"[21] and "Their minds are in bondage . . . brittle and changeable, tossed up and down by windy doctrines."[22]

2

It would be wrong, however, to infer that the uniformity of these first forty journals precludes any diversity. Writers, born as were Thomas Story[23] (1672-1742) and Thomas Chalkley (1675-1741) in the last part of the seventeenth century, constant travelers between the new and the old world, interested in agriculture, and the government of Pennsylvania, could not be expected to write as did the First Publishers of Truth in the 1650's. In general the tone of the later writers is more circumscribed and conventional, while that of the earlier ones, especially in the fragmentary autobiographies of confessional nature, is less restrained, more emotional, and often prophetic.

A Book of Some of the Sufferings and Passages of Miles Halhead, published in 1690, is one of the very early complete journals and perhaps the most ingenuous of all. Miles Halhead, an early convert of 1652, who styled himself "a plain simple man," had in his own mind been assured beyond question that the inner Voice was constantly present in his walks, work, and writings. "The Word of God," he wrote, had once been to him "as a two-edged Sword, and a Hammer" but became "by the love of God sweeter than Honey and the Honey Comb." This weight of God's power, according to his account, frequently oppressed him; on one occasion it had directed him to preach "in the steeple-house at Kendall"[24] where he knew that his presence would be objectionable; again it carried him through harrowing imprisonments;[25] once it urged him to warn the wife of Thomas Preston against the iniquity of pride.[26] He followed its admonition by calling her a Jezebel. And once "after being beaten, bruised and left for dead" by his persecutors, the Word came to him again, saying, "Arise and go to yonder little Chappel and speak my word freely that I shall give thee, and I will make thee a sound man."[27] At yet another time the Word of God promised him safety if he would wade a river in Scotland to escape a stoning,[28] and on another occasion it enjoined upon him a fourteen day fast.[29] Simplicity characterized this autobiographical record of Miles Halhead, who painstakingly explained in a note to the reader that after God had sent him one of these messages he had informed the Master that he was "an unlearned man, not versed in the Scriptures, and for wisdom had but little."[30]

In comparison with a revelation of this character, the information,[31] detailed in the life *of Thomas Chalkley*,[32] traveler, planter, author, and Quaker minister, presents the extremes to be found in the autobiographies of the early Friends. Though Chalkley also reports visions and premonitions,[33] he seems to have been less conscious of mystical guidance than Halhead, and to have relied more than the former on the faculties of intellect.[34]

And yet even allowing for variations in time and temperament, the likenesses within the journals far exceed the differences. The insertion of numerous papers previously published[35]— epistles,[36] legal documents,[37] and court trials[38] repeated verbatim—sadly interferes with unity in autobiographical writing, where the interest is expected to center about the life and thought of the author. On the other hand, though the insertions obstruct the narrative, these documents of legal and illegal procedures, and these letters of protest and admonition, were part and parcel of both individual and group experiences and causes of anguish and anxious hours.

CHAPTER XVII

FROM CONFESSION TO JOURNAL

The Quaker journal was preëminently the outgrowth of the Quaker group mind. Through the religious confession and the autobiography proper, the Friends evolved a means for expressing their emotional life and their religious experiences, and also a means for communicating to their constituency and outsiders Quaker ideas of practical Christianity. To a casual observer it might seem that the Quaker journal sprang into being full grown, for between the years 1689 and 1694 four memoirs of representative early Publishers of Truth were given to the public. These, the journals of William Caton, John Burnyeat, Stephen Crisp, and George Fox, apparently established the *genre*, and set a mold which with comparatively little variation was followed for fifteen decades. The pattern of the Quaker journal certainly became standardized after the printing of these autobiographies, but the sources of the peculiar characteristics of Quaker memoir writing must be sought in the mental habits of the primitive Friends. Every phase of life and thought, portrayed in these four pioneer journals—the home environment,[1] religious crises,[2] psychopathic states,[3] adoption of Quaker tenets,[4] imprisonment,[5] domestic affairs,[6] travels in the ministry,[7]—all had previously found expression in Quaker literature before 1689.

The Friends had very early felt the necessity for self-expression. This need was partly psychological and partly a defense measure. Numerous elements in their experiences had predisposed them to write both subjectively and objectively of themselves. Reliance upon the inner Light rendered them more introspective than many of their religious contemporaries; the habit of looking upon life as sacramental caused them to consider all acts of importance *per se.* Attacks upon the doctrine of the inner Light often impelled them to defend their beliefs through the revelation of their own personal experience. Persecutions called for defense of another type. Religious zeal, bordering on and sometimes passing into fanaticism, induced others to unfold in vision and prophetic literature, their mental states of apprehension, uneasiness, and alarm. The fact, too, that Friends through their scruples against oaths were deprived of court privileges rendered them extremely careful to preserve all records of the history of the Society and of their personal and family life.

Some of their personal experiences found their way into daybooks. Though few diaries appeared in print, internal evidence shows that many of the journals were compiled from diurnal jottings. John Whiting, for example, recorded that his sister Mary, on a missionary journey of nearly five hundred miles, kept "a journal of all meetings she was at, and the distance one from the other."[8] The enumeration of certain dates and places, noted in missionary travel, indicates that the reviews of life were often compiled from notes and diaries. That such is the case is clear from entries like the following taken from a single paragraph in *The Truth Exalted,* the autobiography of John Burnyeat: "We took boat and went over to Long Island, to Oyster Bay . . . being clear of those parts [we] came to New York. . . . We set sail from New York the first day of ninth month, 1672. . . . The third day . . . we met with rough weather . . . but the sixth we got in at the Capes of Virginia, and on the ninth we came to anchor in Patuxent River in the province of Maryland."[9]

William Penn wrote one of the few Quaker diaries printed in the seventeenth century,—his *Travails in Holland and Germany* in 1677—an account of efforts to spread Quakerism in Teutonic countries. Elias Osborne, on the contrary, declared that he had kept "no regular journal" of his life "with respect to the order of time."[10] John Kelsall's manuscript diaries contain many First Day entries, in which he detailed the number of ministers taking part in the service, the central subject or "opening" for the hour, and often a brief résumé of the topic on which the diarist himself had been "led to speak." The extant manuscripts of "The Itinerary Journal" and the "Haistwell Journal,"[11] from which Thomas Ellwood drew for the details of Fox's experiences in America, in editing the autobiography of Fox,[12] give indisputable witness of their original diary form.

Quaker journalists, however, did not rely upon diaries alone when they set about the task of "putting their papers in order." Many of the collected works of the Friends show clearly the source material at hand, upon which the Quaker autobiographer drew in order to survey the history of his thoughts and actions. Often he could turn to "sufferings" tracts that he himself had written,[13] to testimonies concerning his friends,[14] to his printed letters, or to those still in manuscript,[15] or perhaps to an earlier religious confession of his own. Harmony of belief, intercommunication between groups, and circulation of tracts—all played their part in molding these elements into a generic type of Quaker autobiography.

Mrs. Anna Robeson Burr is only correct in saying, "The stamp of George Fox is upon every one of the differing metals [the Quaker journals] and we are led, therefore, back to Fox's Journal,"[16] in so far as she refers to the general conceptions of life and religion taught by Fox, and not to the type form of autobiography used by the early Friends. The fact that three important and two minor[17] Quaker journals preceded his is evidence that the typical journal did not originate in the mind of George Fox, but was the outgrowth of the group mind, dominated, it will be readily admitted, by George Fox. The *genre* itself, however, cannot be considered a literary invention of his.

The collected works of the Friends contain a large percentage of material personal in nature and capable of lending itself to memoir writing. In fact, over a fifth of the first four hundred and forty writers have left some writings of autobiographical nature. A little octavo volume, called *Truth Vindicated by the Faithful Testimony and Writings of Elizabeth Bathurst* (1691), though never transformed into memoirs, illustrates Quaker autobiography in the making. The collected *Works* of Elizabeth Bathurst fill one hundred eighty-seven small pages, eleven of which contain testimonies and ten, a personal appeal made to the communicants of the church of Samuel Ansley.[18] Twelve unnumbered pages are used as a preface of personal nature to *Truth Vindicated*, one hundred sixty to the title rôle of her *Works*, and twenty-four to *The Sayings of Women*. All but the last contain personal material. Her individuality is likewise shown both in the preface and the exhortation, and particularly in her transitions from main point to main point. *Truth Vindicated*, an apologia for Quaker beliefs, represents Elizabeth Bathurst through her own experience pleading for the group. *The Written Gospel Labours* of John Whitehead, it will be recalled, contained three articles of personal nature, a trial in which he was defendant,[19] a treatise on the Quaker ministry,[20] and a vivid autobiography, *The Enmity between the Two Seeds*.[21] The *Works* of Humphrey Smith, to cite another case, contain six articles of personal nature which could easily have formed the basis of a complete autobiography. These essays range from visions, sufferings, and meditations, to an account of his own "conviction." The religious confession of all these was the most direct forerunner of the formal Quaker journal. Through this type of revelation men and women, as the next chapter will show, sought to bring to people a revelation of the miracle that the inner Light had created in their lives.

Chapter XVIII

THE RELIGIOUS CONFESSION
ACCEPTING THE LIGHT

1

The Friends found their supreme opportunity for self-expression in the religious confession. For them vitality in religion lay in experience. Meditations, visions, openings, periods of depression and of exaltation, moments of "centering down into the silence" and of "hearkening to the inner Voice," all became way marks of their spiritual pilgrimage. Assured by intuition of the validity of the inner Light and strengthened by the contagion of religious enthusiasm they felt themselves impelled to give expression to their mystic and spiritual emotions. The confessions, therefore, form the most complete revelation of their desires to present the mystic and spiritual at-oneness existing between their finite selves and the Infinite One, and to express the personal aspects of religion common to all members of the group.

From the standpoint of psychology, a confession, either oral or written, is generally looked upon as relief from pent up thoughts and emotions;[1] from the standpoint of religion, it usually implies a statement of faith or admission of sin. From the psychological point of view the Quaker confessant, though he probably never realized the fact, was finding mental relief in confiding his thoughts and experiences to possible future readers. From the viewpoint of religion the Quaker scribe was in one sense declaring his faith, but only in a minor sense writing an admission of sin. Primarily the religious confessions include a record of the successive steps by which Friends attained a spiritual sense of harmony. They comprise, therefore, a narrative account of the acceptance of Quaker beliefs and practices, the acquiring of mental peace, and a subsequent life of activity in the work of the Quaker ministry.

After the inner Light had once been accepted as the personal Guide in life, the sense of sin, dominant in contemporary Calvinistic and later Methodist teachings, held but a minor place in Quaker autobiography. Most of their confessions portray a religious crisis, a cataclysmic period, in which the writers acknowledge that they were shaken to the depths of their being. These stages never seem to be presented as ends in themselves but as steps toward securing a satisfactory solution for religious questionings and for spiritual distress. The prevailing motive was the revelation of the mystic peace that could be obtained and kept if the worshiper would constantly "keep in the Light." This condition of unrest, oftentimes an abnormal one and in some cases protracted over several years, is dwelt on with great detail, and contrasts sharply with the subsequent years in which the writer, even in times of persecution, found mental poise, and in which, at personal sacrifice, he performed the duties of an itinerant "public" Friend.[2] After attempting to walk in the Quaker way of life many converts apostatized, either on intellectual or social grounds, and returned to other sects or to the Established Church.

In the attainment of mystic peace lies the principal line of demarcation between the journal of George Fox and the recorded spiritual anguish of John Bunyan in *Grace Abounding to the Chief of Sinners*. The latter temporarily secured peace of mind, but never retained it for any length of time. Quite differently and with great uniformity, the confessions of the Friends indicate that the writers, ideally at least, after they had once definitely accepted the inner Light as a guiding gleam, did not consume their energies with questions of future rewards or the fatalities connected with the unpardonable sin, but employed them almost wholly with carrying out the commands of the Spirit.

A state of mind, allied to that of the Seekers, is apparent in the confessants who became upholders of Quaker principles during or immediately after the period of the Commonwealth. In adolescence or early maturity they had felt the effects of the disruption of the Anglican Church, and also the increasing antagonism between the Presbyterian and Independent leaders, and had witnessed the rapid springing up of the sectaries.[3] Many like George Fox, Francis Howgill, and Isaac and Mary Penington, passed through a state of religious melancholy. Edward Burrough wrote that he had been brought up in the Established Church "to be exercised in the formal worship, which was then upheld, to read, to sing, to rabble over a prayer"; and that later he had rejected these services to "follow after the Presbyterians"; that in turn he left them "to follow after the highest notionists" among the sectaries, but that at last he "grew weary of hearing any of the priests," because "something which shined into me, shewed me ignorance in all profession." Through George Fox he learned to understand the significance of the inner Light, and in his confession, *A Warning from the Lord to the Inhabitants of Underbarrow*, he declared with the intense conviction of a new and youthful convert, that he bore witness against "all forms of religion, and false hirelings, and . . . those who were never sent of God to declare his Word."[4]

2

Confessions up to the Act of Toleration generally appeared in the form of tracts, ranging from four to sixty pages in length; after 1689 they were incorporated and given the place of greatest importance in the journals. The confessions of the early converts who came into the Society from other religious bodies portray vividly two stages—the search for and the attainment of peace. In these the steps are more sharply distinguished than they are in the memoirs of the later Quaker confessants, reared under Quaker influences. The first stage shows definitely the influence of the prevailing puritanism of the mid-decades of the seventeenth century; the second emphasizes the attainment of mental poise and the subsequent launching forth upon the active work of the Quaker ministry.

Like the later journals, the early confessional tracts tend to run in rather set grooves; they repeat certain phrases and dwell upon a uniform series of experiences. These tracts include first, the writer's earliest intimations of God and of religious questioning;[5] second, an earnest endeavor to ascertain from the variety of prevailing teachings—Anglican, Presbyterian and Puritan—an adequate basis for a religious life;[6] next, a record of the writer's first knowledge of the Quakers[7] or of the Publisher of Truth who "convinced" him; fourth, the struggle in the individual soul against surrender;[8] fifth, the final submission, and last, the entry into the activities and the defense of the Society.[9]

With a man like Whiting,[10] who was "cradled in conventicles," or like Croker, whose early memories held uppermost the imprisonment of his parents, the approach varied less in kind than in degree.[11] Considered, however, after examination of the autobiographical records left by religiously minded contemporaries, such as John Bunyan's revelling in the weight of his sins, Richard Baxter's straightforward account of his life, Lady Anne Halkett's musings, Sir Tobie Matthew's *apologia* for transferring his allegiance from the

Church of England to the Church of Rome, and Simonds D'Ewes's and John Evelyn's profound regard for the Established Church, and even the Scotch Covenanters' spiritual diaries, the similarities among these eighty and more Quaker confessions stand out with remarkable emphasis.

The earliest confessions, such as William Ames's *A Declaration of the Witness of God in me* (1656) and Richard Farnsworth's *The Heart Opened by Christ* (1654), were defenses pleading for the reality of mystical experience, and had been written in the hope that readers would understand and desire to find in inward guidance the peace and rest which these writers had long sought, and finally found. The later confessions, appearing as part of the complete journals, were obviously designed by their authors to serve didactic ends,[12] to show the high tide of the religious wave that swept the early Friends into recognition as a group force, as well as to portray the fluctuations through which the writers had passed in discovering and surrendering themselves to a religious life that demanded an escape, or "separateness from the world." In comparing the work of the first and second generations of writers one finds the earlier confessions to be more volatile, and more mystical in expression, and the later ones somewhat more studied and adhering more closely to a type form.[13]

3

The grand total of religious confessions written by the first two generations of Friends approximates ninety. The number is almost equally divided between the confessional tracts and the complete journals. Nearly forty of the former appeared in print before 1680. The following tabulation lists the confessions in the chronological order of publication. In some cases it has been difficult to draw a sharp line of distinction between the journal, as it was defined and described in an earlier chapter,[14] and the confession. In cases of doubt the accounts have been judged as confessions when the period of conviction to Friends' principles dominated other interests.

RELIGIOUS CONFESSIONS

(Exclusive of those incorporated in the journals)

1652: Nayler, James, *An Examination . . . at Sessions; Works;* 11-16.

[1653]: Hubberthorn, Richard, *A True Testimony;* Repr: *Works;* 1-7.

1654: Burrough, Edward, *A Warning to Underbarrow;* Repr: *Works;* 13-17.

1654: Farnsworth, Richard, *The Heart Opened;* 13.

1655: Dewsbury, William, *The First Birth;* Repr: *Works;* 44-57.

1655: Whitehead, John, *The Enmity between the Two Seeds;* Repr: *Works;* 1-42.

1656: Ames, William, *A Declaration of the Witness of God;* 8.

1656: Howgill, Francis, *The Inheritance of Jacob Discovered;* 28.

1656: Lilburne, John, *The Resurrection of John Lilburne;* 14.

1656: Symonds, Thomas, *The Voice of the Just;* 8.

1656: Rofe, George, *The Righteousness of God;* 18.

1656: Whitehead, George, *Jacob Found in a Desert Land;* 20.

[Bet. 1657 and 1674]: Zachary, Thomas, *A Word,* etc.; 15.

1658: Smith, Humphrey, *Man Driven Out of the Earth;* Repr: *Works;* 52-68.

1659: Nayler, James, *To the Life of God in All;* 10, Repr: *Works;* xxxix-xlix.

1659: Bache, Humphrey, *A Few Words in True Love;* 12.

1659: Green, Thomas, *A Declaration,* etc.; 32.

1660: Britten, William, *Silent Meeting;* 14.

1660: Beevan, John, *A Loving Salutation;* 8.

1660: Smith, Humphrey, *To All Parents of Children;* Repr: *Works;* 123-135.

1663: Robinson, George, *An Additional Account;* 13.
1663: Coale, Josiah, *A Song of the Judgments;* 14.
1668: Carleton, Thomas, *The Captives Complaint;* 142.
1669: Bennitt, William, *The Work and Mercy of God;* 44.
1673: Dundas, William, *A Few Words of Truth;* 22.
1676: Forster, Thomas, *A Guide to the Blind;* 16.
1676: Barclay, Robert, Introduction to *Universal Love;* 5.
1677: Steel, Lawrence, *Jacob the Plain Man;* 28.
1680: Curwen, Alice, *A Relation of the Labour,* etc.; 55.
1684: Laythes, Thomas, *The Inward . . . Christian;* 70.
1685: Briggs, Thomas, *An Account of;* 20.
1691: Bayly, William, *Account,* prefixed to *Works;* 28.
1695: Brush, Edward, *The Invisible Power of God;* 28.
1702: Green, Theophilus, *A Narrative,* etc.; 32.
1708: Gates, Nicholas, *A Tender Invitation;* 28.
1709: Burnyeat, Jonathan, *Some Account of;* 57.
1710: Fell, Margaret, *A Relation of;* Repr. in *Works;* 1-7.
1710: Lurting, Thomas, *Thomas Lurting, or The Fighting Sailor,* etc.; 60.
1712: Webb, Elizabeth, Letter; Pr. in *Friends' Library,* XIII, 163-172.
1720: Gwin, Thomas, *The Will and Testament;* 60.
1801: Andrews, Isaac, *A Short Account of;* 14.
1834: Skene, Lilias, Autobiographical letter of 1678; Pr. in *Jaffray and the Friends in Scotland;* 575-583.

An analysis of this table shows that the desire of giving expression to religious moods, states, and conditions remained a constant aim with the Friends. Of these forty-eight confessional memoirs, only four brief records antedate 1655. Two belong to the year 1655; seven to 1656; three to 1659; eleven fall between 1660 and 1669, three in the next decade, and three in the 1680's prior to 1689, the publication year of the life of William Caton, the first of the formal journals. In the last decade of the century, including both tract and journal accounts, eight confessions were published; ten in the next; ten between 1710 and 1720, and six more before 1725. Ten more were previously listed among the journals, the maturity of whose authors fell within the 1650-1725 period.[15] In addition to these a half dozen confessions might be added which also narrate a "storm and stress" crisis occurring well within the period under study.[16] The writers of these lived well into the eighteenth century. The tables show an early high water mark for the year 1656, when "the spiritual contagion of zealous enthusiasm" was sending out home and foreign missionaries. Following the publication of the life of William Caton in 1689, these confessions in order of publication indicate a regular sequence of about ten to a decade.

4

The confession of Francis Howgill *The Inheritance of Jacob Discovered after his Return out of Egypt* graphically portrays the successive stages in the religious life of one of the finest spirits attracted to early Quakerism. Francis Howgill (1618-1668/9), university trained and for a short time in orders for the Established Church,[17] had after years of troubled searching been "reached" in 1652 by George Fox at Sedburgh in Westmorland.[18] Previous to that event, he had with the deepest concern endeavored to orientate himself to the theology of various religious groups in England. After his full surrender to Quaker beliefs, he engaged for the rest of his life in the work of the itinerant ministry. His last five years were spent in Appleby Gaol, where up to the time of his death he continued to write in behalf of Friends.

Howgill in his *Inheritance of Jacob* (1656), a tract of twenty-eight pages, and an early example of Quaker confessional writing, vividly presents the points upon which most converts dwelt. In cadence and diction it was never surpassed in Quaker autobiographical writing, and in emotional strength until *The Journal of George Fox* was issued in 1694. Howgill's confession represents an earnest seeker losing himself in the tangle of religious opinion of his day at the very time that the puritan ascendency in church and state had supplanted royalist and Anglican control. Howgill at the age of thirty-eight, two years after he had allied himself with the Friends, reviewed the spiritual turnings in his path and identified his experience with that of Jacob at Bethel. He expressly designed the revelation of his "seeking" and "finding" for men and women who were as lost in the turmoil of the times as he had been.

In this fragmentary autobiography Francis Howgill recalled that at the age of twelve he had "set his heart to know God," that he read the Old Testament, and "fell into the strictest worship" observed in the vicinity of Grayrigg in Westmorland. It is evident that from earliest childhood he possessed an extremely sensitive conscience, for he often questioned the rightfulness of personally engaging in the sports and pastimes of youth, sometimes deciding that they represented the sinful vanity of the world, and yet at others bemoaning the fact that he had been drawn into them. A period of self-recrimination always followed until, in final desperation, he declared, "I had a desire to be alone that I might not see or hear any folly acted." Even though he prayed three and four times a day, God seemed far off. As at a later period he introspectively analyzed the situation, he came to see that "the admiration of the world" for his intellectual prowess in these earlier days had been the chief cause for his failure to realize the nearness of God.

He also stated that for five years he had "posted up and down" on foot, eager to hear all the eminent ministers within walking distance, yet even in so doing he felt himself under constant "condemnation."[19] With the deepest concern he carried his problems to these preachers who told him that this self-judgment was conscience; and greatly as he at this time respected their authority, he began to distrust their beliefs and to feel that conscience represented but one share in his general condemnation of self. At this stage he shared all the fears that belonged to the prevailing temper of Puritanism. He zealously studied the views of the divines concerning imputed righteousness, partook of the sacrament but always with the fear that he was an unworthy communicant, gave himself up to a study of the New Testament, despaired concerning his inability to reconcile conflicting texts, feared that he had sinned against the Holy Ghost, and finally spent hours in prayer and in fasting. "He ran," as he said, "from one man to another," and like George Fox he too found them "physicians of small value."[20] In company with most of the confessants, he claimed that from childhood he had been aware of a guiding yet scarcely recognized force within—a force apart from conscience which kept him from "gross evils" and which he later identified with indwelling divinity.

In spite of his eager and constant inquiries of self and of divines, he wrote that he "was tossed from mountain to hill." Driven almost into despair, he finally ceased to consult or listen to ministers. At this stage he found great solace in silent meditation, and came close to an understanding of the inner Light. He wrote,

I kept still at home in desert places, solitary, weeping. Everything I had done was laid before me, in so much that every thought was judged; and I tender, and my heart was broken; and when I could sorrow most I had most peace; for something spake to me from the Lord; but I knew Him not then.[21]

Finding no help in the Established Church, in which he had been educated, he turned, as did John Gratton, Richard Hubberthorn, and William Bayly,[22] to the Independents, hearkened to their preachers, and purchased their books.

After discovering that they, too, were powerless to contribute to his needs, Howgill allied himself with the Anabaptists, in whose church government he discovered a close adherence to the scriptural accounts of the apostolic church; but even though he encountered dismay when he found them criticizing and quarreling with one another, he admired a few of the members. On occasions he was conscious of a rebuking voice within saying, "His servant thou art whom thou obeyest." In his despondency he decided that there were no teachers who understood or preached Christ.[23] From that period on he became, in fact if not nominally, a Seeker, for he wrote,

Now it was revealed in me that the Lord would teach his people himself;[24] so I waited. . . . And the word of the Lord was within me that the time of the Lord was at hand . . . and it burned in me as a fire that the day was near. . . . I had, as my mind was turned to the Light, pure openings and prophecies of things to come; and a belief that I should see the day and bear witness of his Name.[25]

After this mystic revelation just before the Protectorate, Howgill began preaching against the organized religion of the day, and attracted to his side several men who, like himself, "had wandered up and down" paths supposedly leading to spiritual peace. In 1652 at Sedburgh Fair, he heard Fox declare in a sermon that "the light of Christ in man is the way to Christ." Here at last he discovered the solution, but the prophetic words for which he had waited so long did not bring immediate peace. His earlier habits of thinking, the older theology which he had endeavored to discard, and former doubts, re-asserted themselves. He, like Bunyan's Christian, had to pass through a valley of humiliation. All things, the petty deeds that he had committed, kept surging through his mind. In the language of David, he wrote,

In the morning, I wished it had been evening, but in the evening, I wished it had been morning; and I had no rest . . . all that I had ever done was judged and condemned. . . . I would have run away to have hid myself. . . . I roared out for the disquietness of my heart. . . . I knew not the right hand from the left: I became a perfect fool . . . and as a man distracted.

At last there came a Voice saying, "Just and true is His Judgment."[26] These words brought to him a calm and lasting state of mind. Having fully attained to the peace of the mystic, Howgill closed the narration of his "conviction" with the following metaphorical and biblical phrasing, "And I have rest and peace in doing the will of God; and am entered into true rest and lie down in the field of God with the lambs of God where the sons of God rejoice together and the saints keep holy days." Though his devotion to the leading of the inner Light kept him far from home, caused him to be apprehended as a Jesuit,[27] later to be banished from Ireland[28] and to spend his final years in Appleby Gaol, not a drop from his pen denotes an iota of regret for his surrender.

After months or years of searching, indicative of the religious unrest of the middle years of the seventeenth century, a complete submission similar to Howgill's is the characteristic note in the Quaker confessions. This submission resulted in bringing together by a centripetal force, the scattered elements in the seeker's personality, and of causing all these to center about one purpose in life.[29] Mary Penington left two letters to which reference has already been made, one for her daughter, who married William Penn, and the other for her grandson, Springett Penn. In these she related steps in her search, similar to those of Howgill, in her own experience and in that of her two husbands, Sir William Springett and Isaac Penington. The former, brought up in the Church of England, died in 1644. In his searching for a religion in which he might believe, he followed the prevailing Puritanism of the day—refused to permit a ring to be used at his marriage, allowed no formal prayers in his home, and refused to have his son baptized by the parish "priest."[30]

In the second letter, particularly, Mary Penington narrated her distress over her failure to secure an answer to the question, "What is prayer?" This anxiety occurred long before she had heard of the Quakers. On account of her growing distrust of formal prayers, she refused, at the risk of family disapproval, to attend Anglican services and went alone to hear a puritan preacher.[31] She, too, prayed several times a day, heard sermons and lectures, fasted and meditated,[32] and frequently sought solitude and conversations with "religious professors." Temporarily she turned to the gayeties of the world, but found that her doubts and fears hounded her there. By herself, in dreams and "openings," without suggestions from others as she thought, she came to a realization that by turning her thoughts inward, she could find God there and receive directions for conduct.

In this state of unrest, she discovered about 1659 that "her love was drawn toward" Isaac Penington, who was also a distressed "seeker after the Lord." Together they continued their search, alternately hoping for the solution of their problems and alternately disappointed. She heard rumors of the Quakers, had read a book, perhaps one of George Fox's written in the plain language which she thought ridiculous, and after her previous failure to find satisfaction in religion, had resolved to abandon useless questioning. She and her husband, however, found themselves unable to resist the truth in the teachings of Thomas Curtis, a Quaker preacher from Reading. And since both Isaac and Mary Penington came from the aristocratic classes, the struggle of resigning old habits of life for the ridiculed customs of the despised

Quakers brought her a new series of conflicts even after she had intellectually acquiesced with the doctrines of the Friends.[33] After both husband and wife had come to a decision, however, they whole-heartedly embraced the Quaker way of life. Their home became a center for Friends,[34] and Isaac Penington one of their most influential writers on the theoretical and mystical phases of their belief.

For Mary Penington the hour of final reconcilement seems to have occurred at the first meeting held in their home at Chalfont. She wrote in her epistolary legacy:

To this day I have a fresh remembrance of it. It was then the Lord enabled me to worship Him in that which was undoubtedly his own, and give up my whole strength. . . . I acknowledged his great mercy and wonderful kindness: for I could say, "This is it which I have longed and waited for, and feared I should never experience!"[35]

Her husband, more mystical in his expression than she, in a short treatise entitled A Brief Account of My Soul's Travel Toward the Holy Land wrote of an experience prior to his meeting with the Quakers. Like Francis Howgill and Mary Penington and many other Quakers he had also come very close to an understanding of the inner Light before he had become acquainted with Quaker teachings. Using the language of the mystic, he wrote

At last when my nature was almost spent, and the pit of despair was even closing its mouth upon me, mercy sprang and deliverance came, and the Lord my God owned me and sealed his love unto me, and Light sprang within me, which made not only the scriptures, but the very outward creatures glorious in my eye, so that everything was sweet, pleasant and lightsome about me.

Of a later experience, when he more clearly comprehended the Quaker message, he thus expressed himself:

The Lord opened my spirit. . . . The Lord caused his Holy Power to fall upon me, and gave me such an inward demonstration and feeling of the Seed of Life, that I cried out in my spirit, "This is He, This is He; there is not another; there never was another." He was always with me though I knew Him not . . . as he now was revealed in me and to me by the Father. O that I might now be joined to him, and he alone might live in me.

In this brief spiritual autobiography, after clearly pointing out that the Quakers possessed the key to the spiritual interpretation of both life and the Scriptures, Isaac Penington closed his narrative with a cry, that no doubt was subconsciously at the basis of all early Quaker confessional writing:

O that others had a true, certain, and sensible Taste of the Life, Virtue and Goodness of the Lord as it is Revealed. . . . This the Lord hath brought us to; and this we earnestly and uprightly desire and endeavor, that others may be brought to it also; that they may rightly (in true Silence of the Flesh, and in pure stillness of the Spirit) wait for . . . which answers the Desire of the awakened Mind and Soul, and satisfies it with the true precious Substance.[36]

CHAPTER XIX

THE RELIGIOUS CONFESSION
APPROACHING THE QUAKER
WAY OF LIFE

1

The written confession allowed the Friends not only release from their pent-up emotions of both despair and aspiration, but an opportunity to demonstrate to the world that they who had been "seekers" were now "finders"[1] of religious truth. The confessants among the Friends were apt to make note of certain scruples which weighed heavily upon their consciences in their pre-Quaker days. They averred that these points of mental debate were instrumental in convincing them of the truth of Quaker practices. Two of these refer to the objection of the Friends to the singing of hymns. John Banks (1638-1710) wrote that as a very young man, acting as school master at Mosser Chapel near Pardlow,[2] he had conscientious objections about conducting morning services which consisted of Scripture reading, formal prayers and psalm singing. William Bennitt, after reaching depths of despair, reported that he had "frequented the Meetings of the Independents," whom he then "thought were the children of God," but left them because he felt it was wrong "to sing what others had prescribed" for him.[3]

The biographers of the pioneer "Publishers," who lived through this early period of strained tension, narrate similar pre-Quaker experiences of the initial stages of Quakerism in the lives which they were depicting. Daniel Roberts related that his father was willing to renounce the established religion immediately after Richard Farnsworth, at that time a prisoner in Banbury jail, "had spoken to his condition as if he had known him [John Roberts] from his youth up."[4] John Richardson wrote that his father had "been educated in the Episcopal way," but that after giving his "mind to retirement, reading the Scriptures and seeking after the Lord especially in the fields," he "saw that the priests were wrong" and he grew weary of following them . . . even before he "had heard the name of Quaker." Richard Hawkins, in the biography of his uncle, Gilbert Latye, related that the latter gave up a profitable position on account of the "emptiness of his master's profession," and went to London in 1648, where he followed "the most zealous masters and preachers of that time, often hearing four sermons a day." Never fully satisfied, Gilbert Latye continued his inquiries until 1654, at which time "he gave up to the leading of the Holy Spirit," as expounded by Edward Burrough, and became both a preacher and an exemplifier of his faith.[5]

Many of these confessants indicate that they were writing for a specific public. The appeal of their confessions was uniformly directed to men and women of strong religious bent, and generally to communicants of other religious bodies. John Beevan addressed his confession of faith, *A Loving Salutation,* to Anabaptists with whom he had previously had fellowship. William Bennitt dedicated his *Work and Mercy of God,* "to all those that have Desires after the way of Truth, and are yet seeking it abroad in their imaginations." William Bayly employed a colophon to set forth his hope that all Seekers through participating in his experience might become finders.[6] He directed his *Testimony of the Working of the Light of Christ in Me from my Childhood* "in true love" . . . "to the yet scattered of the Flock, whom my soul desires may Rest at noon in the Life of the Sun of Righteousness."[7]

2

The confessions of the Friends from 1655 to 1725 indicate that interest in religious matters quite definitely began in childhood. Frequently in the complete autobiographies three crises are shown, one occurring as early as the seventh year, one about the twelfth, and a later and more variable one, sometimes mentioned as early as the fifteenth but with others delayed until maturity. Such was the case, as we have just seen, with John Gratton and Francis Howgill. In the later confessions a probable reason for the greater emphasis upon religious precocity is the fact that the autobiographies were penned by authors who were designedly hoping that reference to their own serious childhoods would have a salutary effect upon the minds of youthful readers.[8] The data, with which these eighty odd confessants depict preoccupations with religious ideas or report stages of religious melancholy or uplifted rapture, corresponds very closely with the researches of recent investigators in the psychology of religion.[9]

The recurring references to precocity in spiritual matters are too numerous to escape mention. Only a few from many examples can be cited. At the age of five or six, Lawrence Steel (1644-1684) felt "the first stirrings of the Spirit" and often left his companions to seek peace in prayer.[10] Stephen Crisp (1628-1692) at the age of seven or eight wondered why children could be wicked and yet unconcerned about wrong doing, and at the age of ten "sought God with prayers and tears."[11] Thomas Thompson when about eight years old heard a Voice sounding within him, "Now is the Axe laid to the root of the tree. . . ."; he immediately began to desire that he "might be found as one of the trees bringing forth good fruit."[12] When but five years old John Barcroft (1664-1723) "was much tendered through the effectual preaching of Samuel Thornton at the home of William Edmundson, and the Lord's power."[13]

3

Since mystical invasions occasionally enveloped the consciousness of these confessants, they made use of their memoirs to convey to others their belief in the guidance of the inner Light and in their moments of rapport with divine Power. Like Francis Howgill and Mary Penington, many of them mention antecedent visions or openings as precursors to the final acceptance, and to submission to the guidance of the inner Light. Reference has already been made to the centralizing of George Fox's energies upon a life purpose[14] after his opening "that Christ could speak to his condition," and also to the mystic enlightenment that flooded the spirit of John Gratton after years of experimenting with Anglican, Presbyterian, and Independent beliefs.[15] Citations can be made to but a few of the mystical visitations, which these confessants believed had suggested Quakerism to them or had served to convince them of the power of the Quaker message. Thomas Wilson[16] (1654-1725), upon attending a Friends' meeting after a long period of experimentation with different creeds and professions, recorded:

The Lord's power rose in the meeting and fell violently upon me, to the breaking and tendering of my heart . . . so that great fear, trembling and shaking seized me, insomuch that the table whereon I leaned, and Friends sat was shaken.

Marmaduke Stephenson, one of the Boston martyrs of 1659, eight days before his death, wrote of a previous mystic invasion where he had felt a greater consciousness impinging upon his own:

In the beginning of the year 1655, I was at the plough in the east parts of Yorkshire in Old England, near the place where my outward being [home] was; and as I walked after the plough, I was filled with the love and presence of the living God, which did ravish my heart when I felt it, for it did increase and abound in me like a living stream, so did the life and love of God run through me like a precious ointment giving a sweet smell, which made me stand still. And, as I stood still, with my heart and mind stayed upon the Lord, the word of the Lord came to me in a still small voice, which I did hear perfectly, saying to me in the secret of my heart and conscience, "I have ordained thee a prophet unto all nations."[17]

Even a cursory search through such confessional passages as these will reveal the fact that Quaker authors, as they recalled the obstacles that had opposed their progress, foresaw that their immediate and future readers might have to pass the same way. Humphrey Smith, for instance, acknowledged that he had delayed his surrender because he dreaded the censure of his associates who would consider him "a mad man" and a "hissing post," and dreaded exposure to "want, hardship, revillings [sic], imprisonment, whippings, and all manner of cruel torture."[18] And yet, while they recognized criticism and persecution as deterrents, they showed them to be surmountable obstacles. For the group and for the individual the religious confession became the supreme means for the expression of the Quaker's search for and acquiring of spiritual peace.

CHAPTER XX

INTROSPECTION

1

The basic mysticism of the Quaker faith everywhere illumines the personal writings of the early Friends. The seeking for divine guidance within one's being, in both major and
minor decisions of life, naturally led to contemplative and
introspective habits of mind. In endeavoring to follow the
gleam, the Quaker became interested in understanding himself and in turning his experiences of religious nature into a
practical mysticism. This attaining of spiritual peace was
not merely the result of a clear and satisfied conscience, but
essentially of a complete submission of individual will to
divine Will.[1]

A definite idea for publication, conformity to pattern in
style and plan, and introspection, have been previously noted
as characteristics of Quaker autobiography. In the third of
these qualities—that is in their subjectivity—resides the only
claim that can be ascribed to the Friends for bringing any
new feature into English autobiography, and this assertion
must itself necessarily be a modest one. Since the journals of
the Friends have been read largely by members of the Society, their marked qualities of introversion have been overlooked by literary critics, and their influence upon memoir
writing outside the Society has been slight. This claim may
perhaps also seem unjustified if these early Quaker self-
reviews are approached after perusing the confessionism of

a Marie Bashkirtsev, or after excursions into modern psycho-analysis. The assertion can be substantiated only after comparing the upwards of ninety Quaker confessions and journals with their coeval autobiographies. These attempts at self-analysis must be judged by seventeenth and early eighteenth-century standards, and not by modern ones.

The spiritual records of the Scotch Covenanters, Blair, Livingstone, Pringle, and Frazer, it is true, contain introspective passages. In comparison, their delineations of self are more largely concerned with questions of conscience and less with analysis than are the Quaker accounts. The Anglican *Diary of the Reverend Ralph Josselin* is highly objective, and with the exception of the author's "Self-Review" the *Reliquae Baxterianae* presents but few definitely subjective passages.[2] Mrs. Burr has pronounced *The Journal of George Fox* the "earliest important self-study in English."[3] The tendencies toward introversion in Quaker memoirs become increasingly apparent when a number of them are examined in close succession.

The early Friends knew nothing of the psychology of the subconscious and were wholly ignorant of mental processes as matters of scientific research. They sought to know themselves that they might be able to conduct their lives in accordance with the light of conscience and intuitional guidance. The chief point to note in evaluating their records is the importance that the autobiographers placed on the constant examination of self.

2

In endeavoring to understand the meaning of life the Quaker was a mystic, a practical, not a philosophical mystic. Whether he came into the Society from another religious body or whether he grew up under Quaker surroundings, he

was trained to keep close watch upon himself and his behaviour. Entry after entry indicates the observance of three
steps which may be termed the Quaker's mystic ladder. All
three involved conscience and inner illumination.[4] First of
all, before making important decisions, the Friend was to
await inner Guidance; next, he was to weigh the inclination
that arose within him—that is, examine his thoughts in a
concentrated effort to find out whether this impulse was
really the Voice of divine direction or merely his own human
desire, or whether it was an evil motive originating with
"the adversary, the father of lies." In the third place, after
due caution, the Quaker was ready to act, or as he phrased
it to "obey." Peace was the recompense for obedience; mental and spiritual distress, for failure to comply with the instructions of this inner Guidance.

Directions for "centering down to That of God in one"
are found in some of the earliest personal writings of the
Friends. As early as 1655, from his prison cell in York
Castle, Roger Hebden sent a letter to Friends suggesting a
method by which they could analyze their motives.[5] "I am
moved to write unto you," he declared, "to put you into a
search in yourselves." With succinctness he proceeded to
outline the three steps described above:

Every motion that calls upon you to act on, do not lend an ear
to it . . . although it seem at first view to be self-denial and
a cross to your wills; but when such a motion doth arise, then
return in again, and examine if there were not first in you a desire to do or speak such a thing, as there is presented to be done
or spoken. If you do not find it so, then wait, and be not hasty
in the acting thereof; if self be seen at the bottom, then the
adversary will be ready to threaten with disobedience, if it be
not presently done . . . but wait that you may know the mind
of God in it, that you may not be deceived.[6]

Other Quaker epistles contain variations of Hebden's directions for cautious search of the secret motives of the

heart. Almost at the same time the boy evangelist, James Parnell,[7] was urging Stephen Crisp, his most influential convert, to understand himself and not to allow his imagination, his learning, or his ambitions to mislead him. He sent Crisp this message:

Friend,—In that [the inner Light] stand, and unto it keep thy mind, which lets thee see thy foes to be of thine own house; thine imagination is an enemy; thy wisdom is an enemy; that which has been thy darling is an enemy.[8]

Francis Howgill, in his dying legacy to his young daughter Abigail, anticipated three questions that she might ask: What shall I seek for? In what way must I wait? How must I seek? "If you inquire," he wrote, "I inform thee, thou must silence all thy thoughts. . . . Take heed unto that [the spirit of Truth], and it will show thee thy evil motions and thoughts; and as thou lovest it, it will subdue them."[9] Though the Friends themselves made no definite effort to reduce their mental processes to a formal code, they more or less consciously evolved a system for minute and methodical self-examination.

3

Some "ministering" Friends attached importance to the process of reviewing the day's work and of recording their feeling of satisfaction or the reverse at its close. John Kelsall speaks of his nightly system of self-examination which included a vigorous searching of conscience. The following entry, written in maturity, retrospectively surveys his early habits of contemplation:

I remember very often when I went to bed at night I would consider within myself what I had been doing that day; yea I would have made narrow search into every particular thing that I could recollect, and if I found that I had not done much amiss, this was still a joy to me; but if otherwise, then I saw it as a dark cloud before me, neither could I make a right search at that time.[10]

The last phrase indicates that he looked upon the inner Light as an aid to conscience, yet something apart from it.

Incidentally in his autobiography, while narrating an incident, Samuel Bownas outlined his general practice of self-review. It happened that while on a missionary journey in Scotland, he had been compelled, on the spur of the moment, to defend the Quaker system of ministry. At bed time he noted that he felt ill at ease and mentally distressed. Before outlining the details leading to this state of mind, he thus indicated his general habit of consistent reliance upon "the instructor in his own bosom":

I had an opportunity to reflect on what had passed and to examine my whole conduct all that day: a practice I frequently used, after a more than common day's service; and indeed after every opportunity of enlargement in my gift [i.e. in the ministry], by experience finding the best instructor in my bosom, to show where I hit the matter or missed it.

On this particular occasion, in the course of a conversation following his defense of spiritual as opposed to scholastic preparation for the ministry, several auditors had questioned Bownas as to his birth, training, and education. He had truthfully acknowledged that he and his father were cordwainers and of humble extraction. That night as he pondered over the conversation, he began to comprehend more fully the criticism which the Scotch interrogators had only partially expressed. He then saw that the Presbyterians valued and depended much "upon literature, a qualification" in which he was admittedly lacking. He continued his analysis until he saw that if a Quaker minister "were divinely fitted by the Spirit yet if he wanted human learning," it "all" amounted "to nothing" with the followers of Calvin. After this colloquy with his inner self, in which he had ascertained the basis of his distressed state of mind, he felt assured that his review had been correct and that his extempore defense had been fully in harmony with and the result of divine prompting. With the following words, he concluded his entry for the day:

Thus the wisdom of truth, which I did not see so plainly at first, appeared to my understanding very clearly; and on a close narrow inspection into this Day's work, I found inward peace.[11]

4

The second step in waiting, watching, and obeying was often elaborated upon by Quaker confessants, who considered it important to note their efforts to discover the "seed of the act," and to trace the motivation of their behaviour to its source. John Richardson explained that his reluctance to yield willingly to a "call" to go on a long missionary tour to the American colonies, was due entirely to the fear that in his absence he would be censured for leaving two motherless children to the care of Friends.[12] At another time he saw that fear of a second stoning from the inhabitants of Coventry had made him rationalize his thinking into the belief that he "had sufficiently freed" or cleared his conscience from responsibility for their spiritual welfare.[13]

Benjamin Bangs included a long review of his reluctance to acknowledge even to himself his interest in Quakerism. Though his analysis now seems amateurish, the recording of it was far more unusual in the late 1600's than it is today. From a mature point of view, which with most autobiographies unconsciously colors the narration of earlier events, he reviewed an incident of his youth. His mother, the daughter of an Anglican clergyman and a woman of unusual intelligence, had moved to Norwich, where she allied herself with Friends. From there she wrote to her son in London, suggesting that he "frequent the assemblies" of the Quakers. He noted that he was so irritated at her request that he crushed the letter into a ball and thrust it into his pocket, but still he felt perplexed because he could not give a reason for his excessive annoyance. Angry at himself, and almost in spite of himself, he determined to study the situation by immediately following some plainly garbed Quakers· from Charing Cross to Westminster, where he soon found himself in one of their meetings.

Taking a retired seat back of a post, he found that his angry mood kept him from concentrating either on his own problem or on what was being uttered. Involuntarily he "stamped upon the floor with his foot" so that "the eyes of some were turned upon him." This act made him ask the question, "What is the matter with me that I cannot master my own mind?" Before the meeting was over, he made the discovery that he needed "inward strength" to help "him to stayedness of mind upon God"; and that this "stayedness" could not be acquired until "the enemies of his soul came to be destroyed"; and furthermore that it was obligatory for him to "get into inward retirement." Before the meeting drew to a close he felt that he had "caught sight of this possibility," and not until then did he perceive that the reason for his irritation lay in his unwillingness to yield to divine impulses. After leaving the meeting he recorded that he drew the crumpled letter from his pocket and read it with care and with humility.[14]

From the standpoint of modern psychology these efforts to trace emotions and perplexities to their sources seem trivial, but before 1725 they were rare in autobiographical writings. Objectivity was the rule, and subjectivity in the realm of conscience, when coupled with a religion based upon experience, was in many quarters in England criticized and labelled as enthusiasm.[15] Such cases of intuition as these demonstrate the efforts of the Friends to turn all forms of intuitive knowledge into a practical Christianity which they sought to preach and to exemplify.

5

Quaker memorandists note several phases of interest in self, to which modern psychology has affixed such terms as conflict and the fear complex; and furthermore, they felt that their mental states were worthy of permanent commemoration. They seemed to be aware of the fact that the conflict of two desires pulling in opposite directions created unhappiness. John Gratton, when he was driven nearly to distraction over religious questionings, and when he found it rare "to find a true hearted man or woman" in "this wicked sinful world,"[16] wrote that he was "sick with Trouble of the Mind." Even more clearly Stephen Crisp recognized that unhappiness often came from conflicting motives. In describing his unwillingness to relinquish his own ambitions for "other worldliness" and the Quaker views of life, he admitted that he "did reason divers ways, too many to name now, against the Truth." His understanding of his state of mind at that time is shown in the following sentences:

And I, poor man, knew not what to do, as to religion. . . . I found two drawings, one strong drawing and enticement was to the world . . . and another was toward godliness, watchfulness, seriousness. . . . I wandered up and down, sometimes to one sort of people, sometimes to another, taking a sharp inspection into their lives and doctrines, though I confess, I left my garden undressed, until many noisome weeds overgrew. . . . My will sought strongly to bridle and keep down that airy part and sinful nature, and for a season strove to uphold and maintain myself to be in a better state than before. . . .

With unspeakable relief, he wrote thus of his release from mental conflict: "As I came willingly to take it up [full surrender of self] I found It to be in me, the thing that I had fought from my childhood, even the Power of God." This realization brought him out onto the highway of mental peace, but he acknowledged "many sore conflicts" before he was able "in all things to distinguish between the workings of the true Spirit of Power" and self.[17]

Stephen Crisp also included an account of his reluctance to surrender before the imperative "call" to the Quaker ministry. Though he had formerly cried out in his own spirit, "Oh, that all men knew Thee and Thy goodness," yet when the command came to him "to part with wife, and children and father and mother, and to go and bear witness to His name in Scotland, to that high professing nation," he discovered that "all enemies were not slain" and that he "had strivings, strugglings, reasonings and disputings against the command of God." With secret hopes that the elders at Colchester would hinder his going, he laid the matter before the Monthly Meeting, "but they on the contrary," he added with apparent disappointment "shewed me it must not be my time, but His: then I would have gone by sea, but the Lord withstood me, and shewed me, it must not be my Way but His way, and if I would be obedient, He would be with me. . . ." "At last," Crisp concluded, "I obeyed, and about the end of the seventh month I went forth, and visited the Churches of Christ."[18] Obedience to these divine calls opened the Quakers' only gateway to harmony of soul.

Desire for peace of mind induced other autobiographers to observe that at times fear had been instrumental in causing inconsistencies in their conduct or behaviour. Thomas Ellwood mentions several occasions. On one, very soon after he had publicly announced himself a Quaker, he was passing through the streets of Oxford. Ahead of him he saw several justices, friends of his father, who, he felt certain, would halt and question him about his change in religion. Instead of meeting them squarely, he turned his horse into a by-street and rode out of town, an act which he later confessed "brought trouble and grief upon my spirit for having shunned the cross."[19] William Dundas discovered after numerous heart searchings that his troubled mental state resulted from the fact that he "durst not own the name of Quaker" even though he could "come with confidence and frequent the assemblies of the Lord." For some time he struggled to avoid this obligation but only after openly acknowledging himself a Quaker could he write, "I found that there is nothing can, nor is able to satisfie my thirsty soul short or beneath the Lord of Life."[20]

Friends not infrequently referred to fear as a hindrance or a cause for disobedience. John Burnyeat at one time "failed to obey" an impulse to speak and condemn a minister in a meeting at Aspetry. He thus analyzed the situation:

I saw how I had let in a fear upon me in which I had shunned the priest and spared him, for fear that I should be sent to prison for speaking to him.[21]

Charles Marshall felt extremely reluctant about making his first "testimony in public" when, as he wrote, "the Lord's Power fell" on him and he felt himself "required to speak a few words in the assembly of the Lord's people in Bristol." He reminiscently enumerated the results of his introspection:

I was tempted to look to my own weakness of body and spirit, and insufficiency for such a great work. . . . I reasoned that they were a wise people, and how could it be I should add to them; that I might hurt myself; that imagination might be the ground of such requiring, and that many wise men might look upon me as a forward lad, and so judge me.[22]

Christopher Story likewise expressed remorse over a similar failure to respond to a call to testify. He wrote of sitting in a silent meeting when "a message for deliverance" came to him. He wrote it

operated in me to that degree that I had much to do to contain; but being fearful to open my mouth in the assembly of the Lord's people, I reasoned until the life and power withdrew. I saw I could do nothing, having quenched the spirit: judgment seized me, and I was under trouble and exercise for my disobedience.[23]

Here again is the triple process reversed: waiting, considering, and failure to obey, with the result—discord and not harmony.

Over and over again these confessants repeat the theme of their basic mysticism. Only after meditative watching of self, only after careful weighing of the message, and only after obedience had been expressed in action, could they obtain peace. This was the process by which they made their mysticism practical. Two centuries later Francis Thompson, though the chances are that he had never held the journal of a Friend in his hand, sums up the thought of scores of Quaker confessants in "The Hound of Heaven":

I fled Him, down the nights and down the days;
I fled Him, down the arches of the years;
I fled Him, down the labyrinthine ways
Of my own mind; and in the mist of tears
I hid from him;

only to hear and after spiritual struggles acknowledge the Voice that said:

Lo! Naught contents thee, who content'st not Me.

CHAPTER XXI

PRACTICAL MYSTICISM

1

From his first entrance into the Society of Friends the convert was trained to be a heart-watcher, and to act upon all impulses which he felt were divine in their prompting. The silent meetings for worship naturally had a very great influence upon the making of the Quaker mind. The pervading mystical atmosphere of these meetings gave the worshiper moments of silence in which he could examine his thoughts, listen to testimonies, or perchance deliver a message that was pressing for utterance. Since all these acts tended toward establishing a habit of reliance upon intuition, the practice of silence was advocated as an initial step in making choices and decisions.[1]

A telepathic power often pervaded these assemblies, whereby the individual needs seemed to merge with those of the group. These silent meetings were a mere matter of "numbing and dumbing" to Roger Williams,[2] a subject for ridicule to hostile critics,[3] of occasional dismay[4] to preachers and clergy who saw their parishioners assuming Quaker garb and refusing to pay even "the tithing goose." William Britten, in turn an Anglican, Baptist, and Quaker preacher, in his confession of Quaker beliefs, pronounced silent meetings for worship "a wonder to the world,"[5] and termed the Friends "heart-watchers." In these meetings "We," he wrote, "become silent thereunto [the vanities of the world]

. . . that we may live unto God . . . in which Holy Silence although the tongue speaketh not, yet the spirit helpeth, which the heart-watcher beholdeth."[6]

In the early days a "spiritual contagion" seems to have emanated from these meetings. Preachers such as Nayler, Dewsbury, Parnell, Howgill, and Fox—men subject to mystic invasions, and endowed with something akin to telepathic power—not only dominated the meetings they attended but their enthusiasm seems to have been communicated to others. In his *An Apology for the True Christian Divinity*, Robert Barclay described the peace that he found in the silent worship of the people of his adoption.

When I came into the silent assemblies of God's people, I felt a secret power among them, which touched my heart, and as I gave way unto it, I found the evil weakening in me, and the good raised up, and so I became thus knit and united unto them, hungering more and more after the increase of this power and life, whereby I might feel myself perfectly redeemed.[7]

The Quaker meetings, with their absence of ritual and music, and with their impressive silences, telepathic communication, and opportunities for introversion, attracted considerable attention. Many hostile critics assailed them, among them George Keith. No more learned man than George Keith had allied himself with the seventeenth-century Friends. He was a friend of Henry More, versed in oriental languages, and acquainted with Platonic and eastern mysticism. For twenty years he had affiliated himself in a very influential manner with the Friends in Scotland, England, and in Pennsylvania, but later withdrew to the Church of England.[8] After his apostasy in a little tract entitled *The Magicke of Quakerism* (1707) he described the telepathic power which he had experienced in these silent meetings.

If they [the Quakers] can get those persons whom they have already persuaded to have a good opinion of them and a bad opinion of all Protestant Ministers, especially of the Church of England, to come to their Meetings, the Power and Life of the Friends, as they call it, will reach and take hold of them, and convert them to Quakerism, sometimes without all outward means . . . viz., neither by words, sound of Voice, nor Sight nor bodily Touch, but simply by a feeling of the mighty power that exerted itself, the first time they came into these silent meetings. . . .[9]

He did not attempt to deny the presence of a prevailing and converting power in silent worship, but bent his energies toward showing that it was not supernatural in its origin. His explanation suggests familiarity with eastern occultism.

It is not the effect of any Miraculous Divine Power, as the Quaker would have us believe, nay, nor yet altogether a Diabolick Power, for the whole matter may be resolved into a natural Enthysiasm, or a sort of natural Magicke or Magnetism, by a certain efflux or effluvium, of certain Animal Volatile Spirits, mightily invigorated by exalted Imagination, in Quakers, that flow from their bodies by the command of their will, into the body of the new Proselytes, that produce the like admiration in their credulous admirers, as like in most cases produces like, in fit disposed subjects, and as Fire by application of dry Wood.[10]

The Quaker of this time, as noted before, knew nothing of the psychology of the subconscious as such, and most certainly would never have ascribed the power of the Quaker meeting to "natural magicke" or to "animal volatile spirits." The attitude of mind which brought the Quakers to these silent meetings, and their confidence in a subliminal Divine Self to direct them accounted in part for the spread of early Quakerism and for the power which these meetings exerted. Revelation to the Quaker was not something belonging wholly to the past, for to him the inward Voice was audible and directive, as it had been to the child Samuel in the house of Eli.

The telepathic power of the silent meeting, which tended to bind the group into a close unity, is observable in other phases of life from the comments of numerous autobiographers[11] who placed high value on their intuitive power. Many believed that they had the ability to interpret moods in others, and some that they were aware of thoughts or sufferings of friends who were far away.[12]

2

With belief in intuition firmly ingrained in them, Quaker memorandists used their pages for declaring the validity of their "calls." To some the Light within was seemingly identifiable with intuition; with others of keenly sensitive temperaments the Word was described as audible, even "thundering in their ears."[13] George Robinson wrote that his final embarking for a voyage to the Holy Land in 1657 was the result of divine assurance, which he described as "a blessed presence filling him." By "the power of the Spirit" he was commanded to go to Jerusalem and was warned, "Thy sufferings will be great, but I will bear thee over all."[14] John Burnyeat wrote that he would willingly have shunned "the exercise of going forth to preach" and would have preferred the "ease, peace, and pleasure unto which the Lord had brought" him, but after weighing the matter, he became eager "to discharge the weight from the Lord" that rested upon him, and which "as a fire burned in his heart."[15] Whether the command or the "call" involved a testimony in a meeting for worship, personal sacrifice, or the delivery of a prophetic warning in a spectacular manner, the writer strove to make clear that the execution of these commands always brought mental peace and a sense of spiritual harmony. "Disobedience to the heavenly vision" uniformly resulted in discord and distress.

In response to the divine necessity of "obeying" the Word,

a number of Friends had felt themselves impelled to perform the duty of prophet to a "froward generation." Records of these events occur more frequently in the earlier than
in the later annals. Some Friends responded to "commands"
to preach in America, some to fast, and some to appear
naked. Apparently they acted upon the theory that the
nakedness of their bodies would make the observers conscious of the nakedness of their souls. To use Dr. Norman
Penney's phrase, supposedly they were "sermons in action."[16]
Miles Halhead, while walking among his sheep, heard "the
word of the Lord come unto him in the government of
O.[liver] C.[romwell] in the year 1652 . . . saying 'Thou
shalt not eat nor drink for the space of fourteen days'."[17]
William Simpson went naked for three years "in the days
of Oliver and the Parliament, shewing how God would strip"
men "of their power."[18] In 1662 Solomon Eccles passed
through Bartholomew Fair at Smithfield "naked, with a pan
on his head full of brimstone, flaming up in sight of the
people, crying repentance among them, and bade them remember Sodom."[19] These were on the whole rather abnormal cases,[20] which have to be judged by conditions where
women preachers were partially stripped and publicly
flogged[21] and where a marked strain of religious excitement
developed under the puritan régime.

Other instances occurred in which commands of exacting
nature were listened to and fulfilled. James Dickinson[22]
wrote in his autobiography that he "witnessed peace to flow
through his soul" only after he had passed through the
streets of London "warning the people to repent. . . . The
word of the Lord," he wrote, "came unto me saying, 'See
thou tell it to no man until thou deliver it as I command
thee'; which was to begin at Whitechapel and go through the
main streets of the city, and proclaim the message, 'Wo!
Wo! Wo! from the Lord to the crown of pride in this place,

for the vials of his wrath will be poured down upon it'!"

One of the sharply etched pictures in *The Journal of George Fox* is that of the young religious enthusiast entering the city of Lichfield, where "the three steeple-house spires," as he said, "struck at his life." Just released from a year of imprisonment at Derby, as Dr. Knight points out, he was in a state of mind wherein the symbol of religious teaching, which he was opposing, could "cut him to the quick," in his own vivid words "strike at all that vitally concerned him."[23] His account will best convey the picture, as well as illustrate his obedience to the command that he felt was a divine emanation:

Immediately the word of the Lord came to me that thither I must go. . . . I went within a mile of Lichfield. I was commanded of the Lord, of a sudden to untie my shoes and put them off. I stood still, for it was winter, and the word of the Lord was like fire in me, so I put off my shoes and was commanded. . . . Then I walked on about a mile till I came into the town, and . . . the word of the Lord came to me again, to cry, "Woe unto the bloody city of Lichfield!" So I went up and down the streets crying with a loud voice, "Woe to the bloody city of Lichfield." It being market-day, I went into the market-place, and to and fro in the several parts of it, and made stands, crying, as before, "Woe to the bloody city of Lichfield." And no-one laid hands on me.[24]

Even the more stable nature of Robert Barclay exhibits one case where, though he fought against "the call" "with agony of spirit," and with tears besought "the Lord that this cup might pass from him," in the end he succumbed and in 1672, in sackcloth and with ashes on his head, cried "Repentance" through the streets of Aberdeen.[25]

3

A deep interest in "understanding states" of mind was closely allied to the efforts of many Friends to know themselves and direct their behaviour. In describing an instance similar to that of Christ's conversation with the woman at the well, George Fox writes thus of his psychic power:

The Lord had given me a spirit of discerning, by which I many times saw the states and conditions of people and could discern their spirits. . . . There came . . . another woman, . . . and I cast my eye upon her, and said, "Thou hast been an harlot"; for I perfectly saw the condition and life of the woman. The woman answered and said that many could tell her of her outward sins, but none could tell her of her inward. Then I told her that her heart was not right before the Lord, and that from the inward came the outward.[26]

From a slightly different angle Theophilus Green attributed to William Dewsbury the qualities that Fox claimed for himself. By a self-analytical process, this confessant noted that in his mental distress he had longed to free his mind by discussing his problems of spiritual nature with William Dewsbury, and that he frequently went to the prison door, only to depart because he "saw something in himself that William would cut down."[27] In similar vein Thomas Chalkley wrote of a meeting at Burlington, New Jersey, in 1725:

We were so extraordinarily opened and guided to speak to the state of people . . . who were unknown to us that some of them were ready to think that we spoke by information, when in truth we were clear of any such thing, and only spoke what was immediately given us, without information from man, or woman.[28]

Less frequently one finds a Quaker confessant believing firmly that his mind was in communication with friends who were undergoing persecution or suffering. George Fox, at the time the officials in Boston were visiting the death penalty upon the four Quaker martyrs, declared, "I had a perfect sense of their suffering as though it had been myself, and as though the halter had been put around my neck, though we had not at that time heard of it."[29] John Richardson wrote that his devoted wife Anne, in spite of her great distance from him,[30] always "sympathized" with him in his "adverse and low estates," and "partook with him in his enjoyments when the power of Truth prevailed over his enemies."

The personal writings of the Friends are the most valuable sources for studying their practical mysticism and the making of the Quaker mind. Opposition and persecution from without, and harmony of belief within, served to deepen group-consciousness. The goal of the individual was the mystic's peace, the belief that man could come in touch with divinity, and that by so doing he could put his whole being into harmony with Reality. Since this goal could not be easily reached, each person had to be constantly on his guard. To do so, he found it necessary to be a "heart-watcher" and to follow George Fox's constant admonition, "Mind the Light."

In its general aspects, the aggregation of nearly three thousand tracts from over four hundred hands rounds out neglected pages of English history. Acquaintance with the motives prompting the Quaker literature of controversy, of "sufferings," and of confessions makes more understandable a seventeenth-century reading public with whom Fuller's *The Holy and the Profane State*, Taylor's *Holy Living* and *Holy Dying*, and Baxter's *Call to the Unconverted* were popular books.

A survey of Quaker literary history represents primarily a literature of controversy, partly aggressive, partly defensive, and partly an effort to demonstrate by personal revelation, the validity of a religion of experience. Though the literary interests of the leaders after 1689 embraced all current forms of writing except satire, drama, and light verse, a growing tendency toward sectarianism and exclusiveness inhibited the development of a literature of universal significance. Such a tendency was also fostered by the failure of the group to make provisions for an educated leadership. By 1725 willingness to be "apart from the world" had stifled the early glow of the First Publishers. Desire to promote sectarianism in large measure accounts for the literary weaknesses in a people whose basic mysticism might have been expected to blossom into impassioned prose.

If the literature of the Friends is to be appraised in terms of their aims and accomplishments, the count is in their favor. They hoped to promulgate their views and to waken the world to its need for spirituality. In seven decades they succeeded in carrying the doctrine of the inner Light to the English-speaking world and beyond; they had amassed a hundred thousand converts, more than four hundred writers, and had circulated over two million tracts, many of which had been translated into French, German, and Dutch. The Friends, however, were not the only sect which was preaching "inwardness" in religious life, and it is therefore difficult to determine with any definiteness the spiritual influence of the Friends alone upon the organized religion of the times. Ninety Quaker confessions, presenting the practical mysticism of the Friends, indicate that a sincere effort was made to inculcate spirituality within the group.

So far as the approximation of fulfilling their critical standards is concerned, they did what they, with more or less consciousness, set out to do. They rigorously excluded from their writings "the learning of the world," they avoided stylistic adornment, and they directed their appeals to spiritual, not to intellectual, interests. They never sought beauty of diction. Their plain and carefully guarded style, except in the earliest stages of religious enthusiasm, did not attain high levels, yet very seldom did it sink to low ones. It was saved from mediocrity by biblical cadences and imagery and by an undercurrent of emotion born of sincerity and conviction. Ruskin may have been right in saying that the Quakers might have carried the world before them if they had not rejected color.[31] Presumably he meant color in a literary sense as well the gray and drab colors of Quaker dress.

With a similar idea in view, Mr. J. Middleton Murry remarked, in an address at Jordans in the summer of 1927, that Quaker qualities reflected both in literature and life were more Wordsworthian than Keatsian. Like Wordsworth, too, the Friends were moral teachers. The mysticism of Friends enabled them to see the power of God over all— over storms, harvests, blessings, bereavements—and to be conscious of it in the depths of their being. The celestial beauty of God as sung by Spenser and Milton did not enter into the Quaker conception of deity.

The Friends addressed their appeals to the "inward" eye and gave expression to their inner states. Their habits of mind resulted in the elevation of intuitive and the subordination of reasoning powers.[32] Nearly a fifth of the writers have left autobiographical accounts in which they have detailed their struggles in finding and in keeping the inner Light. These confessions transcend the sectarian field because they reveal men and women facing life problems and struggling toward a goal—the goal of inward peace.

Even though the seemingly endless Quaker controversies of the seventeenth century are no longer vital issues, yet the writings of the Friends are important documents in the sum total of English literature. They represent the ideals of a nonconformist group, impregnated with concepts of the spirituality of life and of religious liberty which they were willing to write for, die for, and live for. Quaker ideals of democracy, of philanthropy, of man's essential goodness, and of peace, have been widely disseminated, and have had an influence upon English thought quite out of proportion to the numerical membership of the sect.

NOTES

CHAPTER I

THE FIRST FOUR HUNDRED AND FORTY

1. W. C. Braithwaite, *Beginnings of Quakerism*, 84.

2. George Fox, *Journal*, 51. All footnotes will refer to the Tercentenary edition of *The Journal of George Fox* unless another edition is specifically noted. E. P. Dutton and Co. 1928.

3. *First Publishers of Truth*, 33, 57, 72, 114.

4. Braithwaite, *Second Period of Quakerism*, 115.

5. Edward Grubb, "George Fox as a Social Reformer," *The Nation and Athenaeum*, June 28, 1924; W. R. Inge, *The Church in the World*, 92, 96.

6. Joseph Besse, *Sufferings*, I, 4; Braithwaite, *Second Period* (The Macmillan Co.), 114.

7. Braithwaite, *Beginnings* (The Macmillan Co. 1914), 512n.

8. *Ibid.*, 205.

9. A few letters and remonstrances were issued in 1652 by George Fox and James Nayler. Quaker literature may be said to begin with the publication of Fox's *To All that would Know the Way to the Kingdom*, 1653.

10. F. S. Turner, *The Quakers*, 237. Mr. Turner based his estimate upon the reports of Charles Leslie, a nonjuring clergyman, and upon a census report inaugurated by King William III.

11. John Stephenson Rowntree, *Life and Works*, 175.

12. John Whiting, *A Catalogue of Friends Books*, 1708.

13. Nathan Kite, *Antiquarian Researches among Friends' Books*, 60.

14. John Whiting, *op. cit.*, 1708.

15. *Journal of George Fox* (Camb. ed., John C. Winston Co.), I, 447n.

16. For this suggestion I am indebted to Dr. W. Haller of Barnard College.

For abbreviations see Bibliography I, p. 274.

17. For a contemporary group of Scotch Covenanters see Robert Wodrow's *Collection upon the Lives of the Reformers and most Eminent Ministers in the Church of Scotland.* A few of the memoirs show introspection but no marks of group reciprocal action. For journals of the primitive Methodists and Mormons, see Mrs. A. R. Burr's *Religious Confessions and Confessants,* 149, 157.

18. *Post,* Ch. XIII, XVIII.

CHAPTER II

THE MYSTICAL SECTS

1. G. B. Tatham, *The Puritans in Power,* 88-92; D. Neal, *The History of the Puritans,* III, 132.

2. Tatham, *op. cit.,* 118-24, 178-81.

3. Francis Howgill, *The Inheritance of Jacob Discovered;* Gratton, *An Account of . . . Exercises when Young;* Fox, *Journal* (Camb. ed., John C. Winston Co. 1911) I, 429n.

4. W. C. Braithwaite, *Beginnings,* 58-65.

5. E. Burrough, *Warning to the Inhabitants of Underbarrow;* W. Dewsbury, *The First Birth;* R. Hubberthorn, *A True Testimony of Obedience to the Heavenly Call.*

6. Robert Barclay, *The Inner Life of the Religious Societies of the Commonwealth,* 176 f. (1876).

7. E. N. S. Thompson, "Mysticism in the Seventeenth Century," *Studies in Philology,* XVIII, 170-231.

8. C. Spurgeon, *Mysticism in English Literature,* 77.

9. Fox, *Journal,* 42; M. L. Bailey, *Milton and Jacob Boehme,* 101; W. Bayly, "To the Reader," *A Collection of the Several Wrightings;* S. Eccles, *Christian Information . . . also Some Prophetical Passages Gathered out of Jacob Boehme's Works,* 1664; Barclay, *Inner Life,* 214, 215.

10. R. M. Jones, *Spiritual Reformers,* 351.

11. John L. Nickalls, "George Fox's Library," *J.F.H.S.,* XXVIII, 3-21.

12. *Ibid.* 4.

13. Barclay, *Inner Life,* 28-30, 83, 84.

14. Thomas Edwards, *Gangraena,* Pt. III, 1.

15. Braithwaite, *Beginnings* (The Macmillan Co.), 14.

16. Barclay, *op. cit.,* 443-48.

17. Jones, *Spiritual Reformers* (The Macmillan Co., N.Y., 1914), 467.

18. Barclay, *op. cit.*, 417-418. See the earlier Barclay's *The Anarchy of Ranters.*

19. *Reliquae Baxterianae* (ed. by Sylvester), I, 77.

20. Fox, *op. cit.*, 46, 98.

21. W. Penn, "Rise and Progress" in *Works*, V, 212.

22. Jones, article on "Seekers" in *Encyclopedia of Religious Ethics; Studies in Mysticism,* Ch. IX.

23. Jones, *Later Periods* (The Macmillan Co., N.Y., 1921), 57, 58.

24. T. Fuller, *The Worthies of England,* III, 434, 435.

25. Jones, *Studies in Mysticism,* 455, 456; John Saltmarsh, *Sparkles of Glory,* quoted. The Macmillan Co., N.Y., 1909. See letter attributed to Richard Hubberthorn in Besse, *Sufferings,* I, 257. This letter has been reprinted in *J.F.H.S.,* XV, 140, 141.

26. Braithwaite, "The Westmorland and Swaledale Seekers," *J.F.H.S.,* V, 3-10.

27. Braithwaite, *op. cit.,* 27.

28. Barclay, *Inner Life,* 160, 270, 274, 279, 281, 292, 294, 435.

29. Caroline Richardson, *English Preachers and Preaching,* 70.

30. G. M. Trevelyan, *England under the Stuarts,* 170, 171.

31. Tatham, *op. cit.,* 16-20.

32. R. Farnsworth, *Light Rising out of Darkness* (1654), 49.

33. Quoted by Braithwaite in *Beginnings,* p. 13. See Evelyn *Diary,* I, 247, 262.

34. Edwards, *op cit.,* Pt. I, 16.

35. J. Gairdner, *English Church in the Sixteenth Century,* Ch. IV.

36. Barclay, *op. cit.,* 18.

37. *Ibid.,* 19.

38. *Ibid.,* 20; Price, *History of Nonconformity,* I, 138; W. H. Frere, *English Church in the Reigns of Elizabeth and James I,* 180-82, 232-34.

39. James Nayler, *Works,* 573, 574.

CHAPTER III

THE INNER LIGHT

1. Fox, *Journal,* 21; Burrough, *Works,* "To . . . Seekers and Waiters," 109; Dewsbury, *Works,* 3-8, 44, 45.

2. Fox in 1653 addressed a tract *To All that Would Know the*

Way to the Kingdom and in 1660 one *To All Nations under the Whole Heavens.*

3. R. M. Jones, *Studies in Mysticism* (The Macmillan Co.), xviii.

4. Caroline Spurgeon, *Mysticism in English Literature,* 22.

5. Fox, *Journal,* 19, 20; Barclay, "Dedicatory Epistle to the King," *Apology.*

6. A. Neave Brayshaw, *The Quakers, Their Story and Message,* 91, 92; Ch. XI; Braithwaite, *Beginnings,* 307. See also Jones, *Later Periods,* 274.

7. Braithwaite, *op. cit.,* 131, 132.

8. Josiah Royce, "George Fox as a Mystic," *Harvard Theological Review,* VI, 31-61.

9. Gerard Croese, *The General History of the Quakers* (1696), 14: "I have heard some of his Friends say (and those not of the Vulgar size, but Men of Learning and Knowledge) that though the Bible were lost, it might be found in the Mouth of George Fox"; Brayshaw, *The Personality of George Fox,* 16, 31, 57, 78.

10. Fox, *Journal,* 14, 15.

11. R. Hubberthorn, *A True Testimony,* 1-17.

12. See Dr. Jones's introductions to Braithwaite's *Beginnings* and *The Second Period of Quakerism.*

13. Barclay, *Apology,* Prop. V, VI, sec. xvi; E. Grubb, *Authority and the Light Within,* Ch. IX.

14. Fox, *Epistles,* CXXX.

15. Jones, "The Psychology of George Fox," *Holborn Review,* LXVI, 320-31; Rachel Knight, *The Founder of Quakerism. A Psychological Study.* Ch. IV, V.

16. Fox, *Journal,* pp. 8, 9. (E. P. Dutton Co.), See also Barclay, *Inner Life,* 214-16; Jones, *Studies,* 495.

17. Fox, *Journal,* 19, 20, 279, 280.

18. *Ibid,* 18-20. See also Fox's *Epistles,* CV, CLV, and *Works,* IV, 282-86.

19. D. Masson, *The Life and Times of Milton,* V, 356.

20. Fox, *Journal* (Bi-Cent. ed.) I, 432-34. For similar admonitions see his *Epistles,* CXLI, CCCV, CCCXXV, CCCXXXV, CCCXLV; Stephen Crisp, *A Memorable Account,* 20, 144, 145, 163.

21. *A True Catechisme of Thomas Richardson* (1664), 26-29; John Richardson, "Life" in *Friends' Library,* IV, 69, 70, 106,

115; *Life of John Roberts*, 10. See also St. Loe Strachey, "The Christianity of Christ," *The Forum*, LXXIII, 343-49.

22. The Friends of the seventeenth century recognized the fact that inward revelation was not new in human experience. In the first decade of Quaker history, Edward Burrough wrote, "Though our name is new, our religion is old" (Burrough, *Works*, 322); and Robert Barclay wrote, "We distinguish betwixt a revelation of a new gospel, and new doctrines, and a new revelation of the good old gospel and doctrines; the last we plead for but the first we utterly deny." (Barclay, *Apology*, Prop. III, sec. ix.)

23. R. Davies, *An Account*, 26-28; W. Edmundson, *A Journal*, 16. See reprint of letter in H. Roger's *Mary Dyer of Rhode Island*, 83-90.

24. Cf. J. Bunyan, *Some Gospel Truths Opened;* Burrough, *Works*, 144; W. Penn, *Sandy Foundation Shaken; Innocency with her Open Face.*

25. Fox, *Journal*, 30; Barclay, *op. cit.*, Prop. V, VI, sec. xxvii.

26. Braithwaite, *Second Period*, 61; News letter in Fleming MSS, 61; Besse, *Sufferings*, I, 5; Sewel, *History*, (Phila. 1823), I, 38, 51, 70.

27. Fox, *op. cit.*, 30, 31; Firth, *The Last Years of the Protectorate*, I, 84-92.

28. Barclay, *op. cit.*, Prop. V, VI, sec. xiii; R. Samble, *A Testimony to the Plainness and Simplicity of the Truth*. James Nayler, *Works*, "Concerning the Fall of Man," 257-61, and "How Sin is Strengthened," 361 f.

29. Nayler, *op. cit.*, "Concerning Election and Reprobation," 309; Fox, *Epistles*, CV, CLV.

30. Fox, *Works*, IV, 282-86.

31. Nayler, *op. cit.*, "Concerning the Baptism of Christ," 317-21, "Concerning the Lord's Supper," 326-32.

32. Fox, *Epistles*, CCLX, "All Outward Things, Figures, Types"; Barclay, *op. cit.*, Prop. XI, on Baptism; Prop. XII on Communion; Jones, *Faith and Practice*, Ch. V; Davies, *An Account*, 15-17.

33. Jones, *op. cit.*, 80.

34. Roger Williams, *George Fox Digg'd out of his Burrowes*, 41, 170, 182; G. Whitehead, *The Real Quaker A Real Protestant.*

35. Nayler, *op. cit.*, 351-55.

36. Fox, *op. cit.*, XXXIV, LXVII; M. Brailsford, *Quaker Women*, 136-42; Gardiner, *History of the Commonwealth and the Protectorate*, 242.

37. Note replies in *The Great Mistery* to Howet's *Quaking Principles Dashed in Pieces by the Standing and Unshaken Truth;* to Timson's *The Quaker Apostasie from the Perfect Rule of the Scriptures Discovered;* to Higginson's *A Brief Relation of the Northern Quakers;* and to Clapham and Jenkin's *A Discovery of the Northern Quakers.*

38. See also Fisher, *Works*, 440-54; Barclay, *op. cit.*, Prop. III, sec. ix; Fox, *Journal*, 20, 78; Burrough, *Works*, 249, 250.

39. Fox, *op. cit.*, 19.

40. Burrough, *op. cit.*, 778; R. Haydock, *Works*, 94; Penington, *Works*, Pt. I, 186; T. Taylor, *Works*, 337-51. For later views see Penn, *Works*, 859; Wyeth, *A Switch for the Snake*, 19.

41. See again Dr. Jones's introductions to Braithwaite's *Beginnings* and *Second Period;* Brayshaw, *The Quakers*, Ch. VII.

42. Braithwaite, *Beginnings*, xxviii, xxxiii.

43. Fox, *Epistles*, LXXXVII, CXVII; *Works*, 322; Jones, *Faith and Practice*, Ch. IV; V. Hodgkin, *Silent Worship;* T. E. Harvey, *Silence and Worship.*

44. Nayler, *op. cit.*, 696; Howgill, *Works*, 14-23; Besse, *Sufferings*, II, 201, 202.

45. Whiting, *Persecution Exposed*, 23; Ellwood, *Life*, 9, 18, 348; Penney, *Experiences in the Life of Mary Penington*, 10-12.

46. Penington, *Works*, IV, 57 f. See also T. E. Harvey's *Silence and Worship*, 32, 33; Barclay, *op. cit.*, Prop. XI; Davies, *An Account*, 27; Burrough, *Works*, 74.

47. Fox, *Works*, I, 365-67; Barclay, *Works*, "Universal Love," 229.

48. Fox, *Works*, V, 171-96; Braithwaite, *Second Period*, xxiv-xxvii; Penn, *Primitive Christianity Revived*, Ch. X; J. Banks, *A Journal*, 130 f.; John Crook, *Life*, 40.

49. For views of Quaker opponents see Roger Williams, *George Fox Digg'd Out of his Burrowes*, 305; Francis Bugg, *The Pilgrim's Progress from Quakerism to Christianity*, 449-88.

50. Fox, *Journal*, 347.

51. Graham, *The Faith of a Quaker*, Ch. X; Braithwaite, *Second Period*, 324-48.

52. Fox, *Battle-door.*

53. Fox, *Journal*, xxxi; Penn, *No Cross, No Crown*, Sec. IX,

X; Braithwaite, *Beginnings,* 139, 140; Brayshaw, *The Quakers,* 101-5.

54. Ellwood, *Life,* 25-27; Davies, *op. cit.,* 19, 20, 23.

55. Fox, *Epistles,* LXXIII; Barclay, *Apology,* Prop. X, sec. xxviii, Ellwood, *The Foundation of Tithes Shaken;* Gratton, *Works,* "The Clergyman's Pretence of the Divine Right of Tythes," 291-354; Burrough, *op. cit.,* 779-81.

56. For Quaker position see Fox, *Journal,* 231; Burrough, *op. cit.,* 773-76; J. Parnell, *Works,* "To All Magistrates, Rulers, and Officers Who Call Men to Swear," 470-72; Fisher, *op. cit.,* 795-809; Barclay, *Truth Triumphant,* III, 522-27; Fox, *Works,* I, 254, 255; J. Whitehead, *Works,* "An Appeal against Injustice," 172-313; Smith, *Balm from Gilead,* "The Cause Plainly Shewed of the Persecution," 121-26.

57. Fox, *op. cit.,* I, 236, 254, 255; II, 59, 60, 183.

58. R. Hubberthorn, *Works,* folios a and a 1 of unnumbered pages.

59. W. Bayly, *Wrightings,* "The Vision . . . written in Newgate Prison"; Fox, *Journal,* 70.

60. S. Eccles, *Signs are from the Lord;* Fox, *Journal* (Camb. ed.), II, 428 n; Barclay, *Truth Triumphant,* I, 195.

61. J. Banks, *Journal,* 110, 111; Fox, *Journal,* 26, 27, 29, 81; See Appendix to Brayshaw's *The Personality of George Fox.*

62. J. Matern, *A Testimony of the Lord's Power; First Publishers of Truth,* 289-91. For anti-Quaker view see Keith, *The Magicke of Quakerism.*

63. Whiting, *Persecution Exposed,* 20; T. Wilson, *Life,* 8, 9.

64. Whiting, *op. cit.,* 24.

65. Joseph Coale, *Some Account of the Life,* 33-63.

CHAPTER IV
CONTROVERSY

1. Braithwaite, *Beginnings* (Macmillan Co., 1912), 283.

2. *Ibid.,* 285.

3. Sewel, *The History . . . of the Christian People Called Quakers* (1823), I, 126.

4. Fox, *Journal* (Camb. ed.), I, 141.

5. See classification made by E. E. Taylor as to education and occupation. *J.F.H.S.,* XIX, 67-82. See also *idem,* "Women

Writers among Friends of the Seventeenth Century and Later,"
ibid., X, 93-96.

6. J. Parnell, *Works*, "Testimony of Stephen Crisp"; J. Backhouse, *Memoirs of Francis Howgill*, 79, 80; J. W. Graham, *William Penn*, 75; Fox, *op. cit.*, I, x; J. Gratton, *Journal of Life and
Collected Works*, 181-211, 335-70.

7. Ellwood, *History of Life*, 431n.

8. Fox, *op. cit.*, 404n.

9. *J.F.H.S.*, II, 105; Whiting, *Persecution Exposed*, 62; Braithwaite, *op. cit.*, 395. When Dr. Owen, Vice Chancellor of Oxford
heard that Taylor, a former Scholar at Oxford was in jail, he
paid Taylor's fees and saw that he was discharged.

10. *F.P.T.*, 161; Wood, *Athen. Oxon.*

11. Taylor, *op. cit.*, 81.

12. A. Neave Brayshaw, *The Personality of George Fox*, 78,
79.

13. *Post*, Ch. XI. A. R. Burr, *The Autobiography* (Houghton
Mifflin), 236.

14. In collaboration with James Nayler.

15. In collaboration with James Nayler and addition by John
Lawson.

16. Firth, *History of the Last Years of the Protectorate*, I,
102 f.; Braithwaite, *Beginnings*, Ch. XI. See also Mabel Brailsford, *A Quaker from Cromwell's Army*.

17. Braithwaite believes that a thousand pages were not published in 1716. Some still remain in manuscript, *op. cit.*, 288.

18. Nayler, *Works*, "Now to those Things which some call
Religious," 632.

19. *Post*, Ch. XVIII.

20. *Athen. Oxon.;* Fox, *op. cit.*, I, 429n.; Braithwaite, *Beginnings*, 288-290.

21. Braithwaite, *op. cit.*, 285.

22. Fisher, *Works*, 32, 33.

23. Barclay, *Truth Triumphant*, III, 186, 187; Whiting, *Persecution Exposed*, 204, 205.

24. Braithwaite, *Second Period*, xxx f.

25. *Ibid.*, 387 f.

26. Voltaire, *Oeuvres Completes*, "Les Lettres sur les An-
glais"; "Enfin Robert Barclay, Éccosais, présenta au roi, en
1675, son *Apologia des Quakers*, ouvrage aussi bon qu'il pouvait
l'être."

27. Brayshaw, *The Quakers*, 52-56. See also Edward Grubb's Introduction to Hine's *Mirror for the Society of Friends*.
28. Braithwaite, *Beginnings* (The Macmillan Co.), 278.

CHAPTER V

THE LITERARY PRINCIPLES

1. John Whitehead, *Written Gospel Labours*, "Preface," 3; MSS Minutes of Morning Meeting, 12th-5 mo. 1703: "And it's proposed that George Whitehead and William Penn or either of them do prepare a title, and a Preface if it be upon their minds or either of their minds." The book was published in 1704.
2. Braithwaite, *Second Period*, 279-281. The Minutes of the Second Day Morning Meeting from 1673-1901 are preserved in the Friends Reference Library in London.
3. Locker-Lampson, *A Quaker Post-bag*, 4, 5.
4. *First Publishers of Truth*, 238n.: "Named 'the younger' or 'junior' to distinguish him from *the* George Fox, although the former was the elder man."
5. Braithwaite, *op. cit.* (The Macmillan Co.), 417-19.
6. Whitehead, *op. cit.*, 3.
7. Fox, *Journal* (Camb. ed.) II, 401n.: "There is no evidence of any relationship to George Whitehead," author of *The Christian Progress*. John C. Winston Co.
8. Whitehead, *op. cit.*, 6, "Testimony of Thomas Thomson," folio a 2 of unnumbered pages.
9. *Ibid.*, 262.
10. *Ibid.*
11. *Ibid.*, 84, 147, 297.
12. *Ibid.*, 243-386.
13. *Ibid.*, 87-110.
14. *J.F.H.S.*, VII, 30; T. Birch, History of Royal Society of London, IV, 99, 100.
15. See letter to Sir John Rodes in Locker-Lampson's *A Quaker Post-bag*, 1-8.
16. Cf. John Locke, *Works*, I, 78 (1801).
17. Braithwaite, *Beginnings* (The Macmillan Co.), xxxviii.
18. Fisher, *Rusticus Ad Academicos*, xviii.
19. Fisher, *Works*, "Testimony of William Penn."
20. Fisher, *op. cit.*, xix.
21. Barclay, *Truth Triumphant*, II, 1.

22. Penn, *No Cross, No Crown,* Ch. XXI, sec. 22.

23. Locker-Lampson, *op. cit.,* 4, 5.

24. Penn, *op. cit.,* Ch. XVIII, sec. 8; Barclay, *Apology,* Prop. XV, sec. vii; Braithwaite, *Second Period,* 507-23.

25. John Crook, *Works,* 315. For a case revealing the Quaker's fear of rhetoric see *Ibid.,* 142.

26. Whitehead, *op. cit.,* Preface, 8, 11.

27. C. Leslie, *The Snake in the Grass,* xxxi, 314 f.; Braithwaite, *Second Period,* 637; Jones, *Later Periods,* 246-59; Hobhouse, *William Law and Eighteenth Century Quakerism,* 203 f.; Turner, *The Quakers,* 266 f.

28. *Post,* Ch. XVIII, XIX.

29. Lydia Ann Barclay, *Selections from the Writings of Patrick Livingstone,* Pref. 1847. A few lines quoted from a nineteenth-century editor will show how these three tenets persisted through later Quaker literature: "And it is hoped that the sincere and honest hearted searcher after Divine Truth and Wisdom will look more at the matter than the manner, that he will look beyond the surface and appreciate the substance, through this testimony to the power and sufficiency of heavenly Truth within, however unpolished the style of composition may seem to the criticizing disposition of the worldly wise, for such valiants as Patrick Livingstone and his fellow-laborers . . . cared not to please the vain mind and corrupt taste in any; but their aim was to satisfy the longing soul and to reach the witness of God in every Conscience."

CHAPTER VI

DISTRIBUTION OF LITERATURE

1. Whiting, *Persecution Exposed,* 130.

2. Margaret Fell, *Works,* "Testimony of George Whitehead"; Crosfield, *Margaret Fox in Swarthmoor Hall,* 38 f.; *Swarthmore* MSS in D.

3. Probably *The Case of the People called Quakers Relating to Oaths and Swearing* (1673). See *Letters of Early Friends,* 195.

4. *Ibid.,* 195, 196. See also Jones, *The Quakers in the American Colonies,* 544.

5. Fox, *Journal* (Camb. ed., John C. Winston Co., 1911), I, 266-67.

6. *Letters of Early Friends,* 282n.; 313-14.

7. Thomas Story, "Life," *Friends' Library*, X, 70.

8. *Account of William Penn's Travails in Holland and Germany*, 38-50; 195-200.

9. *Ibid.*, 44, 47; 53, 194, 205, 209.

10. Besse, *Sufferings*, II, 397; Sewel, *The History . . . of the Christian People Called Quakers* (1823), I, 453.

11. Braithwaite, *Beginnings*, 429 and n.3; Fox, *op cit.*, 380n.: *Pro Presbytero Johanne . . . a Populo Dei in Anglia, vocato Anglice Quakers*.

12. Besse, *op. cit.*, II, 420.

13. Wood, *Athen. Oxon.* III, 70.

14. Dundas, *A Few Words*, 16, 17.

15. Stephen Crisp, *Works*, 32, 34.

16. Caton, "Life," *Friends' Library*, IX, 458; Crisp, *op. cit.* 58. Works of Ames, Caton, Crisp, Fox, Higgins, and Hendrick were translated into Dutch. Fox, *op. cit.*, II, 411n.

17. S. Watson, *A Short Account*, 36-40.

18. Swarthmore MSS IV, 20, in Friends Reference Library, London. Reprinted in *Letters of Early Friends*, 84.

19. Fox, *op. cit.*, II, 499, 500; *J.F.H.S.*, I, IV, VI, VII. See indexes.

20. F. Bugg, *The Pilgrim's Progress*, 142.

21. *Ibid.*, "An Address to Private Gentlemen and Tradesmen" preceding the Table of Contents.

22. Bugg, *The Quakers' Yearly Meeting*, 8.

23. *Ibid.*, 2.

24. Locker-Lampson, *A Quaker Post-bag*, 154.

25. *Ibid.*, 156, 158.

26. *Friends' Library*, XI, "Epistle CXVII," 425.

27. Jones, *The Quakers in the American Colonies*, 544.

28. *Yearly Meeting Epistles*, I, 8.

29. Locker-Lamson, *op. cit.*, 164.

30. *Y.M.E.*, I, 22.

31. *Ibid.*, 77.

32. A reprint of a tract by James Nayler, 1657. Reprinted five times.

33. *The Friend* (Phila.), LX, 349. Reprinted from the records of the Aberdeen Monthly Meeting.

34. Kite, *Antiquarian Researches*, 20, 21.

35. Tract volume 114, No. 36 (in D.).

36. *An Account of a Divine Visitation,* "To the Reader," 5 (1680 ed.).

37. *J.F.H.S.,* X, 139, and XVI, 2.

38. *An Account of a Divine Visitation* belongs essentially to the mystical writings of the early Friends. It represents an entire group of young people shaken by a spiritual manifestation, 6, 7, 15.

39. *Ibid.,* 51.

40. *Ibid.,* 18. See also *Friends' Quarterly Examiner,* XXVIII, 429-35; *The Friend* (London, 1862), 180 f.; Gough, *History of the Quakers,* III, 309.

41. *An Account of a Divine Visitation,* 72, 73.

Chapter VII

THE LITERATURE OF "SUFFERINGS"

1. MS copy of *An Addition to The Spirit of the Martyrs Revived* in Library of Haverford College.

2. Braithwaite, *Second Period,* 281, 284, 286; MS *Yearly Meeting Records,* 1680.

3. Fox, *Journal,* 89, 90, 121, 128-30.

4. Ellwood, *History of the Life of,* 154-73; 128-31.

5. J. Banks, *A Journal of the Life of,* 98-100, 102-4. See also Davies, *An Account of,* 60.

6. George Whitehead, *Christian Progress,* 500, 506, 514, 543, 583, 598; Gratton, *op. cit.,* 70, 78, 81, 83; Davies, *op. cit.,* 111, 119. See also *Extracts State Papers,* 298-301, 310, 313.

7. *E.S.P.,* 303, 307, 308; J. Brown, *John Bunyan,* 203, 217, 223; Masson, *Life and Times of Milton,* VI, 250, 259; *J.F.H.S.:* XVII, 100; XIX, 137; XXVIII, 88.

8. Whitehead, *op. cit.,* 502, 503.

9. Whiting, *Persecution Exposed,* 33. See also Braithwaite, *Second Period,* 114, 115.

10. See reference to work of genealogist Joseph J. Green in Braithwaite, *op. cit.,* 115.

11. Besse, *Sufferings,* I, 146-48; Braithwaite, *Beginnings,* 446; V. H. Holdsworth, *Loveday Hambly, A Quaker Saint of Cornwall.*

12. Miles Halhead and Thomas Salthouse, *The Wounds of an Enemie in the House of a Friend.* Rare tract in Jenks Collection, Haverford College Library.

13. *A Brief Relation of Some Part of the Sufferings . . . of the People of God . . . from 1660 until 1671.* Collected by T. H[olme] and A. F[uller]. (1672).

14. Braithwaite, *Second Period,* 382.

15. James Dickinson, *Journal,* 168.

16. *Ibid.,* 169.

17. *Letters of Early Friends* (ed. Barclay), 118, 119.

18. *Ibid.,* 309; William Crouch, *Friends' Library,* "Memoirs," XI, 308.

19. Braithwaite, *op. cit.,* 285. See also the Introduction to *The First Publishers of Truth.*

20. Braithwaite, *op. cit.,* 285.

21. Luke Howard, *Love and Truth Manifested in Plainness,* 309.

22. Masson, *op. cit.,* VI, 326-32.

23. *F.P.T.,* 346.

24. *Ibid.,* 350.

25. *Ibid.,* 354.

26. *Ibid.,* 356.

27. W. Smith, *Balm from Gilead.*

28. *Ibid.,* Statement of Ellis Hookes, following table of contents.

29. *E.S.P.,* 15.

30. Fox, *Journal* (Camb. ed.), I., 453.

31. *E.S.P.,* 52.

32. Besse, *op. cit.,* I, 389, 709.

33. Kite, *op. cit.,* 17; *E.S.P.,* 148.

34. *Ibid.,* 16; *J.F.H.S.* IV, 4; XVII 7, 9. Cf. John Dunton, *Life and Errors.*

35. Kite, *op. cit.,* 17.

36. Fox, *op. cit.,* II, 470, 471; Gough, *History of the Quakers,* IV, 9. See also *E.S.P.,* 126.

37. Braithwaite, *op. cit.,* 418-19. The subject of the "seditious Quaker press" is one that would bear further investigation.

38. *E.S.P.,* 228-29; *S.P.D.,* CIX 44 Cal. 1644-5.

Chapter VIII
CENSORSHIP

1. Braithwaite, *Second Period,* 280 f.

2. *Ibid.,* 280 MS Yearly Meeting Minutes.

3. Beck and Ball, *London Friends' Meetings,* 336-42; Anna L. Littleboy, *A History of Friends Reference Library,* 1-31.

4. MS Morning Meeting Minutes, 15, vii, 1673.

5. Beck and Ball say that as many of the submitted manuscripts received adverse criticism as those that were approved. *London Friends' Meetings,* 342. For the period from 1673-1725 this statement seems too broad.

6. For full treatment of the action of the Morning Meeting in this case see T. Edmund Harvey's introduction to the Cambridge edition of *The Journal of George Fox.*

7. MS M.M.M., 10, 6 mo. [8] 1685.

8. *Ibid.,* 21, 2 mo. [4] 1684. The MS of *A Serious Remembrancer* is in D. All the serious and religious matters are retained except one on the transitoriness of life. A few personal touches are omitted. See Robson MSS No. 80.

9. MS M.M.M. 13, 10 mo. [12] 1675. See also *Ibid.,* 23, 9 mo. [11] 1685 and 30, 9 mo. [11] 1685.

10. *Ibid.,* 14, 4 mo. [6] 1703: A Treatise of John Whitehead's having been under consideration 'tis agreed for finishing thereof to adjourn till tomorrow evening 6th hour.

11. Fox, *Journal* (Camb. ed.), I, xii-xx.

12. MS Portfolio I, No. 101. The name is also spelled Allethorpe.

13. MS M.M.M. 27, 3 mo. [5] 1678.

14. Fox, *op. cit.,* II, 430.

15. MS M.M.M. 7, 2 mo. [4] 1673. The entire entry has been reprinted in Bailey's *Milton and Jacob Boehme,* 102.

16. See Ch. II, n. 9; Jones, *Spiritual Reformers,* 220-234.

17. MS M.M.M. 25, 5 mo. [7] 1686.

18. The MS copy of *The Lament* over England is in D. So far as I can find, it did not appear in print until 1751, when it was incorporated with some alterations in Rutty's *A History of the Rise and Progress of the People called Quakers in Ireland.* The name is spelled Bowlbie, Boulbie, and Bulby.

19. MS M.M.M. 7, 11 mo. [1] 1687/8.

20. *Ibid.,* 18, 4 mo. [6] 1690.

21. *Ibid.,* 8, 6 mo. [8] 1681.

22. Dr. Penney has retained the original spelling. For a complete analysis of Ellwood's excisions see T. Edmund Harvey's introduction to this edition. John C. Winston Co. Phila., 1911.

23. Fox, *op. cit.,* I, xvi-xviii.
24. Braithwaite, *op. cit.,* 304 f.
25. William Rogers, *The Christian Quaker,* 30-32.
26. J. S. Rowntree, *Life and Work.* "Micah's Mother, A Neglected Chapter in Church History," 142-76; *J.F.H.S.,* I, 57.
27. T. Ellwood, *An Antidote,* 127; *Life,* 267-70.
28. *Op. cit.,* 127, 128; *Life,* 267-70.

Chapter IX

VENTURES IN HISTORY AND BIOGRAPHY

1. First published in Dutch in Amsterdam in 1717.
2. Fox, *Journal,* xviii-xxii.
3. Charles Lamb, *Essays of Elia,* "A Quaker's Meeting."
4. Brailsford, *Quaker Women,* 239, 240.
5. John Dunton, "Pietist and Impostor," *Studies in Philology,* Oct. 1925.
6. See reprint of minutes of Second Day Morning Meeting for 1695 in Smith's *Descriptive Catalogue,* I, 481.
7. Ellwood, *Sacred History* (1778), I, v.
8. *Ibid.,* I, vii, viii.
9. *Ibid.,* II, v.
10. *Ibid.,* III, 671. Ellwood cites Henry Hammond's *Paraphrase of the New Testament* (1653) on the meaning of the term "elect lady" in the third epistle of John.
11. *Ibid.,* III, 628. He quotes Wilson's *Christian Dictionary* to show that the word translated as "preaching" meant "prophesying."
12. *Ibid.,* III, 563. He states that Saul lost his old name, which meant inquietude, and was given the new name, Paul, which in Greek signified quiet or rest, and in Latin little or small.
13. Ellwood, *Life,* 188-90, 270.
14. Ellwood, *op. cit.,* III, 522.
15. Ellwood, *Sacred History,* III, iv.
16. *Ante,* Ch. V.
17. Burrough, "Testimony," *Works;* II *Sam.* I, 19-27.
18. Burrough, *Ibid.,* 4.
19. Richard Hawkins, *Life of Gilbert Latye.*
20. Thomas Aldam, *A Short Testimony.*
21. Daniel Roberts, *Life of John Roberts.*

22. Whiting, *Early Piety Exemplified . . . in Mary Whiting.*

23. Marshall, *Sion's Travellers Comforted,* "Testimony of Hannah Marshall"; *Friends' Library,* III, 71 f.

24. John Richardson, *A Short Account . . . of Anne Richardson.*

25. Repr. in *Experiences in the Life of Mary Penington* (ed. Norman Penney).

26. See Richard Claridge's preface to the *Works* of William Crouch and Besse's to *The Life and Works of Richard Claridge.*

27. Hawkins, *op. cit.,* 19.

28. Roberts, *op. cit.,* 32, 39, 41, 43.

29. Caton, *An Abridgment of Eusebius Pamphilus's Ecclesiastical History* (1698), 202.

30. *Ante,* 90-92.

31. Whiting, *Persecution Exposed,* 115.

32. *Ibid.,* 168.

33. *Ibid.,* 228.

34. *Ibid.,* 334.

35. *Ibid.,* 178; cf. p. 184 under Alexander Parker.

36. Isaac Sharp, "John Whiting," *J.F.H.S.,* VII, 7-16.

37. Whiting, *op. cit.,* "Preface" 1, 2.

38. See also Beck and Ball, *London Friends' Meetings,* and printed *Minutes of Yearly Meeting.*

39. A.R.B. Coll'n and Swarthmore Coll'n in D. For description of letters see Braithwaite's *Beginnings,* App. B. Cf. *Letters of Early Friends* (ed. Barclay).

CHAPTER X

QUAKER ESSAYS

1. M. E. Hirst, *Quakers in Peace and War,* 153 f.

2. William Penn, *The Peace of Europe* (Everyman ed.), 7.

3. *Ibid.* (E. P. Duttton and Co.), 3, 18.

4. E. H. Hankin, "Mental Ability of the Quakers," *Science Progress,* XII, 304-6, and XVI, 654-64; *J.F.H.S.,* VII, 30-32.

5. John Bellers, *Essays upon the Poor, Manufactures, Trade, Plantations, and Immorality* (1699); *An Essay towards the Improvement of Physick* (1714); *An Essay for Imploying of the Poor to Profit* (1723).

6. Thomas Fuller, *Church History* (Ed. by Nichols), III, 363-67.

7. *Ibid.*, *The Holy and the Profane State*, "The Good Sea Captain."

8. Fox, *Epistles*, CLIII (1657).

9. Cf. John Hammond, *Leah and Rachel* (1656). Repr. in *Force Tracts*, No. 14. A plea to urge colonists to settle in Virginia and Maryland.

10. T. Budd, *Good Order Established in Pennsilvania and New Jersey*, 9-19. Budd later affiliated with the Keithian separation. Fox, *The Short Journal*, 334, 5.

11. Budd, *op. cit.*, 43 f.

12. *Ibid.*, 48 f.

13. The most accessible reprint is in the Everyman Library, entitled *The Peace of Europe*. E. P. Dutton Co.

14. Penn, *op. cit.*, 281-82.

15. Cf. Fox, *Journal*, 300.

16. The composition of this tract was at one time assigned to Fox. The style and the allusions are, however, unlike his.

17. *J.F.H.S.*, XIII, 87; Fox, *Short Journal*, 330n. The Historical Society of Pennsylvania possesses a copy of this tract.

18. Penington, *Works*, Pt. I, 338-41, 349, 356, 489-96 (1681).

19. Crook, *Works*, 325-35.

20. William Shewen, *Counsel to the Christian-Traveller; Also Meditations and Experiences* (2nd ed.) 21.

21. Chalkley, *A Journal*, 25.

22. *Ibid.*, *Works*, 23-29.

23. William Thompson, *Some Fruits of Solitude: in Reflections and Maxims.*

24. Bennitt, *Works*, 108-42.

25. Thomas Taylor, *Truth's Innocency*, 337f.

26. J. Gratton, *Journal . . . with a Collection of his Books and Manuscripts*, 355-70.

27. *Ibid.*, 360, 362.

28. H. Smith, *Works*, "An Alarum Sounding Forth Unto all the inhabitants of the Earth," 19-28; Burrough, *Works*, "A Trumpet of the Lord Sounded forth of Sion"; Eccles, *Signs Are from the Lord;* Nayler, *Works*, "A Lamentation by one of England's Prophets over the Ruins of this Oppressed Nation" (1653).

29. Howard, *Truth in Plainness,* "A Warning from the Lord unto the Rulers of Dover," 99-103; Burrough, *Works,* "A Warning from the Lord to the Inhabitants of Underbarrow," 1-18; J. Whitehead, *Works,* "A Reproof from the World . . . to Certain Professors . . . about Hull and Beverly," 43-59.

30. Bayly, *Collection of Wrightings,* 225 f. See also *ibid.,* "Some Words Given forth in the Spirit of Truth," 238-42; H. Smith, *op. cit.,* "The Vision . . . Concerning London," 193-200 (1660).

31. Billing, *An Alarm to All Flesh,* 1.

32. *Ibid.,* 9, 10.

Chapter XI

SUNDRY VENTURES—VERSE AND ALLEGORY

1. See also Ellwood, *Rogero Mastix, A Rod for William Rogers in Return for His Rhiming Scourge,* 1685.

2. The Friends Reference Library possesses four large volumes of Quaker broadsides.

3. Jenks Collection, Haverford Library.

4. "Elegy for George Whitehead," Box C, No. 41 Friends Reference Library; "Carmen Spirituale" by Richard Claridge (1723).

5. Crook, *A True and Faithful Testimony Concerning John Samm;* Elizabeth Smith, Testimony for William Smith; *Piety Promoted by Faithfulness, Manifested in . . . Anne Whitehead,* 32, 39-41, 91, 92, 93-5, 103.

6. The first edition was printed by Luke Hinde, a printer of Friends' books in the first half of the eighteenth century.

7. See Smith *Catalogue,* Vol. II, 155, 156.

8. MSS in Friends Reference Library. Octavo volume of poems by John Kelsall (1683-1743).

9. *J.F.H.S.,* XII, 17; Rutty, *History of the . . . Quakers in Ireland,* 138-41.

10. H. T. Wake, Notes to Raunce MSS.

11. This poem does not appear in *Balm from Gilead,* the collected works of William Smith. I believe it has never been published.

12. This poem completes the introduction to *The Great Mistery of the Great Whore.*

13. This poem, so far as I have been able to ascertain, has never been printed. The spelling is unchanged but the punctuation has been modernized.

14. Smith, *Catalogue*, II, 152, 153. Little is known of this author. The last date given in his epistles is 1671.

15. Martin Mason MSS in Friends Reference Library. Punctuation has been modernized.

16. Kelsall MSS, Diary, I, 127. For similar thought see Preface to Thomas Ellwood's *Davideis*.

17. Kelsall MSS, Poems.

18. Clayton Hamilton, *The Manual of the Art of English Fiction*, 29.

19. Jonathan Dickenson, *Protecting Providence* (4th ed.), 28.

20. Fell-Smith, *Stephen Crisp and his Correspondents*, 35, 36; *British Quarterly*, July, 1873; Bunyan, *Grace Abounding* (Camb. 1907) 21; cf. Sir Thomas Browne, *Works*, (ed. John Grant) III, 550-55.

21. Fox, *Journal*, 258, 272-73; Robert Fowler, *A Quaker's Sea-Journal* in Caroline Hazard's *Narragansett Friends' Meetings*, 182-83; *John Adams, Vision of*, Repr. in *J.F.H.S.*, XI, 74-78.

22. Banks, *Journal*, 66, 67, 84; Halhead, *Some Passages*, 4, 6; Chalkley, *Journal*, 25-27.

23. Fell-Smith, *op. cit.*, 35, 44, 45.

24. H. Smith, *Works*, 193.

25. Fell-Smith, *op. cit.*, Intro., 50.

26. Stephen Crisp, *A Short History*, 14.

27. *Ibid.*, 13.

28. *Ibid.*, 21.

29. Cf. Thomas Lawson's *A Mite into the Treasury*, 46-47.

30. For the attitude of the Friends toward music, see F. J. Gilman, *The Evolution of the English Hymn*, 177 f.; 184 f.; 192 f., 232; Lawson, *op. cit.*, 41-43; H. Smith, *Works*, 108 f.

31. Eccles, *A Musick-Lector*, 28.

CHAPTER XII
SERMONS, PROVERBS, AND ADVICES

1. Burnyeat, *Truth Exalted*, 1, 7, 17; Gratton, *Life*, 41, 42, 51, 66.

2. J. Faldo, "A Key to the Quakers Usurped and Most Un-

intelligible Phrases" in *Quakerism, No Christianity*, 303-30; K. Tibbals, "The Speech of Plain Friends," *American Speech*, I, 200; T. E. Harvey, *Quaker Language*.

3. Barclay, *Inner Life*, 215. For similarity of titles of non-Quaker religious works see advertising section of *Sermons of Stephen Crisp* (1693 ed.) p. 176 f.

4. Caroline Richardson, *English Preachers and Preaching*, 28.

5. John Kelsall systematically recorded his own "openings" in meetings for worship, and made brief entries concerning the subject matter of others. MS diaries in D.; T. Wilson, "Life" in *Friends' Library*, II, 322.

6. Samuel Bownas, "Life," *Friends' Library*, III, 57.

7. *Ibid.*, 57.

8. This information is given in editorial forewords to the printed sermons. See Fox, *Journal* (Camb. ed.), I, 455; II, 460 for sermons of Fox.

9. Evans and Evans in reprinting this sermon in 1838 in *The Friends' Library* appended a note of apology saying that it was the editorial opinion that "the practice of taking down sermons or prayers delivered in assemblies or worship" . . . is improper." *Friends' Library*, II, 292-97.

10. Sewel, *op. cit.*, II, 458-466 (1823).

11. Stephen Crisp, *Works*, 33; Fell-Smith, *Stephen Crisp and His Correspondents*, xxvii, xxxiii. Dutch translations of ten of Crisp's works are noted in Smith's *Catalogue*.

12. Nathaniel Crouch wrote "books on miscellaneous subjects under the pseudonymn of Richard or Robert Burton." He published also cheap editions, which sold at a shilling apiece. John Dunton pays him this tribute: "I think I have given you the soul of his character when I have told you that his talent lies at collection. He has melted down the best of our English histories into twelve penny books, which are filled with wonders, rarities, and curiosities." *D.N.B.* See note "To the Reader" preceding the 1693 edition of *Several Sermons of Mr. Stephen Crisp:* "If any desire to be further satisfied by speaking with the writer [the short-hand reporter], they may be gratified by applying to the Bookseller."

13. Kite, *Antiquarian Researches*, 35; Littleboy, *A History of Friends Reference Library*, 9, 10.

14. Kite, *op. cit.*, 33.

15. This volume contains ten sermons, seven by Penn, and one each by Samuel Waldenfield, Benjamine Coole [Coale], and George Whitehead.

16. After the Keithian separation (1692) Crouch published in 1694 a group of eleven sermons entitled *The Great Doctrines of the Gospel of Christ . . . or Sermons of the Christian Quakers*. See also J. Smith, *op. cit.*, II, 36, 37.

17. Other preachers included were John Boweter, William Bingley, John Butcher, Francis Camfield, Richard Ashby, Samuel Waldenfield, James Parke, John Vaughton, and Francis Stamper. Crouch had also included the sermon on "Regeneration" by William Dewsbury. See no. 9 *supra*.

18. Richardson, *op. cit.*, 77, 80.

19. Whiting, *Persecution Exposed*, 175-77; Fox, *The Short Journal*, 312; Braithwaite, *Beginnings*, 242.

20. *Concurrence and Unanimity*, 168.

21. *Letters of Early Friends;* J. Kendal, *Letters on Religious Subjects;* Fox, *Epistles*.

22. John Whitehead, *Gospel Labours*, 214-21; Luke Howard, *Works*, 226-72.

23. *Yearly Meeting Epistles*, 1685, 1688.

24. Burrough, *Works*, 588; J. Coale, *Works*, 236-38.

25. Gratton, *Works*, 127-31; Burnyeat, *Truth Exalted*, 147-59.

26. W. Smith, *op. cit.*, "Universal Love," 75-96; and 1-48 under the year 1663; T. Taylor, *Truth's Innocency*, "Some Prison Meditations . . . being a Free-Gift Sermon," 39-49 and 53-70.

27. Fox, *Epistles*, CCLXII, CCLIV; Josiah Newman, *The Quaker Records*, 37-65; Braithwaite, *Beginnings*, 144, 145, *Epistles from the Yearly Meeting*, 1681-1682.

28. F. Jeffrey, *Edinburgh Review*, July, 1813. Quoted by Janney in *History of . . . Friends*, III, 187.

29. Cf. Henry Percy, *Advice to a Son;* Phineas Fletcher, *Advice of a Father;* Francis Osborne, *Advice to a Son;* Pepys, *Diary*, I, 247; II, 9; IV, 213 (ed. Baybrooke); George Saville, *A Lady's Gift, or Advice to Her Daughter*. These are non-Quaker contemporary "advices."

30. Repr. in Backhouse's *Memoir of Francis Howgill*, 85-92.

31. Crook, *Works*, 409.

32. W. Smith, *Balm from Gilead*, 73 for year 1663.

33. *Ibid.*, 88, 89.

34. For additional advices see: H. Smith, *Works*, "To all Parents of Children upon the Face of the Whole Earth," 125, 127, 129; T. Thompson, *An Encouragement*, 86-96; Croker, *Brief Memoir*, 323; Dewsbury, *Epistle*, reprinted in *Friends Library*, II, 291; Chalkley, *Works*, Pt. II, 30-38; Caton, "A General Epistle to Young Schoolars and Little Children" prefatory to his *Abridgment of Eusebius;* J. Pike," "Life," *Friends' Library*, II, 353, 355, 358; Joseph Sleigh, *Good Advice and Counsel* (1691); Gershon Boate's, "A Father's Advice to his Child or the Maiden's Best Adorning"; J. Banks, *A Journal*, "A Rebuke to Unfaithful Parents," 341-52; Thomas Gwin, *The Will and Testament . . . being some Religious and Serious Considerations*, 4.

35. W. Smith, *op. cit.*, 115, 116 for year 1664.

36. Fell-Smith, *op. cit.*, 26, 27.

37. Judith Zins-Penninck, *Some Worthy Proverbs of* (1663), 3.

38. *Ibid.*, 5.

39. Braithwaite, *Second Period*, 417; *J.F.H.S.*, VI, 2, 25, 26; *Life of John Roberts*, 35.

40. Martin Mason MS in Friends Reference Library. For description of contents see Smith, *Catalogue* II, 155-56.

41. S. M. Janney, *Life of William Penn*, 14.

42. Penn, *Fruits of a Father's Love*, Ch. II, Sec. I; Locker-Lampson, *A Quaker Post-bag*, "Letter to Sir John Rodes," p. 6. "Observe to put down in a pocket book, for that purpose all openings which are usually short, but full and lively; for I have few things to remember with more trouble than forgetting of such irrecoverable thoughts and reflections. I have lost a whole volume of them."

43. *More Fruits of Solitude* by Penn appeared in 1702.

44. Penn, *Some Fruits of Solitude*, Maxim 30.

45. *Ibid.*, Maxim 108.

46. *Ibid.*, Maxim 337.

47. *Ibid.*, Maxim 380.

48. For other popular conduct books of this *genre* see Dent's *Plain Man's Pathway to Heaven;* Drelincourt's *Defence against the Fear of Death;* Bayly's *The Practice of Piety;* and Law, *A Serious Call.*

49. Penn, *No Cross, No Crown* (1682), Preface, 1, 2.
50. *Ibid.,* 102-48; 208-20; 226-37.
51. *Ibid.,* "The Character of a Proud Man," 159 f.
52. *Ibid.,* 226 f.
53. *Ibid.,* 258-339.
54. *Ibid.,* 339-378.
55. *Ibid.,* 378-404.
56. *Ibid.,* 161.
57. *Ibid.,* 180.
58. *Ibid.,* 99.
59. *Ibid.,* 167.
60. *Ibid.,* 202.

CHAPTER XIII

THE QUAKER AND THE "WORLD'S" JOURNALS

1. Anna Robeson Burr, *Religious Confessions* 145; *The Autobiography,* 184.
2. Note especially Thomas Story (1660-1742), Thomas Chalkley (1675-1741), and Samuel Bownas (1676-1753).
3. *A True Relation Undertaken by one Robert Fowler.* For other examples cf. Smith's *Catalogue* under William Dundas, Barbara Blaugdone, Katharine Evans.
4. R. Hubberthorn, *A True Testimony;* Nicholas Gates, *A Tender Invitation;* R. Steel, *Jacob, the Plain Man Wrestling with God.*
5. Ellwood, *Life,* 17, 18; Edmundson, *Journal,* 14, 59.
6. Gratton, *Journal,* 177.
7. Edmundson, *Life,* 21; *Life of John Roberts,* 5, 6, 10.
8. Burnyeat, *Life,* 56.
9. Banks, *Journal,* 131, 139.
10. George Whitehead, *Christian Progress* (1725), 22, 24-31. Cf. Beck's *George Whitehead and His Work,* 125-29.
11. Whitehead, *op. cit.,* 353 f.
12. Sewel, *History,* 550, 571, 596 (1823).
13. Barclay, *Inner Life,* 413-22.
14. Anna Trapnel, according to Champlin Burridge was claimed by Baptists, Fifth Monarchy, and Quakers. *Baptist Historical Society,* VII, 235. Probably she belonged to all in turn.
15. Braithwaite, *Second Period,* 228-50, 295, 482 f.
16. *Ibid.,* 542-44; Stephen Crisp, *Works,* 22.

17. Burr, *The Autobiography*, 131-38. Introspective journals had appeared on the continent. Cf. The Life of St. Teresa of Jesus; Cardan, *De Propria Liber*.

18. Publications of the Wodrow Society. Note lives of Robert Blaire, John Livingstone, James Frazer, James Melville, and Robert Pringle in Tweedie's *Select Biographies*.

19. See Bibliography I.

20. Bunyan's *Grace Abounding* was published in 1666; Baxter's life in 1696.

21. Herbert's life was published in 1764; Digby's, 1868; Lady Fanshaw's, 1829; Evelyn's *Diary* in 1818; Pepys's in 1825; D'Ewes's in 1845.

22. See prefaces to lives of William Caton, John Banks, and William Crouch, and openings of journals of Elizabeth Stirredge, Thomas Story, and Joseph Pike.

23. *Post*, 202-205.

24. To these should be added three atypical journals: *A Short Account of the Life of Mr. John Pennyman* (1628-1706), who after "disownment" by Friends wrote his book as an *apologia* for his actions (1696); the hostile *Pilgrim's Progress from Quakerism to Christianity* of Francis Bugg, also an "apostate," printed in 1698; and *A Brand Snatched from the Burning* by Samuel Keimer, printed in 1718, which mingles a little Quakerism with French prophetism. Smith, II, 17: "In *Memoirs of Religious Impostors*, it is stated he became a Friend."

25. *Diary of Alexander Jaffray*, iii, 10.

26. The tables concerning the autobiographies of the seventeenth-century Friends in Mrs. Burr's *The Autobiography*, which Mr. Waldo Dunn, with acknowledgment, follows in his *English Biography*, are inaccurate. Samuel Fisher, Richard Farnsworth, Edward Burrough, and William Dewsbury have left only fragmentary accounts. Dr. John Rutty (1698-1775) is placed among the seventeenth-century writers, as is William Evans, a nineteenth-century Friend. Gilbert Latye's *Life* is a biography written by his nephew, and only correspondence of Alice Ellis exists. I have not been able to find any trace of the John Wibur, whom she lists. A John Wilbur who died in 1856 left a journal but obviously he cannot belong in this list.

27. Croker, *Brief Memoir*, 293-97.

28. *Autobiography of Henry Lampe*, 16, 23.

29. Much variation, particularly in the exclusion of poetry and references to literature and personal matters, occurs in the MS life of Thomas Chalkley housed in the Historical Society of Pennsylvania, and the first edition in 1751, and the later cutting by William and Thomas Evans for volume VI of *The Friends' Library*, published 1842.

30. *Diary of Alexander Jaffray*, 70, 110.

31. *Ibid.*, 52, 129.

CHAPTER XIV

QUAKER JOURNALS AND QUAKER LIFE

PRE-QUAKER EXPERIENCES AND MARRIAGE

1. E. Colby, "The Essence of Autobiography," *The Open Court*, XXXVII (1923), 483.

2. Alice Hayes, *A Legacy*, 1; Joseph Pike, *Life*, 1.

3. Davies, *An Account*, 1; Fox, *Journal*, 1.

4. Davies, *op. cit.*, 1-17; Fox, *op. cit.*, 1-12; Banks, *A Journal*, 4-12.

5. Davies, *op. cit.*, 28, 29; Stephen Crisp, *Works*, 23-25.

6. Quoted from Monyash M. M. Minute Book, Feb. 1673, by Braithwaite, *Second Period*, 371.

7. Gratton, *Life*, 1, 2.

8. *Ibid.*, 2.

9. *Ibid.*, 3.

10. Bunyan, *Grace Abounding*, 15, (Camb., 1907).

11. Gratton, *op. cit.*, 5-19.

12. *Ibid.*, 20.

13. *Ibid.*, 34, 53.

14. For a similar statement see Patrick Livingstone in *Selections from his Writings*, 24-44.

15. *Ibid.*, 39.

16. *Ibid.*, 133.

17. *Ibid.*, 95.

18. *Ibid.*, 355-70.

19. Margaret Fell, *Works*, 1.

20. Croker, *Brief Memoir*, 283.

21. *Ibid.*, 284.

22. Whiting, *Persecution Exposed*, Introd.

23. Ellwood, *Life*, 20-40.

24. Cf. *Piety Promoted by . . . Anne Whitehead*, and prelimi-

nary testimonies to journal of Richard Davies, and to E. Bathurst's *Truth Vindicated,* and Lawson's *Serious Remembrancer.*

25. Earthly as opposed to divine fatherhood. *Journal,* Fox,
317, 318; cf. Locker-Lampson, *Quaker Post-bag,* 174-75.

26. Chalkley, "Journal" in *Friends' Library,* VI, 39.

27. Halhead, *Some Passages,* 9.

28. Brailsford, *Quaker Women,* 133-87.

29. Fox, *op. cit.,* 262.

30. Davies, *op. cit.,* 36.

31. *Ibid.,* 42, 46, 54.

32. *Ibid.,* 37.

33. *Ibid.,* 37. For other cases see Caton, *Life* (Barclay Series
VI), 110, 113; Brailsford. *op. cit.,* 231-37.

Chapter XV
QUAKER JOURNALS AND QUAKER LIFE
CUSTOMS AND LETTERS

1. Davies, *An Account,* 28, 29.

2. *Ibid.,* 25. Cf. the treatment received by Ellas Hookes, who
was beaten by a woman for not removing his hat. *J.F.H.S.,* I,
13.

3. Fox, *Journal* (E. P. Dutton Co., 1928), 318 f.

4. Alice J. Whitmore, "The River at the Spring: A Study
of Beginnings," *The Bellman,* June 8, 1898.

5. Fox, *op. cit.,* 121, 122.

6. Edward Pyot, *The West Answering North;* A. F. Robbins,
"Fox and his Friends at Launceston," *Friends Quarterly Examiner,* 1896; T. Hodgkin, "George Fox at Launceston," *Ibid.,*
1895.

7. J. Backhouse, *Memoirs of Francis Howgill,* 17-19.

8. Carleton, *The Captive's Complaint,* 29; cf. Hayes, *A Legacy,*
38, 46.

9. Chalkley, "Life," *Friends' Library,* VI, 2.

10. *Life of John Roberts,* 6, 7.

11. T. Thompson, *An Encouragement,* 19; Banks, *A Journal,*
12-14; Brayshaw, *Personality of George Fox,* ix, f.

12. Fox, *op. cit.,* 31.

13. Brayshaw, *op. cit.,* x.

14. *Ibid.*

15. Brayshaw, *op. cit.*, xi.

16. Fox, *op. cit.*, 205.

17. *Ibid.*, 187.

18. Cf. G. Whitehead, *Christian Progress*, 85: "The turnkey threatened to take away our ink horns and did take away one."

19. Sansom, "Life," in *Friends' Library*, XIV, 28.

20. Banks, *op. cit.*, 98-104; 114-15; Davies, *op. cit.*, 60.

21. Ellwood, *Life*, 84, 129 f., 145, 194, 203.

22. Fox, *op. cit.*, 83, 95, 119 f., 243 f., 315 f.

23. *Ibid.*, 83, 95.

24. G. Whitehead, *op. cit.*, 79, 80, 83, 85-95.

25. *Ibid.*, 91, 92.

26. *Ibid.*, 82.

27. Fox, *Journal* (E. P. Dutton Co. 1928), 237-38.

28. *Ibid.*, 29, 30, 42, 78; Whitehead, *op. cit.*, 208 f., 224 f.; Edmundson, *Life*, 83-85, 88-90; Burnyeat, *Truth Exalted*, 23, 56.

29. Whitehead, *op. cit.*, 295, 301, 373, 379.

30. Fox, *Works*, VII, VIII (Phila. 1831); cf. Claridge, *Life and Works*, 135-65; Banks, *op. cit.*, 59, 82, 87, 111, 134-38, and his formal letter "A Rebuke to Unfaithful Parents," 341-52; Crook, *Works*, 341-52. For additional advices see essays of Samuel Hunt, *Instructions for Children and Others;* and William Thompson, *The Care of Parents is a Happiness to Children.*

31. Cf. *Letters of Early Friends*, illustrative of the primitive period, and Locker-Lampson's *A Quaker Post-bag*, which prints letters of William Penn, Martha Rodes, Henry Gouldney, and Silvanus Bevan, written between 1690 and 1742.

32. A. Clark, *Working Life of Women in the Seventeenth Century*, 12.

33. Halhead, *Some Passages*, 8. See also Gratton, *Life*, 155, 196.

34. "Life of William Dewsbury," in *Friends' Library*, II, 271.

35. Wilson, "Life," in *Friends' Library*, II, 332.

36. *Ibid.*, 314.

37. William Wilson, *The Memorial of the Just shall not Rot;* "Testimony." See also Penn, *An Account of the Blessed End of Gulielma Maria Penn.*

38. H. Tuke, *Biographical Notices*, II, 100.

39. John Lilburne, *The Resurrection of* (1656), 4-6.

40. From photographic reproduction of original in D.

Chapter XVI
THE LANGUAGE OF THE JOURNALS

1. Fowler, *A True Relation*, 182.
2. Lurting, *The Fighting Sailor Turn'd Peacable Christian*, 8, 10, 11.
3. Ellwood, *Life*, 130, 132, 141, 148-51.
4. Thomas Story, *Life*, 125-27.
5. Fox, *Journal*, 81, 104 f., 118, 168.
6. *Ibid.*, 8.
7. *Ibid.*, (5th ed.), II, 29.
8. *Ibid.*, 45.
9. *Ibid.*, 46.
10. Knight, *The Founder of Quakerism*, 57-73.
11. *Ibid.*, 60.
12. Fox, *op. cit.*, 10.
13. *Ibid.*, 17.
14. *Ibid.*, 257.
15. *Ibid.*, 173.
16. F. Aydelotte, "George Fox's Style," *B.F.H.A.*, XII, 69-78.
17. Fox, *Journal*, (5th ed.), I, 404; *Isa.*, 58:5.
18. Fox, *Journal*, 10; *Mal.* 3:2.
19. Fox *Journal*, (5th ed.), I, 322.
20. Fox, *Journal*, 120.
21. *Ibid.*, 303.
22. *Ibid.*, 93.
23. *Logan-Story Correspondence*, (Ed. by Norman Penney).
24. Halhead, *Some Passages*, 3.
25. *Ibid.*, 4, 17.
26. *Ibid.*, 5, 6.
27. *Ibid.*, 8.
28. *Ibid.*, 13.
29. *Ibid.*, 6.
30. *Ibid.*, 12.
31. Chalkley, *Journal*, 269, 238-39; quotes all of Addison's hymn "How are my servants blessed, O Lord." See also 36, 91, 93, 100, 101, 111.
32. Bowden, *History . . . of Friends*, 264-66. See Whittier's poem "Chalkley Hall."
33. Chalkley, *op. cit.*, 83.

34. *Ibid.*, 24, 26.

35. Banks, *Journal*, 68-77; Fox, *op. cit.*, 168.

36. Chalkley, *op. cit.*, 155; Sansom, *Life*, 83-9.

37. Sansom, *op. cit.*, 126-28, 284-86, 329.

38. *Ibid.*, 347 f.; Fox, *op. cit.*, 225 f.

Chapter XVII

FROM CONFESSION TO JOURNAL

1. H. Smith, *Man Driven out of the Earth and Darkness* (1658), repr. in *Works*, 52; and *To All Parents* (1660), repr. *idem* 123.

2. Howgill, *The Inheritance of Jacob* (1656), repr. in Backhouse, *Memoirs of Howgill*, 20-23; *Humphrey Bache, or Restitution the Fruit of Conversion* (1659); Carleton, *The Captive's Complaint*; Dewsbury, *Works*, "The First Birth," (1655), 44-57; Theophilus Green, *A Declaration* . . . (1659).

3. Hubberthorn, *A True Testimony*, (1653), repr. in *Works*, 1, 2.

4. Bennitt, *The Work and Mercy of God* (1685), repr. in *Works*, 174-177.

5. Dundas, *A Few Words of Truth* (1673), 18.

6. Carleton, *The Captive's Complaint* (1668), 29.

7. Dundas, *op. cit.*, 10-28.

8. Whiting, *Early Piety* . . . *of Mary Whiting*, 11.

9. Burnyeat, *Truth Exalted*, 58, 59.

10. Osborne, *A Brief Narrative*, 54.

11. Fox, *The Short Journal and Itinerary Journals*, xxii, xxviii.

12. For editing of contemporary non-Quaker memoirs see C. H. Firth, "Some Seventeenth Century Diarists," *Scottish Historical Review*, July 1913.

13. Cf. Tract *The Tree Known by its Fruits* (1710) with insertion in "Life of Oliver Samson," in *Friends' Library*, XIV, 39-40.

14. Burrough, *Works*, 1672, "Testimonies" of Francis Howgill, Josiah Coale, and George Whitehead.

15. Cf. Fox, *Works*, VII, VIII and *Journal* (Camb. ed.) 1, 5, 79, 87, 101, etc.

16. Burr, *The Autobiography*, 236.

17. Miles Halhead and Joan Vokins.

18. Ansley or Annesley was a puritan nonconformist, the maternal grandfather of Charles and John Wesley, *D.N.B.* Nichols, *Literary Anecdotes,* V, 232.

19. J. Whitehead, *Written Gospel Labours,* 243-86.

20. *Ibid.,* 87-110.

21. *Ibid.,* 1-43.

Chapter XVIII

THE RELIGIOUS CONFESSION
ACCEPTING THE LIGHT

1. G. M. Stratton, *The Psychology of the Religious Life,* 215 f.

2. John Fothergill, *Account,* 1, 2; Howard, *Love and Truth,* 1-3; Gratton, *Life,* 1, 2; H. Smith, *Works,* 52, 289.

3. Patrick Livingstone, *Selections* "Concerning the Heavenly Seed," 31; Thomas Wilson, *Life,* 1-4; Burnyeat, *Life,* 149-160; Burrough, *Works,* 13.

4. Burrough, *op. cit.,* 13-15; cf. Thomas Aldam, *A Short Testimony.*

5. Wilson, *Journal,* 1, 2; T. Thompson, *An Encouragement,* 11, 12; Livingstone, *op. cit.,* 21, 22; Stirredge, *Strength Manifest,* 2-8; Hayes, *A Legacy,* 15, 16; Edmundson, *Life,* 2.

6. Wilson, *op. cit.,* 2, 3; Thompson, *op. cit.,* 13; Livingstone, *op. cit.,* 23-29; Stirredge, *op. cit.,* 10-14; Hayes, *op. cit.,* 22-34; Edmundson, *op. cit.,* 3-7.

7. Wilson, *op. cit.,* 4; Thompson, *op. cit.,* 14, 16, 17; Livingstone, *op. cit.,* 29; Stirredge, 15-18; Hayes, 17-34; Edmundson, 7; Burnyeat, *Life,* i.

8. Wilson, *op. cit.,* 5-8; Thompson, 15-17; Livingstone, 30-46; Hayes, 34-40; Stirredge, 20-29; Edmundson, 11-16; Burnyeat, 2-10.

9. Wilson, *op. cit.,* 9; Thompson, 18, 19-40; Stirredge, 29 f.; Hayes, 34 f.; Edmundson, 21 f.; Burnyeat, 10 f.

10. Whiting, *Persecution Exposed,* Author's introd., 1.

11. Croker, *Brief Memoir,* 283, 284.

12. Gratton, *op. cit.,* 1; Pike, *op. cit.,* 1; Hayes, *op. cit., Friends' Library* II, 68; Blaugdone, *Account,* 7.

13. Samuel Bownas, *Account,* 5-7; Fothergill, *op. cit.,* 2, 3.

14. See Ch. XIII.

15. See Ch. XIII.
16. Cf. Lydia Lancaster, *Epistles* 1684-1761; Susanna Morris, 1682-1755; Jane Hoskens, 1693-(?) Margaret Lucas, 1701-1769; Isaac Sharples, 1702-1784; William Reckitt, 1706-1770; Sophia Hume, *An Exhortation to the People of South Carolina* (1748).
17. Backhouse, *Memoirs*, 1.
18. Fox, *Journal*, 61, 62; cf. (Camb. ed.), I, 404n.
19. Howgill, *The Inheritance of Jacob*, 14, 15.
20. *Ibid.*, 16.
21. *Ibid.*, 17, 18.
22. Gratton, *op. cit.*, 4-28; Hubberthorn, *Works*, 1-3; W. Bayly, "Life" prefixed to *Works;* Bennitt, *Works*, 171; Sansom, *Life*, 3, 4; Howard, *A Few Words*, 8.
23. Cf. Farnsworth, *Heart Opened*, 11, 12; Aldam, *A Short Testimony*, 4; Dewsbury, *Works*, 46; Richardson, "Life," *Friends' Library* IV, 61; Marshall, "Life," *Friends' Library*, IV, 128.
24. Cf. Howard, *op. cit.*, 6.
25. Howgill, *op. cit.*, 20.
26. *Ibid.*, 21, 22; Fox, *op. cit.*, 62, 69; Backhouse, *op. cit.*, 24-28.
27. Backhouse, *op. cit.*, 35.
28. *Ibid.*, 52.
29. E. A. Ames, *The Psychology of Religious Experience*, 253, 264.
30. Mary Penington, Letters written *ca.* 1680. First published in 1797 and 1821, respectively.
31. *Ibid.*, 24.
32. *Ibid.*, 29, 30, 36, 37.
33. *Ibid.*, 38-44.
34. Ellwood, *Life*, 13-21, 101, 111-14.
35. M. Penington, *op. cit.*, 45.
36. I. Penington, *Works*, II, 48-51 (1784).

CHAPTER XIX

THE RELIGIOUS CONFESSION
APPROACHING THE QUAKER WAY OF LIFE

1. W. Bayly, *Wrightings*. Close of unpaged section of his "Life"; Blaugdone, *An Account*, 39.
2. Banks, *Journal*, 4; Livingstone, *Selections*, 3-5.

3. W. Bennitt, *Works*, 171.

4. *Life of John Roberts*, 5, 6; cf. John Richardson, "Life," *Friends' Library*, IV, 61; *F.P.T.*, 54.

5. Davies, *An Account*, 6. For adverse view see Josselin, *Diary*, 112, 118, 130; Roger Williams, *George Fox Digg'd out of his Burrowes*, 248.

6. W. Ames, *A Declaration*, 8.

7. Bayly, *op. cit.*, last of unpaged section.

8. Sansom, *Life*, 8; Marshall, "Life," *Friends' Library*, IV, 127; Pike, "Life" *ibid.*, II, 351, 357, 358; Livingstone, *Selections*, 3-5.

9. E. D. Starbuck, *The Psychology of Religion*, 188-212; G. A. Coe, *The Psychology of Religion*, 152-74; W. B. Selbie, *The Psychology of Religion*, 166-88.

10. Steel, *Jacob the Plain Man*, 6; *Experiences in the Life of Mary Penington*, 17, 18.

11. Crisp, *Life and Works*, 17, 18.

12. Thompson, *An Encouragement*, 11.

13. John Barcroft, *A Brief Narrative*, 2; cf. Kelsall MS I, 6.

14. Fox, *Journal*, 8; ante, Ch. III.

15. Gratton, *op. cit.*, 20, 34-36.

16. Wilson, *Life*, 4; cf. H. Smith, *Works*, 19, 60; Halhead, *Some Passages*, 2, 3; Burnyeat, "Life," *Friends' Library*, XI, 164.

17. Repr. in *Christian Life and Thought*, 32; Besse, *op. cit.*, II, 201. Cf. Richardson, *op. cit.*, IV, 64; Marshall, "Life," *Friends' Library*, IV, 130; Burnyeat, *Works*, 179.

18. H. Smith, *Works*, 18-20.

Chapter XX
INTROSPECTION

1. Barclay, *Apology*, XI, 6.

2. Baxter, *Autobiography* (ed. Thomas), Ch. X.

3. Burr, *The Autobiography* (Houghton Mifflin Co.), 236.

4. Marshall, *Sion's Travellers*, 4; Fox, *Journal* (Camb. ed.), I, 28; *F.P.T.*, 22, 43, 110, 115; Hodgkin, *Silent Worship*, 42-62.

5. Cf. Fox's letter to Lady Claypoole, *ante*, Ch. III.

6. Roger Hebden, *A Plain Account*, 29, 30.

7. Fell-Smith, *Stephen Crisp and his Correspondents*, 5.

8. Colchester MSS. Repr. in Callaway, *Memoir of James Parnell*, 71.

9. Rep. in Backhouse, *Memoirs of Francis Howgill*, 87.
10. Kelsall MS Diaries, 28.
11. Bownas, *Account of*, 48, 49.
12. Richardson, "Life," *Friends' Library*, IV, 76.
13. *Ibid.*, 70. See also p. 62.
14. Bangs, "Life," *Friends' Library*, IV, 216-17.
15. Faldo, *The Dangers of Enthusiasm*, 13, 14, 29, 40.
16. Gratton, *Life*, 7, 18.
17. *Ibid.*, 8-20. Cf. Ellwood's question of conflict over fear of offending his father and desire to attend a Quaker meeting. *Life*, 47.
18. Stephen Crisp, *Life*, 21, 22.
19. Ellwood, *Life*, 44, 45.
20. Dundas, *A Few Words.*, 18, 19. Chalkley, "Life," *Friends' Library*, VI, 17, 18. Thomas Chalkley inserts a story of a Quaker woman on the western frontier of New England, who perished in an Indian raid by leaving her home to reach a fort because she had admitted to her mind "a slavish fear."
21. Burnyeat, *Truth Exalted*, 174.
22. Marshall, "Life," *Friends' Library*, IV, 130.
23. C. Story, "Life," *Friends' Library*, I, 148, 149. See also Stirredge, "Life," *Friends' Library*, II, 198, and Hayes, *A Legacy*, 35, 36.

CHAPTER XXI

PRACTICAL MYSTICISM

1. H. Smith, *Works*, 128, 129; Dewsbury, "Life," *Friends' Library*, II, 291.
2. Williams, *George Fox Digg'd out of his Burrowes*, 134-35; 210.
3. Bugg, *Pilgrim's Progress*, 8-22.
4. Locker-Lampson, *Quaker Post-bag*, 149; G. Whitehead, *Christian Progress*, 234-36.
5. Britten, *Silent Meeting*, 3, 4.
6. *Ibid.*, 3, 4.
7. Barclay, *Apology*, Prop. XI, sec. 7.
8. Braithwaite, *Second Period*, 483 f.; Marjorie Nicholson, *The Conway Letters*, 413; Fox, *Journal* (Camb. ed.) II, 455; Croese, *History*, 150.
9. Keith, *The Magicke of Quakerism*, 68.

10. *Ibid.*, 50-53.

11. Richardson, "Life," *Friends' Library*, IV, 86, 89, 96, 107; *Memoirs of Rise of Quakers . . . in the North of Scotland.* Bound with *Diary of Alexander Jaffray*, 466.

12. Wilson, *Journal*, 57; Davies, *An Account*, 126; Pike, "Life," *Friends' Library*, II, 353.

13. *George Fox: Some Modern Appreciations.* See Dr. Jones's article on "The Psychology of George Fox," 71.

14. G. Robinson, *An Additional Account*, 278.

15. Burnyeat, *Truth Exalted*, 21. Cf. Caton, *Life*, 51.

16. Fox, *Journal* (Camb. ed.) I, 462. See Roger Williams, *op. cit.*, 44.

17. Halhead, *Some Passages*, 6; Braithwaite, *Beginnings*, 372; Fox, *op. cit.*, I, xvi, 51, 105; II, 184.

18. *F.P.T.*, 365; *A Short Relation Concerning the Life and Death . . . of William Simpson*, "Testimony of George Fox."

19. Braithwaite, *Second Period*, 25; *A Brief Relation of the Persecutions . . . since 1662*, 5; Pepys, *Diary*, 9th July, 1667; Fox, *op. cit.*, II, 428.

20. Cf. Norman Penney's addendum to *First Publishers of Truth*, 364-69.

21. E. Manners, *Elizabeth Hooton*, 39-40.

22. Dickinson, *Journal*, 70, 71.

23. Knight, *The Founder of Quakerism*, 223, 227.

24. Fox, *Journal* (E. P. Dutton Co., 1928), 39, 40.

25. Barclay, *Works*, I, 194, 195. Cf. Marmaduke Stephenson, "Account" of Robinson bound with *A Call From Life unto Death*. In 1659 William Robinson, shortly before he was hanged in Boston wrote: "The presence of the Lord filled me" and both "constrained and commanded me to pass to the town of Boston my life to lay down in his will for the accomplishing of his services"; *Memoirs of John Exham, Friends' Library*, III, 488: With "his head covered with sack cloth and ashes," John Exham passed through the streets of Cork in 1667 to proclaim "the necessity of repentance and amendment of life"; H. Smith, *Works*, 24.

26. Fox, *op. cit.*, 85, 86.

27. Green, *A Declaration to the World of my Travel and Journey out of Aegypt*, 6.

28. Chalkley, "Life," *Friends' Library*, VI, 52.

29. Fox, *op. cit.*, 196; Dr. Knight lists eight telepathic cases in her *Founder of Quakerism*, 184-89.

30. Richardson, "Life," *Friends' Library*, IV, 110.

31. J. W. Graham, *The Faith of a Quaker.*

32. E. H. Hankin, *Science Progress*, XVII, 304 f.

BIBLIOGRAPHY I

EARLY QUAKER AUTOBIOGRAPHICAL RECORDS

ABBREVIATIONS

D for Friends Reference Library.

E.S.P. for Extracts State Papers.

J.F.H.S. for Journal Friends Historical Society (London).

B.F.H.A. for Bulletin Friends Historical Association (Haverford, Penn.).

M.M.M. for minutes of the Morning Meeting Minutes.

Y.M.M. for minutes of the Yearly Meeting Minutes.

Y.M.E. for Yearly Meeting Epistles.

ADAMS, JOHN, Vision of John Adams, *J.F.H.S.* XI, 74-78. *Irish Friend.* IV (1841), 150.

AMES, WILLIAM, A Declaration of the Witness of God Manifested in me from my Youth. London, 1656.

ANDREWS, ELIZABETH, An Account of the Birth, Education and Suffering of. *J.F.H.S.* XXVI (1929), 3-8.

ANDREWS, ISAAC, A Short Account of. London, 1801.

BACHE, HUMPHREY, Humphrey Bache, or Restitution the Fruit of Conversion. Manchester, 1847.

——— A Few Words in True Love. London, 1659.

BANGS, BENJAMIN, Memoirs of the Life and Convincement of. 1757.

BANKS, JOHN, A Journal of the Life, Labours, Travels, and Sufferings of that Faithful Minister of Jesus Christ. London, J. Sowle, 1712.

BARCROFT, JOHN, A Brief Narrative of the Life, Convincement, Conversion, Labours of Love in the Gospel Ministry. Dublin, 1730.

BAYLY, CHARLES, A True and Faithful Warning. London, 1663.

BAYLY, WILLIAM, A Short Relation or Testimony of the Working of the Light of Christ in me from my Childhood, 1659. Repr. and prefixed to *A Collection of the Several Wrightings of William Bayly,* 1676.

BEEVAN, JOHN, A Loving Salutation to all People who have any Desires after the Living God. London, 1660.

BELL, DEBORAH, A Short Journal of the Labours and Travels in the Work of the Ministry of that Faithful Servant of Christ. 1762.

BENNITT, WILLIAM, The Work and Mercy of God Conduceth to His Praise; or a Demonstration of the Visitation of God's Love to my Soul in the Days of my Youth. London, 1669.

BEWLEY, GEORGE, A Narrative of the Christian Experiences of George Bewley. Dublin, 1750.

BLAUGDONE, BARBARA, An Account of the Travels, Sufferings, and Persecutions of Barbara Blaugdone. London, T. Sowle, 1691.

BOWNAS, SAMUEL, An Account of the Life, Travels, and Christian Experiences. London, Luke Hinde, 1756.

BRIGGS, THOMAS, An Account of Some of the Travels and Sufferings of that Faithful Servant of the Lord, Thomas Briggs. 1685.

BRITTEN, WILLIAM, Silent Meeting. London, 1660.

BRUSH, EDWARD, The Invisible Power of God Known in Weakness with a Christian Testimony. London, T. Sowle, 1695.

BURNYEAT, JOHN, The Truth Exalted in the Writings of that Eminent and Faithful Servant of Christ, John Burnyeat. London, T. Northcott, 1691.

BURNYEAT, JONATHAN, Some Account of the Gospel Labourers of Jonathan Burnyeat. London, 1857.

BURROUGH, EDWARD, A Warning from the Lord to the Inhabitants of Underbarrow, 1654. Repr. in *Works*, 1672, pp. 13-16.

CARLETON, THOMAS, The Captive's Complaint . . . with a True Relation of the Prisoner's Spiritual Progress and Travel toward the New and Heavenly Jerusalem. London, 1668.

CATON, WILLIAM, A Journal of the Life of that Faithful Servant and Minister of the Gospel of Jesus Christ. London, T. Northcott, 1689.

CHALKLEY, THOMAS, A Journal . . . of Thomas Chalkley, A Minister of the Gospel in the Society of Friends. Phila., 1749.

COALE, JOSIAH, A Song of the Judgments. London, 1663.

CRISP, STEPHEN, The Memorable Account of the Christian Experiences of. London, 1694.

CROKER, JOHN, Brief Memoir of John Croker (Barclay Series VI). London, 1839.

CROOK, JOHN, A Short History of the Life of John Crook containing some of his Spiritual Travels and Breathings after God. London, T. Sowle, 1706.

CROUCH, WILLIAM, Posthuma Christiana; or a Collection of some Papers of William Crouch. London, 1712.

CURWEN, ALICE, A Relation of the Labour, Travail, and Suffering of that Faithful Servant of the Lord, Alice Curwen. 1680.

DAVIES, RICHARD, An Account of the Convincement, Exercises, Services, and Travels of that Antient Servant of the Lord. London, J. Sowle, 1710.

DEWSBURY, WILLIAM, The First Birth, 1655. Repr. in The Faithful Testimony, etc., 1689, pp. 44-57.

DICKENSON, JONATHAN, God's Protecting Providence. Phila., Reinier Jansen, 1699.

DICKINSON, JAMES, A Journal of the Life, Travels, and Labour of Love in the Work of the Ministry. London, 1745.

DUNDAS, WILLIAM, A Few Words of Truth from the Spirit of Truth. 1673.

EDMUNDSON, WILLIAM, A Journal of the Life of that Worthy Elder and Faithful Servant of Jesus Christ. Dublin, 1715.

ELLWOOD, THOMAS, The History of the Life of Thomas Ellwood; or, An Account of the Birth, Education, etc. First ed. 1714 (ed. by S. Graveson). London, Headley Bros., 1906.

FARNSWORTH, RICHARD, The Heart Opened by Christ or The Conditions of a Troubled Soul. London, Giles Calvert, 1655.

FELL, MARGARET, A Relation of Margaret Fell . . . pp. 1-14 of A Brief Collection of Remarkable Passages . . . J. Sowle, London, 1710.

FORSTER, THOMAS, A Guide to the Blind . . . or a True Testimony to the Light Within. 1659.

FOTHERGILL, JOHN, An Account of the Life and Travels in the Work of the Ministry of John Fothergill. London, Luke Hinde, 1753.

FOWLER, ROBERT, A True Relation of the Voyage Undertaken by one, Robert Fowler, with my Small Vessell, called the Woodhouse but Performed by the Lord like as did Noah's Ark, London, 1658. Repr. in Reports of Narragansett Friends' Meetings as "A Quaker's Sea Journal," 1900.

FOX, GEORGE, A Journal or Historical Account of the Life, Travels, Sufferings, Christian Experiences and Labour of Love in the Ministry, of that Antient, Eminent, and Faithful Servant of Jesus Christ, George Fox. London, Thomas Northcott, 1694.

GATES, NICHOLAS, A Tender Invitation to all to Embrace the Secret Visitation of the Lord to their Souls. London, J. Sowle, 1708.

GRATTON, JOHN, John Gratton Giving an Account of his Exercises when Young, . . . with a collection of his Books and Manuscripts. London, J. Sowle, 1720.

GREEN, THEOPHILUS, A Narrative of some Passages of the Life of Theophilus Green from his Youth. London, T. Sowle, 1702.

GREEN, THOMAS, A Declaration to the World of my Travel and Journey out of Aegypt into Canaan Through the Wilderness, etc. . . . London, T. Simmons, 1659.

GWIN, THOMAS, The Will and Testament of Thomas Gwin of Falmouth: Being Some Religious and Serious Considerations, which he Recommends to his Children and Friends. London, T. Sowle, 1720.

——— MS Diary in possession of A. Pearse Jenkin of Redruth. (Unread).

HADWEN, ISAAC, A Brefe Jurnall of a Voige Into Amiricay together with Jn. Lawson. (1718-1719). MS in possession of J. Theodore Hadwen of Northwich, Cheshire. (Unread). (Extracts ed. by Norman Penney in B.F.H.A., XV, 29-32).

HALHEAD, MILES, A Book of Some of the Sufferings and Passages of Miles Halhead of Mountjoy. . . . London, A. Sowle, 1690.

HALL, DAVID, Some Brief Memoirs of the Life of David Hall; with an Account of the life of his Father, John Hall. London, Luke Hinde, 1758.

HAYES, ALICE, A Legacy or a Widow's Mite: Left by Alice Hayes. London, J. Sowle, 1723.

HEBDEN, ROGER, A Plain Account of Certain Christian Experiences and Labours . . . of Roger Hebden. London, 1700.

HOLME, BENJAMIN, A Collection of the Epistles and Works of Benjamin Holme. To which is Prefixed an Account of his Life and Travels in the Work of the Ministry. . . . London, Luke Hinde, 1754.

HOSKENS, JANE, The Life and Spiritual Sufferings of that Faithful Servant of Christ. Phila., 1771.

HOWARD, LUKE, Love and Truth in Plainness Manifested . . . with an Account of his Convincement, Labours and Sufferings for the Truth. London, T. Sowle, 1704.

HOWGILL, FRANCIS, The Inheritance of Jacob Discovered after his Return out of Aegypt. . . . London, Giles Calvert, 1656.

HUBBERTHORN, RICHARD, A True Testimony of Obedience to the Heavenly Call (1655). Repr. in *Works*, 1663, pp. 1-7.

HUME, SOPHIA, An Exhortation to the Inhabitants of the Province of South Carolina. Phila., Franklin and Hall, 1748.

JAFFRAY, ALEXANDER, Diary of Alexander Jaffray, Provost of Aberdeen . . . To which are added Particulars of his Subsequent Life, given in Connexion with Memoirs. . . . London, 1833.

JEFFRYS, JOHN, A Serious Address to the People of the Church of England. To which are Prefixed Some Passages of his Life, Written by Himself. Dublin, 1739.

KEITH, GEORGE, A Journal of Travels from New Hampshire to Caratuck on the Continent of North America. London, 1706.

KELSALL, JOHN, MS Diary in Friends Reference Library. London.

LAMPE, HENRY, *Curriculum Vitae* or the Birth, Education, Travels and Life of Henry Lampe, M.D. London, Headley Brothers, 1895.

LANCASTER, LYDIA, Extracts from the Letters of Lydia Lancaster. London, 1840. MSS in D.

LAYTHES, THOMAS, The Inward and Spiritual Christian. . . . London, 1684.

LILBURNE, JOHN, The Resurrection of John Lilburne. London, Giles Calvert, 1656.

LIVINGSTONE, PATRICK, Selections from the Writings of Patrick Livingstone. Manchester, 1847.

LURTING, THOMAS, The Fighting Sailor Turn'd Peaceable Christian; Manifested in the Convincement and Conversion of Thomas Lurting. London, J. Sowle, 1710.

MARSHALL, CHARLES, Sion's Traveller Comforted and the Disobedient Warned. London, T. Sowle, 1704.

MELLIDGE, ANTHONY, A True Relation of the Former Faithful and Long Service, etc. 1656.

MORRIS, SUSANNAH, Journal of her Life and Travels. *Friends Miscellany.* (ed. by Comly), Phila., 1834, I, 143-192.

OSBORN, ELIAS, A Brief Narrative of the Life, Labours, and Sufferings of Elias Osborn. London, J. Sowle, 1723.

PARNELL, JAMES, Fruits of a Fast. 1655.

PENINGTON, ISAAC, An Account of My Soul's Travail toward the Holy Land, in *Works.* Part II (1681), pp. 48-51.

PENINGTON, MARY, Some Experiences in the Life of Mary Penington (ed. by Norman Penney). London, Headley Bros., 1911.

PENN, WILLIAM, MS of the Irish Journey in Library of Haverford College.

PENN, WILLIAM, An Account of W. Penn's Travails in Holland and Germany anno MDCLXXVII. London, T. Sowle, 1694.

PENNYMANN, JOHN, A Short Account of the life of Mr. John Pennymann . . . and Appendix, London, Job and John How, 1696.

PETERS, JOHN, A Brief Narration of the Life, Service and Sufferings of John Peters, London, 1709.

PIKE, JOSEPH. Some Account of the Life of Joseph Pike. Barclay Series, Vol. V, London, 1837.

RAYLTON, THOMAS. Some Account of the Birth, Education, and Convincement of that Faithful Minister . . . *Piety Promoted.* (Phila., 1854), II, 235-242.

RICHARDSON, JOHN, An Account of the Life of that Ancient Servant of Jesus Christ, John Richardson, London, Luke Hinde, 1757.

RIGGE, AMBROSE, Constancy in the Truth Commended; Being a True Account of the Life, Sufferings, London, J. Sowle, 1710.

ROBINSON, GEORGE, An Additional Account of George Robinson: Showing his Call to go to Jerusalem. . . . Bound with *An Account of the Voyage of Sarah Cheevers and Katherine Evans to the Island of Malta.* (1715), pp. 297-316.

ROBINSON, WILLIAM, See Marmaduke Stephenson.

ROFE, GEORGE. The Righteousness of God to Man . . . a True Declaration of how I lived before I knew the Truth and overcame the Deceit, London, Giles Calvert, 1656.

SANSOM, OLIVER, An Account of Many Remarkable Passages of The Life of Oliver Sansom, shewing his Convincement of the Truth, etc., London, J. Sowle, 1710.

SMITH, HUMPHREY, To the Parents of Children upon the Face

of the Whole Earth, 1660 Repr. in *Works*, 1683, pp. 123-125.

—— Man Driven out of Darkness. Repr. in *Works*, 1683, pp. 52-68.

STEEL, LAWRENCE, Jacob the Plain Man Wrestling with God until the Break of Day, etc. London, 1677.

STIRREDGE, ELIZABETH, Strength in Weakness Manifest. London, J. Sowle, 1711.

STORY, CHRISTOPHER, A Brief Account of the Life, Convincement, Sufferings, etc. London, J. Sowle, 1726.

STORY, THOMAS, A Journal of the Life of Thomas Story: Containing, An Account of his Remarkable Convincement . . . Newcastle upon Tyne. 1747.

STOUT, WILLIAM, Autobiography of William Stout of Lancaster, Wholesale and Retail Grocer and Ironmonger. (ed. by Harland from MSS), London, 1851.

SYMONDS, THOMAS, The Voice of the Just Uttered: His Passing out of Aegypt through the Red Sea. . . . London, Thomas Simmons, 1656.

TAYLOR, JOHN, An Account of Some of the Labours, Exercises, Travels, and Perils by Sea and Land. . . . London, 1710.

THOMPSON, THOMAS, An Encouragement Early to Seek the Lord . . . in an Account of the Life and Service of that Ancient Servant of God, Thomas Thompson, London, J. Sowle, 1708.

VOKINS, JOAN, God's Mighty Power Magnified, London, T. Northcott, 1691.

WEBB, ELIZABETH, A letter from Elizabeth Webb to Anthony William Boehm, Chaplain to Prince George of Denmark, and his reply, 1712. Evans: Friends' Library, XIII, 163-173. Philadelphia, 1849.

WHITEHEAD, GEORGE, Jacob Found in a Desert Land. . . . London, Giles Calvert, 1656.

—— The Christian Progress of that Ancient Servant and Minister of Jesus Christ, London, J. Sowle, 1725.

WHITEHEAD, JOHN, The Enmitie between the Two Seeds. Wherein is Discovered the Subtilty and Envie of the Serpent's Seed, 1655. Repr. in *Written Gospel Labours . . . of John Whitehead*, London, 1704, pp. 1-42.

WHITING, JOHN, Persecution Expos'd in Some Memoirs Relating to the Sufferings of Jno. Whiting, and Many Others of the People called Quakers, London, 1715.

WILSON, THOMAS, A Brief Journal of the Life, Travels, and Labours of Love in the Work of the Ministry. Dublin, 1728.

ZACHARY, THOMAS, A Word to those who have been Convinced of the Truth. . . . No place or printer, ca. 1660.

BIBLIOGRAPHY II

GENERAL

Account of a Divine Visitation and Blessing Attending the Religious Care and Exercise of the Teachers of Waltham Abbey School. 1680.

ALDAM, THOMAS, A Short Testimony Concerning that Faithful Servant of the Lord, Thomas Aldam. 1690.

ALDINGTON, RICHARD, A Book of Characters. London, 1924.

ALEXANDER, WILLIAM, Collectitia, or Pieces, Religious, Moral, and Miscellaneous. York, 1824.

ALLPORT, FLOYD H., Social Psychology. Boston, 1924.

ANTROBUS, BENJAMIN, Some Buds and Blossoms of Piety, London. 1684.

AUBREY, JOHN, Brief Lives (ed. Andrew Clark), 1898.

AUDLAND, JOHN, The Memory of the Righteous Revived; Being a Brief Collection of the Books and Written Epistles of John Camm and John Audland, London. 1689.

BACKHOUSE, JAMES, Memoirs of Francis Howgill. York, 1828.

BAILEY, MARGARET L., Milton and Jacob Boehme. Oxford Press, 1914.

BAILLIE, ROBERT, Letters and Journals. London, 1841.

BARCLAY, JOHN (editor), Letters . . . of Early Friends; Illustrative of the History of the Society, 1841.

———— Memoirs of the Rise, Progress, and Persecution of the People Called Quakers in . . . Scotland. 1833.

———— Select Anecdotes and Instructive Incidents Taken from Publications of Several Members of the Society of Friends. 1822.

———— Select Series A, Biographical, Narrative, Epistolary, and Miscellaneous. 6 vols.

BARCLAY, ROBERT, Truth Triumphant through the Spiritual Welfare . . . of Robert Barclay. 3 vols. London, 1718.

———— Reliquae Barclayanae, MS in D.

BARCLAY, ROBERT, The Inner Life of the Religious Societies of the Commonwealth. London, 1876.

BARNARDISTON, GILES, Memoir, *Friends' Library* (1840), Vol. IV.

BATHURST, ELIZABETH, Truth Vindicated by the Faithful Testimony . . . of Elizabeth Bathurst. London, 1691.

BAXTER, RICHARD, Autobiography (ed. J. M. Lloyd Thomas). London, 1926.

―――― A Call to the Unconverted. London, 1718.

―――― The Saints' Everlasting Rest. London, 1650.

BAYLY, WILLIAM, A Collection of the Several Wrightings. . . . London. 1676.

BECK, WILLIAM, The Friends; Who They Are and What They Have Done. London, 1892.

―――― George Whitehead. 1901.

BECK, WILLIAM, and T. F. BALL, The London Friends' Meetings. 1869.

BELLERS, JOHN, Some Reasons for a European State. London, 1710.

BENEZET, ANTHONY, A Short Account of the People Called Quakers. Phila., 1780.

BERKLEY, SIR JOHN, Memoirs; Select Tracts Relating to the Civil War in England. London, 1815.

BESSE, JOSEPH, A Collection of the Sufferings of the People Called Quakers from 1650 to 1689. 2 vols. London, 1753.

BEVAN, EVAN, Memoir of Evan Bevans. *Friends' Library,* Vol. XIII, 1849.

BEVAN, JOSEPH GURNEY, A Short Account of the Life and Writings of Robert Barclay. London, 1802.

BILLING, EDWARD, An Alarm to all Flesh. London, 1660.

BISHOP, GEORGE, New England Judged. London, 1661.

BLAIR, ROBERT, Life (Wodrow Society Pub.), ed. by W. K. Tweedie. 1834-1848.

BOCKETT, RICHARD, JR., Fruits of Early Piety. London, 1722.

BOLLES, JOSEPH, An Addition to the Book Entitled *Spirit of the Martyrs Revived.* N.Y., 1738.

BOWDEN, JAMES, History of the Society of Friends in America. 2 vols., London, 1850, 1854.

BOWETER, JOHN, Epistles, Travels . . . of John Boweter, London, 1705.

BRAILSFORD, MABEL, A Quaker from Cromwell's Army: James Nayler. N.Y., 1927.

―――― Quaker Women. London, 1915.

BRAITHWAITE, W. C., Beginnings of Quakerism, London, 1912.
―――― The Second Period of Quakerism, London, 1919.
BRAYSHAW, A. NEAVE, The Personality of George Fox, London, 1918.
―――― The Quakers. Their Story and Message, N.Y., 1927.
BUDD, THOMAS, Good Order Established in Pennsylvania and New Jersey in North America, 1685, No. 4 of Gowan's *Bibliotheca Americana* (ed. Edward Armstrong).
BUDGE, FRANCES, Annals of Early Friends. Phila., 1883.
BUGG, FRANCIS, The Pilgrim's Progress from Quakerism to Christianity. London, 1700.
BUNYAN, JOHN, *Works* (ed. Offor), 6 vols., London, 1869.
―――― Grace Abounding to the Chief of Sinners. Camb. Press, 1907.
BURNETT, GILBERT, History of his Own Time. 7 vols. (ed. Routh), 1823.
BURNYEAT, JOHN, His Collected Works . . . The Truth Exalted, London, 1691.
BURR, ANNA R., The Autobiography. Boston, 1909.
―――― Religious Confessions and Confessants. Boston, 1914.
BURRIDGE, CHAMPLIN, Early Dissenters in the Light of Recent Research. Camb. Press, 1912.
―――― The Antecedents of Quakerism, *English Historical Review.* CXVIII (Jan. 1915), 78-91.
BURROUGH, EDWARD, The Memorable Works of a Son of Thunder and Consolation. 1672.
BURTON, ROBERT, The Anatomy of Melancholy (ed. A. R. Shilleto), 3 vols., London, 1896.
BUTLER, SAMUEL, The Genuine Remains (ed. R. Thyer). 2 vols., 1759.
―――― Hudibras and Other Works (ed. A. Ramsey). 1759.
CADBURY, CHRISTABEL, Robert Barclay: His Life and Work, London, 1912.
CALLAWAY, HENRY, Memoir of James Parnell. London, 1846.
CANBY, HENRY SEIDEL, The People Called Quakers. *Century,* LXXXIV (June, 1912).
―――― Quakers and Puritans. *Saturday Review of Literature,* Jan. 2, 1926.
CARTWRIGHT, THOMAS, Diary (ed. Jos. Hunter). Camden Soc., 1843.

CHALKLEY, THOMAS, A Collection of the Works of, Phila., 1749.
CHEEVERS, SARAH, This is a Short Relation of Some of the Cruel
    Sufferings . . . of Katherine Evans and Sarah Cheevers in
    the Inquisition in the Isle of Malta. London, 1662.
CHESTER, EDWARD, A Narrative of the Life and Death of Ed-
    ward Chester. London, 1709.
Christian Life and Thought in the Society of Friends. Being
    the First Part of the Christian Discipline of the Religious So-
    ciety of Friends. London, 1922.
CLARENDON, EDWARD HYDE, Earl of, The History of the Rebel-
    lion. 7 vols., Oxford, 1839.
CLARK, ALICE, Working Life of Women in the Seventeenth
    Century, N.Y., 1920.
CLARK, WILLIAM HENRY, History of Non-Conformity from Wic-
    lif to the Close of the Nineteenth Century. 2 vols., London,
    1913.
CLARIDGE, RICHARD, The Life and Posthumous Works of Rich-
    ard Claridge (Collected by Besse). London, 1726.
CLARKSON, THOMAS, Portraiture of Quakerism. 3 vols., London,
    1806.
―――― Memoirs of the Private and Public Life of William Penn.
    2 vols., Phila., 1814.
COALE, JOSEPH, Some Account of the Life, Service, and Suffer-
    ing . . . of Joseph Coale. London, 1706.
COALE, JOSIAH, The Books and Divers Epistles of . . . Josiah
    Coale. 1671.
COALE, WILLIAM, A Testimony Concerning . . . William Coale.
    London, 1682.
COATE, MARY, Social Life in Stuart England. London, 1924.
COE, GEORGE A., The Psychology of Religion. U. of Chicago
    Press, 1916.
COLBY, ELBRIDGE, The Essence of Autobiography. *Open Court,*
    July, 1923.
COMPSTON, F. B., GEORGE FOX. Prophetes Hebraeus Redivivus.
    English Review, XLVI. (Feb. 1928.)
CROESE, GERARD, The General History of the Quakers. London,
    John Dunton, 1696.
CROOK, JOHN, The Design of Christianity. London, 1701.
CROSFIELD, HELEN, MARGARET FOX. London, 1914.
CURTEIS, GEORGE HERBERT, Dissent in its Relation to the Church
    of England. London, 1911.

DALE, R. W., History of English Congregationalism. London, 1907.

DAVIES, JOHN H., Bibliography of Quaker Books. *J'n'l of Welsh Bibliog. Ass'n.,* Aug. 1914.

DEACON, JOHN, An Exact History of James Naylor with his Parents, Birth, Education, Profession, and Blasphemies. 1657.

D'EWES, SIR SIMONDS, The Autobiography and Correspondence of. London (ed. Halliwell), 1845.

DEWSBURY, WILLIAM, The Faithful Testimony of that Antient Servant . . . Collected and Printed for Future Service. London, 1689.

DEXTER, H. M., The Congregationalism of the Last Three Hundred Years as Seen in its Literature. N.Y., 1880.

——— Congregationalism. What it is, Whence it is, How it works. Boston, 1871.

DIXON, HEPWORTH, A History of William Penn. 1902.

DUNN, WALDO, English Biography. N.Y., 1916.

DUNTON, JOHN, Life and Errors. 2 vols., London, 1818.

ECCLES, SOLOMON, Signs are from the Lord to a People or Nation to Forwarn Them. London. 1663.

——— A Musick-Lector. London, 1667.

ELLIS, WILLIAM, A Brief Account of the Life and Death and Some of the Gospel Labours. London, 1710.

ELLWOOD, THOMAS, A Collection of Poems on Various Subjects (n.d. for the first and second editions).

——— Sacred History. London, 1709.

——— Davideis, The Life of David, King of Israel: A Sacred Poem in five books. London, J. Sowle, 1712.

Epistles of the London Yearly Meeting. 1675-1759. London, 1760.

EMMOTT, E. B., A Short History of Quakerism. London, 1923.

ESTAUGH, ELIZABETH, Testimony to the Memory of Her Beloved Husband, John Estaugh. 1744.

EVANS, CHARLES, Friends in the Seventeenth Century. 1875.

EVANS, THOMAS and EVANS, WILLIAM, Editors of *The Friends' Library* Comprising Journals, Doctrinal Treatises, and Other Writings of the Religious Society of Friends, 14 vols., Phila. 1837-1850.

EVELYN, JOHN, Memoirs (ed. Wheatley). 4 vols., 1879.

EYRE, ADAM, Diurnal. 1646-47 (ed. Morehouse). Surtees Soc. 1877.

Examples for Youth in Remarkable Instances of Early Piety. (ed. William Raws), N.Y., 1802.

FALDO, J., The Danger of Enthusiasm Discovered, 1674.

FANSHAWE, LADY, Memoirs. London, 1830.

FELL, SARAH, The Household Account Book of Sarah Fell of Swarthmore Hall (ed. Norman Penney). Camb. Press, 1920.

FELL, MARGARET (Fox), A Brief Collection of Remarkable Passages and Occurrences. London, 1710.

FELL-SMITH, CHARLOTTE, Stephen Crisp and his Correspondents. London, 1892.

FIENNES, CELIA, Through England on a Side-Saddle in the Time of William and Mary, 1888.

First Publishers of Truth (ed. Norman Penney). London, 1907.

FIRTH, CHARLES, Last Years of the Protectorate. 2 vols., 1909.

———— Some Seventeenth Century Diarists, *Scottish Historical Review,* July, 1913.

FISHER, SAMUEL, The Testimony of Truth Exalted by the Collected Labours . . . of Samuel Fisher. 1679.

FOX, GEORGE, Works. 8 vols., Phila., 1831.

———— A Battle-door for Teachers and Professors to Learn Singular and Plural. London, 1660.

———— Journal (ed. Norman Penney). Cambridge, 1911.

———— Journal, Tercentenary. Abr. London, 1924.

Fox, George. Some Modern Appreciations. London, 1925.

FRAZER, JAMES, Memoirs of the Rev. James Frazer of Brea (Wodrow Society). 1838-1840.

FRERE, W. H., The English Church in the Reigns of Elizabeth and James I. 1904.

GAIRDNER, J., English Church in the 16th Century. N.Y., 1904.

GARDINER, S. R., History of the Commonwealth and Protectorate. 3 vols., 1894.

GOADBY, J. J., The Baptists and Quakers in Northamptonshire (1650-1700). Northampton, 1882.

GOULD, DANIEL, Photogravure of the Original Letters of the Four Quaker Martyrs. *Pub. of Mass. Hist. Soc.*

GRAHAM, JOHN, William Penn, Founder of Pennsylvania. London, 1916.

———— The Faith of a Quaker. Camb. Press, 1920.

———— Reply to "Mental Ability of the Quakers." *Science Progress,* XVII.

GRUBB, EDWARD, What is Quakerism? London, 1929.
———— Quaker Thought and History. 1924.
GRUBB, ISABEL, Quakerism and Industry before 1800. London, 1930.
GUMMERE, MRS. AMELIA MOTT, The Quaker, A Study in Costume. 1901.
———— The Quaker in the Forum. Phila., 1910.
———— The Journals and Essays of John Woolman. N.Y., 1922.
HALKETT, LADY ANNE, Journal (ed. J. G. Nichols). Camden Soc., 1875.
HALLOWELL, R. P., The Quaker Invasion of Massachusetts. Boston, 1883.
HAMILTON, C. L., A Psychological Interpretation of Mysticism. Distributed by University of Chicago Libraries. 1916.
HANKIN, E. H., Mental Ability of the Quakers. *Science Progress*, XVI, 654-664; XVII, 304 ff.
HARVEY, T. EDMUND, The Rise of the Quakers. London, 1921.
———— Silence and Worship, 1923.
HAWKINS, RICHARD, A Brief Narrative of the Life and Death of Gilbert Latye. London, 1707.
HAYNES, E. S. P., Religious Persecutions, A Study in Political Psychology. London, 1904.
HAZARD, CAROLINE, Narragansett Friends Meeting in the Eighteenth Century with a Chapter on Quaker Beginnings in Rhode Island. N.Y., 1899. (Appendix contains an account of Robert Fowler's journey in the Wodehouse.)
HEBDEN, ROGER, A Plain Account of Certain Christian Experiences, Labours . . . of Roger Hebden. London, 1700.
HERBERT OF CHERBURY (Lord), Autobiography (ed. Sidney Lee). London, 1886 and 1906.
HINE, REGINALD L., A Mirror for the Society of Friends. Being the Story of The Hitchin Quakers. London, 1929.
HIRST, M. E., Quakers in Peace and War. N.Y., 1923.
HOBHOUSE, STEPHEN, William Law and Eighteenth Century Quakerism. N.Y., 1928.
HODGKIN, VIOLET (Holdsworth), A Quaker Saint of Cornwall: Loveday Hambly and her Guests. 1927.
———— Silent Worship: The Way of Wonder. 1919.
HODGSON, WILLIAM, Select Historical Memoirs of the Religious Society of Friends, Commonly Called Quakers. Phila., 1844.

HOLDER, CHARLES FREDERICK, The Quaker in Great Britain and America. 1905.
—— The Quaker and Puritan; A Thrilling Passage in Colonial History. *Arena*, XXXIII (1905), 382-392.
HOOKES, ELLIS, The Spirit of the Martyrs Revived. n.d. Repr., 1682.
HOWITT, WILLIAM, Life of John Roberts of Siddington. *Edinburgh Review*, 1834.
HOWGILL, FRANCIS, The Dawnings of the Gospel Day. 1676.
HUBBERTHORN, RICHARD, A Collection of the Several Books and Writings of . . . Richard Hubberthorn. London, 1663.
HUTCHINSON, LUCY, Memoirs of the Life of Colonel Hutchinson. London, 1848.
JANNEY, SAMUEL, The Life of William Penn. Phila., 1852.
JENKINS, HOWARD M., The Family of William Penn. Phila., 1898.
JONES, RUFUS M., Spiritual Reformers of the XVI and XVII Centuries. 1914.
—— The Mystic's Experience of God. *Atlantic Monthly*, CXXVIII (Nov., 1921).
—— Studies in Mystical Religion. 1909.
—— The Quakers in the American Colonies. 1911.
—— The Later Periods of Quakerism. 1921.
—— The Faith and Practice of the Quakers. 1927.
JOSSELIN, REV. RALPH, Diary (ed. E. Hocliffe). London, 1908.
KEITH, GEORGE, The Magicke of Quakerism. London, 1707.
KELTY, MARY, Early Days in the Society of Friends. London, 1840.
KENDAL, J., Letters on Religious Subjects. London, Vol. I. (1802) ; Vol. II (1805).
KITCHEN, GEORGE, Sir Robert L'Estrange; A Contribution to the History of the Seventeenth Century Press. London, 1913.
KITE, NATHAN, Antiquarian Researches among Early Printers and Publishers of Friends' Books, Manchester. 1844.
KNIGHT, RACHEL, The Founder of Quakerism; a Psychological Study. N.Y., 1923.
KRAPP, GEORGE PHILIP, The Rise of Early English Prose. N.Y., 1915.
LAWSON, THOMAS, A Mite into the Treasury. London, 1680.
—— A Serious Remembrancer. London, 1684.
LESLIE, CHARLES, The Snake in the Grass. London, 1696.

LEUBA, JAMES H., A Psychological Study of Religion. N.Y., 1912.

——— The Psychology of Religious Mysticism. N.Y., 1925.

LITTLEBOY, ANNA L., A History of Friends Reference Library with Notes on Early Printers in the Society of Friends. London, 1920.

LIVINGSTONE, JOHN, A Brief Historical Relation (Wodrow Society).

LODDINGTON, WILLIAM, Plantation Work. London, 1682.

LOCKER-LAMPSON, A Quaker Post-Bag. N.Y., 1910.

LOGAN, JAMES, The Correspondence of James Logan and Thomas Story (1724-1740). Phila., 1927.

MACKAY, LYDIA M., The England of George Fox's Journal. *Blackwood's Mag.* CXC (Oct. 1911), 557-565.

MANNERS, EMILY, Elizabeth Hooton, First Quaker Woman Preacher. With notes by Norman Penney. Sup. XII to *J.F.H.S.*

MARKHAM, THOMAS, An Account of the Life and Death of Our Faithful Friend . . . Thomas Markham. London, T. Sowle, 1695.

MARSH, T. W., Early Friends in Surrey and Sussex. 1886.

MASON, MARTIN, MSS in D. containing letters, verses, and maxims.

MASSON, DAVID, The Life of Milton. 7 vols., London, 1877.

MATERN, JOHN, The Testimony of that Dear and Faithful Man, John Matern. London, 1680.

MELVILLE, JAMES, The Autobiography and Diary of Mr. James Melville (Wodrow Society).

MILTON, JOHN, Prose Works (ed. George Burnet). 2 vols., 1809.

MOLLINEUX, MARY (Southworth), Fruits of Retirement, or Miscellaneous Poems, Moral and Divine. London, 1702.

MOORE, WILLIAM, Newes out of the East . . . a True Account count of the Tryals and Sufferings, Jeopardies, and Torturings which John Philly and William Moore Passed through . . . 1664.

MORE, HENRY, The Life of the Learned and Pious . . . (ed. R. Ward). 1710.

MORRISON, C. C., The Quakers. An Outside View. *Christian Century,* Nov. 8, 1923.

NAYLER, JAMES, A Collection of Sundry Books, Epistles and Papers written by James Nayler. London, 1716.

NEAL, DANIEL, The History of the Puritans, 5 vols. Bath, 1793-1797.

NEWCASTLE, MARGARET, Duchess of, Life of the Duke of Newcastle (ed. C. H. Firth). London, 1886.

NICOLSON, MARJORIE, The Conway Letters. New Haven, 1930.

NICHOLSON, REBECCA, Contributions to the Biography of Elizabeth Estaugh. Phila., 1894.

NIGHTINGALE, BENJAMIN, Early Stages of the Quaker Movement in Lancashire. London, 1921.

—— The Ejected of 1662, Manchester. 2 vols., 1911.

NORRIS, W. G., John Ap John and Early Records of Friends in Wales. London, 1907. Suppl. VI to *J.F.H.S.*

PARNELL, JAMES, Works. London, 1675.

PENINGTON, ISAAC, The Works of the Long-Mournful and Sorely Distressed Isaac Penington. London, 1681.

—— Letters of Isaac Penington (ed. John Kendall). London, 1796.

PENN, WILLIAM, Works of William Penn. 5 vols., 1782.

—— Some Fruits of Solitude. London, 1693.

—— The Harmony of Divine and Heavenly Doctrines. London, 1696.

—— No Cross, No Crown. London, 1682.

PEPYS, SAMUEL, Diary (ed. E. H. Wheatley). 10 vols., N.Y., 1895.

PERROT, JOHN, A Sea of the Seed's Sufferings through which Runs a River of Rich Rejoycing. London, 1661.

PETERS, JOHN, A Brief Narration of the Life . . . of John Peters. London, 1709.

Piety Promoted . . . (ed. John Field). 5 vol. 1711-1728.

Piety Promoted in a Collection of Dying Sayings of the People with a brief Account of some of their labours in the Gospel . . . 4 vols. Comprises eleven previously printed parts (ed. by William and Thomas Evans. Phila., 1854). Vol. 5, 1890.

PONSONBY, ARTHUR, English Diaries. London, 1923.

—— More English Diaries. London, 1927.

POWICKE, F. J., A Life of the Reverend Richard Baxter. London, 1924.

—— A Life of the Reverend Richard Baxter under the Cross. London, 1927.

PRATT, JAMES BISSET, The Subconscious and Religious, *Harvard Theological Review*, VI (1913), 209-228.

The Psychology of Religious Belief, N.Y., 1907.

PRINGLE, WALTER, The Memoirs of Walter Pringle of Green-knowe (Wodrow Society).

PRYNNE, WILLIAM, Histrio-Mastix. London, 1633.

Quakerism and the Church of England. *Church Quarterly Review,* XXX, 352-364.

REES, THOMAS MARDY, A History of the Quakers in Wales and their Immigration to North America. 1925.

RERESBY, SIR JOHN, The Memoirs of (ed. J. J. Cartwright). 1875.

RICHARDSON, CAROLINE, English Preachers and Preaching, 1640-1670. N.Y., 1928.

RICHARDSON, JOHN, A Short Account of the Life . . . of that Faithful Handmaid of the Lord, Anne Richardson. 1828.

ROBERTS, DANIEL, The Life of John Roberts, a Gloucestershire Farmer of the Time of Charles II, by his Son, Daniel Roberts. 1745. Repr. with original spellings under title of Ye Quaker of Ye Olden Time. 1898.

ROUS, JOHN, Diary (ed. Mary Green). London, 1856.

ROWNTREE, J. S., Quakerism Past and Present. London, 1859.

—— Life and Works. 1908.

ROYCE, JOSIAH, George Fox as a Mystic, *Harvard Theological Review,* VI, 31-60.

RUTTY, DR. JOHN, A History of the Rise and Progress of the People Called Quakers in Ireland. London, 1811.

SAMBLE, RICHARD, A Handful after the Harvest-Man. London, 1684.

SELBIE, W. B., The Psychology of Religion. Oxford, 1924.

SEWEL, WILLIAM, History of the Rise, Increase, and Progress of the Christian People Called Quakers. London, 1722.

SHERMAN, STUART P., What is a Puritan? *Atlantic Monthly,* CXXXVIII, 342-356.

SIXMITH, WILLIAM, Some Fruits Brought Forth through a Tender Branch. 1679.

SIMPSON, WILLIAM, A Short Relation Concerning the Life and Death of . . . William Simpson. (Appended is his tract on Going Naked a Sign). 1671.

SMITH, HUMPHREY, A Collection of the Several Writings of . . . Humphrey Smith. London, 1683.

SMITH, JOSEPH, A Descriptive Catalogue of Friends' Books. 2 vols. London, 1867.

—— Supplement. 1893.

—— Bibliotheca Anti-Quakeriana; or a Catalogue of Books Adverse to the Society of Friends. 1873.

SMITH, WILLIAM, Balm from Gilead. London, 1675.

SPENCE, CHARLES J., A Brief Account of the Manuscript Journal of George Fox. *Essayist and Friends' Review*, 1893.

SPINGARN, J. E., Critical Essays of the Seventeenth Century. 3 vols. Oxford, 1908.

SPURGEON, CAROLINE, Mysticism in English Literature. Camb., 1913.

STARBUCK, EDWIN, The Psychology of Religion. N.Y., 1901.

STEVENSON, JOHN, A Rare Soul Strengthening and Comforting Cordial for Young and for Old (Wodrow Society).

STEPHENSON, MARMADUKE, A Call from Death to Life and out of the Dark Ways and Worships. London, 1660.

STORY, JOHN, The Memory of that Servant of God, John Story, Revived. 1683.

TATHAM, G. B., The Puritans in Power. Cambridge, 1913.

TAYLOR, E. E., Francis Howgill of Grayrigg. A Sufferer for the Truth. London, 1906.

—— The First Publishers of Truth. *J.F.H.S.* XIX, 66-81.

TAYLOR, THOMAS, Truth's Innocency and Simplicity Shining through the Conversion. London, T. Sowle, 1697.

THOMAS, ANNA L., The Quaker Seekers in Wales. London, 1924.

THOMPSON, E. N. S., Literary Bypaths of the Renaissance. Yale Press, 1924.

THORESBY, RALPH, Diary (ed. Jos. Hunter). London, 1880.

THORNTON, MRS. ALICE, Autobiography. London, 1873.

TICKELL, HUGH, Some Testimonies Concerning the Life and Death of Hugh Tickell. London, 1690.

TRAHERNE, THOMAS, Centuries of Meditation (ed. Sidney Dobell). London, 1908.

—— Poetical Works (ed. Sidney Dobell). 1903.

TREVELYAN, G. M., England under the Stuarts. 1904.

TUKE, HENRY, Biographical Notices of Members of the Society of Friends. York, 1813-15.

TURNER, F. S., The Quakers. London, 1st ed., 1889. 2nd ed., 1911.

UNDERHILL, EVELYN, Practical Mysticism. A Book for Normal People. N.Y., 1915.

WAGSTAFFE, THOMAS, Piety Promoted, etc. London, 1774.

WATSON, GRACE, A Narrative and Testimony Concerning Grace Watson. London, 1690.

WATSON, SAMUEL, A Short Account of the Convincement of . . . Samuel Watson. London, 1712.

WEBB, MARIA, The Fells of Swarthmoor Hall. London, 1867.

—— The Penns and Peningtons of the Seventeenth Century. Phila., 1868.

WHITE, WILLIAM, Friends in Warwickshire. Birmingham, 1873.

WHITEHEAD, ANNE (Downer), Piety Promoted by Faithfulness Manifested by Several Testimonies Concerning that True Servant of God, Anne Whitehead. 1686.

WHITEHEAD, JOHN, The Written Gospel Labours of that Ancient and Faithful John Whitehead. London, 1704.

WHITLEY, W. T., Bibliography of Baptist Books. 1916.

WHITING, JOHN, A. Catalogue of Friends Books. London, 1708.

—— Early Piety Exemplified in the Life and Death of Mary Whiting. London, 1711.

WHITMORE, ALICE, The River at the Spring, *Bellman*, June, 1918, pp. 627-633.

WHITROWE, JOAN, The Work of God in a Dying Maid. 1677.

WIDDERS, ROBERT, Life, Death, Travels, and Sufferings of. London, 1688.

WILLIAMS, ROGER, George Fox Digg'd out of his Burrows. Boston, 1676.

WILSON, WILLIAM, The Memorial of the Just Shall Not Rot, or a Short Collection of Letters of . . . William Wilson. London, 1685.

WODROW, ROBERT, Collections upon the Lives of the Reformers and most Eminent Ministers in the Church of Scotland. Glasgow, 1834-1848.

WOOD, ANTHONY À., Athenae Oxonienses (ed. Philip Bliss). 3 vols., London, 1817.

WYETH, JOSEPH, ANGUIS FLAGELLATUS, or A Switch for the Snake. London, 1699.

GENERAL INDEX